ESSAYS ON CONTEMPORARY GERMAN LITERATURE

German Men of Letters, Volume IV

ESSAYS ON
CONTEMPORARY
GERMAN LITERATURE

German Men of Letters, Volume IV

edited by

BRIAN KEITH-SMITH

OSWALD WOLFF
London, W.1
1969

First published 1966

© 1966 OSWALD WOLFF (PUBLISHERS) LIMITED, LONDON

2nd Impression 1969

MADE AND PRINTED IN GREAT BRITAIN BY
THE GARDEN CITY PRESS LIMITED
LETCHWORTH, HERTFORDSHIRE

CONTENTS

INTRODUCTION

THERE are several limitations in presenting a volume of essays on contemporary German literature, from which grows the danger that the purpose and scope of this book may be misunderstood. It has always been a doubtful cause to publicly comment on the works and opinions of writers who are still alive and actively articulate, not least because it is almost impossible to establish what are the significant values to be applied to any choice of contemporary writings. It may be embarrassing for some to openly criticize a living writer, for others a delightful trap in which to practice out personal aesthetic theories, often leading to a situation where the critic tells the writer what he ought or ought not to have just written or be about to write. One is, or perhaps ought to be aware of the more than usually subjective nature of any such undertaking. Academically the study of contemporary literature is often suspect on these grounds alone. For how does one avoid either gullible acceptance of publishers' propaganda—culled excerpts from the first reactions of critics to a new book—or the temptation to only read those works which appear sufficiently obscure to ensure that no one else around is as well informed? One obvious answer is to read the major critics' pronouncements on such works some months after they have appeared, but here one is immediately confronted with the jungle of private theory and public bitterness and animosity that so characterizes many German critics today. Rightly some of the most sensitive critics will not express themselves in public on every new "major" publication, nor accept a "duty" to give oracular advice on the relative significance of current publications. Indeed perhaps more than ever the student of German finds it difficult to gain a first-hand knowledge of significant current German literature, overwhelmed by the sheer quantity of both "serious" and "popular" books written by today's German men of letters. He can either at the best try to follow the development of one particular author, or spend his time becoming a specialist in the field. The wide variety of viewpoints expressed by post-war German writers denies any simple categorization of them into literary movements or trends. Some writers express a harmonious spiritual attitude seemingly detached from or in spite of the treacherous nature of the times; others reveal an uncertainty

7

in the face of experience that seems to confirm them as most truly representative of their day.

The essays in this volume, if they confirm anything collectively, spotlight the essentially divided character of German writing today. It would have been easy to select a number of contemporary German writers who have purposely denied the value of traditional literary themes and forms as having anything to say to us today, and present them as representative. Nor would it have been difficult to have found some traditionalists with whom to oppose them. There is, however, no central theme to this volume—for each writer in it has essentially different attitudes and means of expressing them. Often one meets the temptation to think of today's writers as somehow belonging to a similar spiritual generation to our own, but this is especially nonsensical in a century where the shifts of values have so rapidly increased in both direction and speed. It would be wrong for instance to expect the attitudes of Wilhelm Lehmann to correspond with those of Uwe Johnson who will be dealt with in a later volume.

In general the reading public, spurred on by the subtler and less subtle devices of what Hans Magnus Enzensberger has dubbed the *"Bewußtseinsindustrie"*,[1] has found itself reading parts of some of the most complex and long prose works in German literature. One is hardly surprised but nevertheless disillusioned to find that certain authors have cut down their novels by as much as 100 or 200 pages when they are to be translated into foreign languages. The reading public has learnt to pay great respect to the "abstract" poem and the "absurd" play—products of a growing unease with the basic structures of a machine-fed society. The simple timeless direct pageantry of nature has been daubed over by the intricate self-conscious metaphorical artistry of writers scared by the possible annihilation man is inflicting on himself. No longer, we are told, is it possible for a German writer to create simple, direct, short, easily understandable works of art that correspond to his understanding of and reaction to the world around him. Why?

The first and most obvious reason is the legacy of two world wars. For instance the theatre of cruelty for many is part of the long process of the psyche working out of it memories and neuroses left over from the war. We cannot expect, nor would playwrights wish their audiences to react disinterestedly to this—they will either turn away revolted, or work out their anger through this medium. West Germans cannot, and very often are not allowed to forget their immediate past. And where there is no direct memory of the worst anguish or atrocities, there is awareness of them flickering through the memories of others. We wish neither to criticize nor appraise this, but simply reiterate that a generation's memories last longer than it or its critics would like to believe. Many of the older generation of writers feel it their duty to record and hand down their reactions to the Nazi period, lest we forget. In this they counter the all too understandable wish of their generation to forget, or at least not to perpetuate what they once witnessed. The younger generation of writers, anxious for the future, are naturally interested in their inheritance, and again are counters against a new generation that wishes to forget, indeed never find out. Distrust in the past and interest in new experiments may be found in the works of young writers throughout Europe. For many this means revolt against the inhumanity of an industrialized society, the apparent impotence of organized religions, the restricting taboos of their forefathers, the suppression of the individual. Some make a genuine attempt to find fresh roots and mould new forms, and show up the increasing decay and impotence of everyday language for complete self-expression. This often leads to a more sophisticated, less altruistic understanding of the self that demands increasingly complex forms to describe a more and more shifting and expanding understanding of man.

The most formative experiences of today's writers have been negative—the war and its aftermath, the onslaught of conflicting ideologies that so often seem removed from the hard facts of everday life, seduction by the promise of material success, and frustration with the apparent blindness of power and its manipulators the planners. Reality has become an infinitely richer and infinitely more ungraspable category than ever before. Thus we read the vivid formula of Heinrich Böll in his essay *Der Zeitgenosse und die Wirklichkeit* (1953) where he examines in detail two concepts—"Aktualität" and "Wirklichkeit", actuality and reality. Reality he explains is the hidden possibility opened up behind the event, to a certain extent controllable by man and possibly facing him with an ethical choice. Thus the death of the Japanese fishermen after the Bikini atomic tests opens up our eyes to the possible reality of fall-out and all that entails. The writer's duty for Böll is to reveal reality by careful choice and depiction of actuality, and his imagination is his ability to do just this. Reality becomes the result of acts of interpretation of actuality, and for this he finds a striking metaphor :

"Das Wirkliche liegt immer ein wenig weiter als das Aktuelle : um einen fliegenden Vogel zu treffen, muß man v o r ihm schießen : man muß dazu die Geschwindigkeit des Vogels, die des Geschosses kennen, zahlreiche Imponderabilen noch : Wind und Luftdruck, Dinge die sich errechnen lassen, und wenn die Berechnung fehlgeht, fliegt der Vogel davon in Entfernungen

hinein, wo er unerreichbar für das Geschoß wird. Auch die
Wirklichkeit bewegt sich."[2]

This dichotomy between actuality and reality informs most of
contemporary German literature. It also provides one reason for
the inclusion in this volume of an essay on East German literature.
Many of the post-war works have titles which bear witness to this
pressing awareness of the intangibility of reality. In many we find
major themes where time or place sequences provide an incomplete
subjective view of what the characters think is reality, but which
turns out to be a mirage of the spirit (e.g. Bachmann—*Die gestundete Zeit*, Böll—*Billard um halb Zehn*, Celan—*Sprachgitter*, Enzensberger—*Blindenschrift*, Frisch—*Mein Name sei
Gantenbein*, Johnson—*Zwei Ansichten*, Kasack—*Die Stadt hinter
dem Strom*, Nossack—*Unmögliche Beweisaufnahme*, Rehn—*Nichts
in Sicht* and many others). In these there is a deep perception if
not terror of the gulf set between what is experienced as the truth
by the individual and what is made out to be the truth by
man in the mass. The problem is made painfully concrete by the
division of Germany and more especially by the Berlin wall.
Hardly any writer in Germany today except those who write
propaganda publicly believes to be relevant what the ruling parties
in either half of divided Germany have to say about their own
merits or the other side's faults. This is not to say that those who
live in the West despise the relative freedom of the individual, nor
that writers in the East condemn a communist régime as barbarous.
Writers on both sides are clearly anxious about the future, about
the encroachment of bureaucracy on private life, about the loss
of any sense of purpose for the individual, about the instincts
released in man immediately his spiritual sensitivity is dulled into
submission to any party line, and about the cruelty man has
recently shown himself capable of inflicting on his fellows. There
are signs that some writers are seeking a way out of the themes of
annihilation and the *memento mori* tradition and into a region
where the deepest concern is for man's way of life in what most
writers see will be an utterly changed world before the end of the
century. There is a sense of responsibility for maintaining and
looking for new stable values whilst rejecting anything that is
bound down to institutions of the past, which finds expression for
instance in the self-critical annual meetings of the Gruppe 47.
Ruthless albeit extempore criticism of the German language,
eroded on both sides by the influences of Eastern communist and
Western capitalist slogans, ensures that no new work is published
by its members that falls short of a certain standard. In theory this
could establish certain linguistic and stylistic values, but in practice

much is allowed to escape due to the difficulty of appreciating, let alone criticizing complex styles at a moment's notice. The Gruppe 47 has become, since it started as a small group of writers seeking for new values in the tabula rasa stage of the immediate post-war years, the most hotly debated literary institution in West Germany. At first condemned for its closed secretive nature, it is now censured for setting itself up as a literary clique. Its strength lies in its apparently independent political and spiritual atmosphere, its weakness in its image of a literary élite which it has done little to discourage. From the outside it looks a strangely German phenomenon, this serious-minded self-examination of expression, and it is by no means isolated. Various academies such as those at Mainz and Hamburg meet regularly and publish works that are supposed to represent the true German spirit, as often as not of little interest to the book trade. Alongside these has developed a proliferation of literary prizes awarded out of different motives and for different reasons by widely contrasting organizations. Most of them confer upon the prizewinners not only a suitable financial incentive to continue as *"freie Schriftsteller"*[3] but a certain cachet of showing particular qualities laid down by the adjudicators.

Many writers have used the work of the academies or the award of prizes as a means to independence, and there is now a marked anti-establishment vein running through the works of the younger generation. For some it is a natural antipathy towards a society ruled by the economics of free enterprise, for others a deep suspicion of the structures of the welfare state. There is a conscious attempt to hold apart the life of the individual and the life of the state expressed in various ways on both sides of the iron curtain. This deep-lying distrust feeds on a sense of duty sharpened by comments from outside and within imploring writers to engage art with the problems of the day. Whereas in general the older generation has steered clear of using the theme of Germany divided as a symbol for works on the human spirit, and has concerned itself more actively with the future of current institutions on both sides of the iron curtain, and man's response to older problems such as faith and guilt, materialism and inheritance, the younger generation is more directly concerned with the obvious problems of the day the political actualities, perhaps even the hope of reuniting a Germany freed from such elements they see to be keeping it apart.

The selection of writers in this volume includes no major dramatist, a feature that corresponds with a few exceptions to the situation in Germany today. For since the death of Brecht in 1956 the German stage has seen but few notable new plays. The names of Dürrenmatt and Frisch, both Swiss, and that of Fritz Hochwälder are the only ones of real consequence to have appeared.

Instead there have been a few sensational temporary successes that have aroused bitter controversy usually on account of their themes. Thus Martin Walser's *Eiche und Angora* and *Der schwarze Schwan*, or Peter Weiss' *Die Verfolgung und Ermordung Jean Paul Marats*. Undoubtedly *Der Stellvertreter* by Rolf Hochhuth with its vivid use of the theme of the responsibility of Pope Pius XII for recognizing the Nazi régime and doing little to prevent its terror against the Jews culminating in a scene representing Auschwitz caused the greatest furore in German literary life since the war. The theme rather than the play's formal literary expressiveness aroused bitter argument on all sides—a chapter that eminently succeeded if we consider the aim of literature to be provocative, but one that revealed a disturbing need for the extreme as suitable matter for theatre audiences. The rôle, or rather taking into account the development of "absurd" theatre, the non-rôle of theatre in modern Germany is a matter of great debate among all those in Germany most intimately concerned with the German theatre's future.

The need for extreme themes is partly explained by the feeling of living under the Damocles sword of a nuclear threat—most clearly shown in Dürrenmatt's *Die Physiker*—which treated as material for drama can make all else seem absurd. But more than this the rôle of the unexpected makes up a large part of the thematic structure and becomes the starting-point for the discussion of ethical and moral values. Such discussion makes stringent demands on the most commonly used literary forms. We find many writers, despairing of the memories of the past, have learnt and preach the lesson that twentieth century man must learn not to rely on established patterns. For established patterns, whether in political structures or in individual planning or in the use of cliché-ridden language, seem to rob the individual of free action. Too carefully worked-out casts of mind, suitable for answering the demands of the day in which they were formed, soon lose their validity and restrict the individual's ability to move with the times, or more important still to move if necessary against them. If reality moves, then so must man and the structures within which he lives. Thus much of contemporary German literature is an extended morality against the restrictive forces of pattern and habit. The processes by which these forces are fed are shown to be not only positive ways through which to comprehend the past and present, but also temptations if applied to the future. Thus the memory or "Erinnerung" process, thus the desire to look for forms and construct them where no forms really exist, thus the acceptance and continued use of jargon and cliché which eventually become so overloaded with meaning as to be incapable of distinguishing the individuality of any single event. There is in the traumatic drum-

ming of Günter Grass' Oskar Matzerath a pathetic reduction of
a human figure into an animal-like object, suppressed by the
taboos, conventionality and appeased acceptance of the world
around them by his family and associates. In the setting-up and
ruthless continuation of a personal myth by Böll's Heinrich Fähmel
—isolated from the possibility of unexpected events and from the
rise of nationalism and terror—the individual falls to the temptation of an artificially self-appointed reality that cannot and will
not move, and neglects to take on the responsibility of helping
others and reacting actively against encroaching evil. The insurance agent in Nossack's *Unmögliche Beweisaufnahme* can only find
his way out into a region of the *"Unversicherbare"*[4] by means of
an unexpected event. The freedom expressed in what André Gide
described as the *"acte gratuit"* is a freedom which to the contemporary German writer is more and more threatened—not solely
by external pressure but also by internal decay. The younger
writers while eager to learn from the immediate past are sensitive
to the fact that tomorrow's past is already with us and needs to
be fashioned by man responsible for all that goes on around him.

With the unexpected event forming an important ethical core
as a warning to overcome appeasement towards the everyday, the
current preference in German for writing Hörspiele and short
stories may be explained. The radio play can with the help of
technical sound devices explore a wider range of experience than
the more artificially formed opera or stage play. It is a form that
is relatively new, hence not bound down by tradition. In this way
it seems far less of a metaphor than a chronicle, is closer to
actuality than forms to which the reader or listener has deeply
trained and often automatic responses. It therefore retains an
element of the experimental, and allows for the treatment of, for
instance, a world after some great catastrophe in the future, or a
situation in which individual predicament can be set against a
far more calamitous background, or in which different levels of
dream and actuality can be brought together and interwoven.

The short story too can narrate a single event without necessarily giving it the artificiality of interpreted form, without the
writer imposing on the reader any symbolic structure, without
making the reader feel (as so often in a *Novelle*) that such an event
only makes sense in this form. The short story's content is closer to
actuality and further removed from art, is not the result of human
interpretative and patterning creation but set as it were at an
earlier stage in the process of comprehension and reaction. Indeed
many contemporary short stories contain within them the theme
of breaking down a myth and laying bare the truth in any event.
It is a form elastic enough to query the validity of the patterning

instinct in man, powerful enough to present the irrational as meaningful without the often erroneous aid of man trying to twist the expressions of irrational event into his rationally constructed but often in fact imaginarily constructed world.

This same concern to portray events or impressions as literally as possible without first translating them into the artificial or habitual framework of well-established literary forms, to portray 'the truth' rather than an image of the truth accounts for non-figurative experiments in lyrical poetry and extended use of all elements that point up the growing sense of disintegration in experience in the epic form, especially with inner monologue in the novel. There are not a few novels where continued emphasis on particular idiosyncracies or traumatic states of consciousness develop an aura of the grotesque that seems particularly well-suited to evoke the absurdity of contemporary life when the political balance of power is brought to mind. So many of the heroes of recent German literature have been outsiders, not just because they are social misfits, but because they still believe in seeking for some form of absolute meaning to life within a society that has learnt to live powerlessly unconcerned with the absurdity of the modern world. Few of these have any transcendental belief —the ugliness in their past and the indifference of ideological struggle towards the individual has seen to that. And so one is tempted to see most contemporary German writers as opposed to the ways of life of their contemporaries. The best of them, however, are able to see through the static at times destructively negative use of such writing, parody their own anger, and instead continue to ask constructive leading questions of man and contemporary institutions. Perhaps for the first time in German literature we may speak of an age where all writers in their sincerest moments are trying by denying the worst of traditional restrictions and values to lay the ground for a revival of humane principles based on accepting the right of each individual to believe in and live out his own separate and not necessarily conformative way of life. Much that we read in German today is based on the use of shock techniques—one essential need if we are to understand them is to consider them as having a positive often didactic purpose to open up the mind to a less rigidly cast attitude towards not just life but literary values as well.

Out of the dichotomies of history and experience seen in Germany today is growing a literature whose major emphasis is not one of withdrawal into a spiritual realm consciously opposed to the driving forces of materialist or totalitarian societies, but rather one that has accepted the responsibility of engaging itself as a champion of freedom within those societies. It is a literature made

for the individual and not the mass, though it is as never before
read by the mass but with as yet vastly differing reactions. That
such a literature should exist and express itself with the vigour
exemplified by the authors who are presented in this volume raises
the hope that the German spirit will not be doomed either to
memories of the past or to subservience to the political ideologies
of the present and future.

TRANSLATIONS

1. The industrialization of consciousness.
2. Reality lies always a bit further than actuality: to hit a bird in
flight, one must shoot in front of him: for this one must know the speed
of the bird and that of the shot, together with countless other imponder-
ables: the wind and barometric pressure, things which can be worked out,
and if the calculation is wrong, the bird will fly off into the distance
where the shot cannot reach him. Reality also moves.
3. Independent writers.
4. Unassurable.

Wilhelm Lehmann

Wilhelm Lehmann

by DAVID A. SCRASE

(University of Zürich)

The first 24 years of Wilhelm Lehmann's life are described in the auto-biographical tract *Mühe des Anfangs*. He was born of North German parents in Puerto Cabello, Venezuela in 1882. At the age of three his Mother took him back to Germany where they settled in Wandsbek near Hamburg, then still a country village. His schooldays became ever more irksome and painful, although he was by no means a bad pupil. His passion from the very first was the natural world; he kept an assortment of animals and birds in the attic, and spent most of his free time in the garden and in the surrounding fields and woods. Not without difficulty he matriculated and went to university, first Tübingen, then Strasbourg, Berlin and finally Kiel, where he studied English and French, but spent much time on botany and natural history in general. In Berlin he met and became a close friend of Moritz Heimann. At Kiel he fell in love with and married Martha Wohlstadt, some fifteen years his senior. He began teaching at a private school in Mecklenburg, where the villagers treated him with scant respect and even open hostility. His relations with his mother, never very good, became even more strained on his marriage, and a most unhappy period of his life ended in complete tragedy when his first child died.

Lehmann later taught at the progressive Freie Schulgemeinde Wickers-dorf, at the Landschulheim Holzminden and at the Gymnasium in Eckernförde where he lives today. He served in the First World War and spent some of it in a British prisoner of war camp. During the thirties Lehmann was regarded with hostility by the authorities, refusing either to conform, join the party, or give up his Jewish friends. However he did not flee the country, nor were his works officially proscribed.

O N April 1st, 1932 Lehmann wrote in his *Bukolisches Tage-buch*:

"Alles in der Natur ist zugleich einfach und vielfach." [1]

We might, in fact, say the same of Lehmann. His vocabulary alone often makes for certain difficulties. What of the word *Lazerte*? What exactly is the *Schwalbenwurz* or the *Tazette*, and who was *Ceridwen* or *Makarie*? A poem like *Traumleib der Wärme* (from the group *Nördlicher Juli* in the book *Antwort des Schweigens*) remains obscure until certain facets of the poet's philosophy of life and art are known. Many other poems require specialized know-ledge before one can begin to appreciate them. Lehmann's know-ledge of natural history is so great that he often feels compelled to add a note so the reader can get through the poem without having to search through a flora or fauna first. From a note we learn that the *Tazette* is a kind of narcissus, and that the word derives from the Italian *tazza* meaning cup. A quotation from Goethe's *Wilhelm Meisters Wanderjahre* tells us who Makarie was, and, more important, her particular relevance for Lehmann. If we know our Latin we can be fairly sure that the *Lazerte* is a lizard, but no note helps us here. For most people, in fact, the notes are not comprehensive enough; although, if we delve deeply enough into the prose works, we find many explanations of not only words and phrases but also whole poems.

This brings us to the more simple side of Lehmann as a poet. Throughout his essays we find his basic poetic philosophy, his philosophy of life and his method of working emphasised again and again. In his essays and other prose works explanations of certain aspects of his work, of basic ideas are given, and, as already mentioned, even of whole poems. One cannot begin to understand Lehmann the poet from his poetry alone, but much more easily once one looks at his work as a whole.

In one short sentence of the essay *Gedicht als Tatsache* we find the quintessence of Lehmann's poetic philosophy :

"Den wahren Dichter kennzeichnet seine enge Beziehung zu den Phänomenen und seine Ueberzeugung vom Können der Sprache." [2]

The poet must form an intimate relationship with the natural world and must be able to use language to express both what he sees and what he experiences in his contact with nature. In *Sprache als Ereignis*, a speech held on the occasion of the 90th anniversary of the Matthius-Claudius Gymnasium at Wandsbek (Lehmann's old school), Lehmann discusses the origin of poems :

"Woher kommen Gedichte? Aus den unzähligen Zeiten des Gelebten, aus den Abertausenden von Kammern und Zellen des Durchempfundenen. In meinem Falle überwiegend aus dem ergreifend-ergriffenen Gefühl sinnlicher Phänomene. Es gibt eine produktive Aneignung durch blosses Sehen. Meine Gedichte sind Taten meiner Augen." [3]

Again we have the insistence on natural phenomena as felt and experienced by the poet. It is important to note the emphasis put on seeing. For Lehmann the eyes are much more important than the mind or the imagination. The poet's task is to see first, and then to describe without delving into inner meanings. From this it will be seen that Lehmann prefers the simile to the metaphor. And

in his poetry the symbol is of secondary importance, the actual
picture produced being of prime importance.

In *Eroberung des Lyrischen Gedichts* Lehmann writes :

> "Verzücktem Hinsehen entspringt mein Gedicht. Es würde sich
> verflüchtigen ohne den Rückhalt des unmittelbar Sichtlichen.
> Kunst ohne Körper ist ein Unbegriff; ein nicht denkender Dich-
> ter ist nicht denkbar, aber ein nur gedachtes Gedicht ist keins . . .
> Mein Gedichte verdanke ich fast alle meinem Blick, dem mit
> meinen leiblichen Augen Geschauten." [4]

Here he is, in fact, talking about his poem *Übern Deich*, but the
same is true of all his poems. Nowhere do we find any sort of abstraction in Lehmann's works : for him it has no place in poetry
at all—"Abstraktion und Utopie sind die Feinde der Dichtung." [5]

In order to avoid any kind of abstraction by referring to the
world of natural phenomena simply as nature, Lehmann insists
that any celebration of nature must take an individual and specialized form. One should not try to describe the cosmos, but instead
what it contains. As he puts it in the essay *Dichtung und Dichter
Heute* :

> "Es braucht in der Tat Erfahrung, um zu merken, dass man
> eines Ganzen nur teilhaftig wird, wenn man eines Teiles sich
> bemächtigt, dass das All nur als ein Etwas sich beschwören lässt
> und Gott und die Welt nur auf den Zuruf geheim bestimmter,
> sorgsam geplanter Silben erscheinen." [6]

This aspect of Lehmann's poetic philosophy is basic for his poetry.
Indeed, he insists, it is basic for all poetry and all time :

> "Ein Literaturhistoriker meint, den Leser des zwanzigsten Jahr-
> hunderts interessierten im Gegensatz zu dem des achtzehnten
> Verallgemeinerungen nicht, sondern ihn hungere nach dem Par-
> tikulären. Dieser Hunger aber hat weniger mit Jahrhunderten
> zu tun als mit dem Wesen des Dichterischen. Der Dichter, wo
> und wann immer, schlägt Obst aus, ihn verlangt nach Kir-
> schen . . . Das Paradoxon, immer das Siegel der Wahrheit, ge-
> schieht : je lokaler, je persönlicher ein Gedicht, desto universaler
> wirkt es." [7]

In the same essay we find :

> "Des Totalerlebnisses werden wir nur mittels des Einzelerleb-
> nisses inne." [8]

The poem *Etwas*, written between 1955–57 both states the theory
and exemplifies it. In the middle of a description of the scene we
find the line :

"Dieses Etwas sei mir alles!"

At this point we must examine the ideas behind the words *Etwas* and *All* a little more closely.[10] The *Etwas* represents one particular natural phenomenon or a specific aspect of creation or the natural world.

The *All*, which in Lehmann's poetry is always represented by the *Etwas*, is often expressed by the words *Sein*, *Weltall* and sometimes *Wesen*. It refers to the world of natural things, to the cosmos, the universe, to being or to the ordered yet mysterious sphere of existence. Everything is ordered because of the cycle of being— birth, life and creation or procreation, death. At death one is absorbed back into the *All*. Similarly the continuance of seasonal change and the procreative cycle is indicative of order. The mystery is not so much why we exist, or how, or who is the prime mover behind it all. Rather it is the fact that man finds it so much more difficult to accept things and simply exist as animals and plants do. Oneness with the world of plants and animals, oneness with the *All* is the aim of the poet. If he achieves this aim then all is ecstasy and timelessness.

If he does not achieve communion with the *All* then he falls into despair. He is then threatened by what Lehmann usually calls the *Nichts* or the *Oede*. This represents the realm of hopelessness, loneliness and barrenness, of being cut off from natural phenomena. The complementary antithesis of communion with the *All*, in fact. It should be noted that man himself, or more specifically the poet, has to make an effort to achieve contact with the *All*. The *All* itself merely exists, is there, and does not concern itself with anything else or any being. Animals and plants are in a permanent state of innocent and natural ecstasy. Further we should not confuse the word *All* with the word *alles*, which merely means everything and may, on occasions (as in the quotation above from the poem *Etwas*), be used with the word *Etwas*. An extract from Lehmann's *Bukolisches Tagebuch*, written on June 15th, 1928, demonstrates how these words may be used in close juxtaposition and also introduces us to the *Nichts*:

"Was man 'Alles' heisst, ist dem 'Nichts' sehr nahe. In der Mitte schwebt das 'Etwas'—im 'Etwas' schwebt das Ganze, wie die ganze Natur in einer einzigen Pflanze, in einem einzigen Tier gegenwärtig ist. Das Etwas trägt wie jene Schildkröte der Inder das Weltall. Der Name aber eines solchen Etwas ist nach uraltem Glauben seine tatsächliche Existenz. Was nicht benannt war, konnte nicht sein. Ein altes Gedicht beginnt: 'Als in der Höhe die Himmel noch nicht benannt waren.' Allah ist die 'Wesenheit' Gottes'. Sie ist unverständlich; damit sie verständlich werde, muss Gott andere Namen haben. Bei den Aegyptern hat er ihrer neunundneunzig—einer, der hunderste, ist verborgen. Ihn kannte König Salomo und war darum der Weise.

Und darum bin ich namengierig. . . ." [11]

What Lehmann is stressing here, is that anything without a name, in other words what one may loosely term *Alles* or everything, has no identity and therefore no meaning. And anything without meaning belongs to the realm of hopelessness—of the *Nichts*. Hence it is of utmost importance to the poet to be able to put a name to what he sees.

We now come back to the importance of language for Lehmann. He often points out that plant names and sometimes those of animals tend to be apt. Somehow, sometime in the past the fitting name of *Shepherd's Purse* was found (German : Hirtentäschelkraut). Somebody must have looked carefully and imaginatively, or perhaps thoughtfully, at this plant and noted that the seed containers looked very much like a shepherd's purse. The name was there. Watching a snipe in flight Lehmann hears and explains the peculiar noise resulting from air passing through the tail feathers

"Gut hat wahrlich zugehört, wer die Schnepfe 'Himmelsziege' getauft hat." [12]

(*Bukolisches Tagebuch*, April 12th, 1931.)

Lehmann is at pains to point out that no one individual coined such words :

"Stumm im Wundern über ihre Gestaltung, kann ich den Gaukelnden nicht die Reverenz erweisen, sie mit Namen anzureden. Ich weiss sie nicht. Und ich tue mir nichts zugute darauf, dass ich weiss, dass ich sie nicht weiss. Nein, ich möchte sie alle wissen, alle 'bestimmen'. Denn die richtigen Namen gehören zum Wesen, nicht der Einzelne schuf sie in schnellem Einfall, die Welt dichtete sie." [13]

The essence of the being itself always gave rise to the name, which evolved over a period of time. Once the name is there the essence of the named object is perceived : and by perceiving it the namer has taken a step in the direction of communion with the *All* through a relationship with the *Etwas*, namely with whatever has been named.

The poet cannot, of course, name natural phenomena now, since the best name has already been found. So his task is to find new phrases and descriptions which are peculiarly apt. In Lehmann's poetry we find a wealth of images—often similes—which are new and fitting :

> So lass uns weiter fliehn,
> Mit runden Schulterknochen
> Wie Eichelhäher ziehn.
> *(Lied des alternden Weingott.)*

> Weinbeerengross
> Schwoll der Leib der Spinne,
> Und mitteninne
> Weinte ich.
> *(Letzter Abend.)*

> Die Karpfen schwimmen sanft umblaut,
> Als hülle sie der Pflaume Haut.
> *(Heisser Herbstabend.)*

> Die Tulpen reichen Urnen,
> Den Sommer einzusargen,
> *(Nachfeier.)*[14]

The prose works too yield numerous examples :

> Er [der Tag] blies die Schatten von den Steinen, so dass sie jung
> und roh wie eben geworfene Hasen lagen.
> *(Der Ueberläufer.)*

> Auf den Telefondrähten reihen sich, wie Notenköpfe auf Linien,
> die Schwalben.
> *(Bukolisches Tagebuch,* September 24th, 1930.)

> Durchdringendes Geschrei der Mauersegler, die gleich eisen-
> farbenen Sicheln um die Türme des Herrenhauses sausten....
> *(Der Provinzlärm.)*[15]

Having established a broad basis of Lehmann's poetic philosophy
we should now examine certain poems and prose works to see more
precisely how he puts this philosophy into action.

In order to achieve communion with the *All* the poet allows
himself to be taken into the realm of nature by means of a kind
of ecstatic trance or dream. This dream only lasts for a short
time during which the passage of time is suspended, but it can be
caught and celebrated in the poem :

> Ich wanderte in die Wesen aus,
> Sie litten mich traumeslang.
> Dann riegelten sie das ängstliche Haus.
>   Wie Zikadenschaum
>   Vertrocknet der Traum—
> Er dauert nur im Gesang.
> *(Uber die Stoppeln.)*

The same idea is expressed in the poem *Zu Zweien* :

> Zuströmendes Licht, wie geselht,
> Weisser Septemberschimmer.
> Zeit, entgehe der Zeit,
> Werde, Augenblick, Immer!

and in *Tiefer Augenblick* :

> Fliege summt und Wasser schätzt,
> Ammer, die den Schnabel wetzt :
> Sagt den Spruch mir, der euch, feit.
> Stille, still, es schläft die Zeit.
> Bleibe, tiefer Augenblick![16]

The poet can allow himself to be taken into this realm by identifying himself with some being. This is the significance of "Ich wanderte in die Wesen aus". Earlier in the same poem the poet tells how he flew through the air astride a flock of partridges :

> Zwölf Rebhühner flogen, als flöge der Lehm—
> Ich bin auf ihrem Nacken geritten.[17]

and in *Reisezeit der Mauersegler* he describes a mythical journey made on a flight with some swifts. After the bliss of such identification with the animal world, however, the troubled existence of mankind is always waiting for the poet's return :

> Ich musste zurück in die Mühsalgestalt,
> Im Ohr die heiligen Lieder.
> Aus dem Gewölk, um die Sonne geballt,
> Fiel eine Feder nieder.[18]

If one offers oneself up to nature identification and contact with it is not always completely onesided. One can be accepted by the particular being, or at least not spurned by it. Astonished, and yet proud, Lehmann tells in his *Bukolisches Tagebuch* how a butterfly fresh from the chrysalis creeps on to his hand.

> In der warmen Hand schlüpft ein Männchen mit dichter Behaarung und russschwarzen Flügelläppchen aus und schwirrt wie toll darauf umher. So fühlte sich das Wesen der Natur der Menschenhand nicht ganz fremd.
>
> (July 2nd, 1930.)[19]

The best set of circumstances for the poet to give himself up to his ecstatic dreams are to be found alone in nature, in stillness and in great heat. Complete stillness is a miracle of creation :

> Wer daran denkt, dass wir Menschenkinder auf einer Kugel

hausen, die durch den unendlichen Raum kreist, wird sich mit
Lichtenberg nicht darüber wundern, dass der Wind über die
Erde geht, wohl aber, dass je Windstille bei uns gedeihen kann.
(*Bukolisches Tagebuch*, October 16th, 1927.)[20]

Not surprisingly, we learn from an essay, *Der Platz, an dem ich
schreibe*, that all Lehmann's works stem from outside :

Alle meine Schriften sind unter freiem Himmel entstanden. . . .
Wenn Schreiben Verfassen bedeutet, ist daher der Platz, an dem
ich schreibe, das Draussen, zumeist unter norddeutschem,
genauer schleswig-holsteinischem, aber auch unter italienischem,
südfranzösischem, dalmatischem, irischem Himmel.[21]

To praise existence is to praise continuance because only through
continuance does anything exist. So we find Lehmann praising
not so much creation as procreation. The actual moment of procreation represents the closest contact one can obtain with the *All*.
To recognize the procreative act in plants and animals is to be
part of it, and to celebrate it in the poem is the poet's way of capturing the sacred moment and re-living it.

Much that is typical of Lehmann's poetry is contained in the
poem *Rosen im Mittagsbrande* :

Der hundertfältige Leib
Blüht auf zur grossen Stunde,
Die mit dem luftigen Munde
Im Wohlgeruch der Glieder wühlt.
Der heisse Buhle nimmt
Die Schönen, bang gekrümmt,
Die Narbe schauert wie ein Weib.

Verschliesst euch denn der Macht
Des grausam weichen Stosses,
Der nach des holden Schosses
Goldbrauner Mitte zielt.

Sie aber folgen lüstern
Den sinkenden Geschwistern—
Um meine Füsse spielt
Der Leichen bunte Pracht.[22]

The vaguely scientific designation of the rose as "der hundertfältige
Leib"—the actual term is *rosa centifolia*—would perhaps confuse
many readers. Likewise the term "Narbe" would not be clear to
everybody at first. The use of erotic words or words erotic in their
connotation like *Leib*, *Mund*, *Buhle*, *Weib*, *Schoss* and *lüstern*

creates the appropriate atmosphere. The sun, at the time of
greatest heat—("*zur grossen Stunde*", or "*Im Mittagsbrande*")—is
the lover who lecherously takes the beautiful roses. The roses cannot resist his might and give in to the love act. And at the poet's
feet are the dead bodies of those roses which have already given
in. The application of the human term *Schoss* to the rose occurs
in other poems by Lehmann, and is also used for other natural
phenomena and the earth in general. Not stated in the poem, but
implicit because of other poems, is that although the roses die they
do so of necessity so as to continue their species and with it existence. This thought is expressed in *Dunkelnde Buchenblätter*. This
time the wind is the seducer and the beech leaves lament that they
are already to lose their youth. But why should they lament?

> Vergängnis schreckt? Lass dich vernichten.
> Die Söhne werden weiter dichten.[23]

The wind appears in the form of an erotic image on many
occasions, sometimes referred to as the *Windgott*, suggesting that
the wind is often responsible for pollination or for distributing the
seeds. The wind is often personified in human terms:

> Im Laube seh ich kramen
> Den Wind, die Eschensamen
> Vorsichtig heben seine Hand,
> Die grünen Troddeln drehn.
> (*Auf den Abgeernteten Feldern.*)

> Er, der Wind, strich durchs All auf flinken Zehn,
> Der Schönheit ins Gesicht zu sehn;
> Vom Rosenbusch, schon herbstgedrückt,
> Hat er den letzten Duft gepflückt.
> (*Spätsommer.*)[24]

The determining factor of the wind in the seasonal rhythm and
in procreation is to be seen in such poems as *Wechsel der Weise*
and *Der Bund*.

Apart from the wind another important determining factor in
procreation and in the world of natural phenomena is a figure
whom Lehmann calls *Merlin*. Merlin is the guiding force and
inspiration *in* rather than behind existence or the *Weltall*. In the
poem *Merlin* he is represented by the cuckoo and this is his usual
guise. But wherever a personification of the creative force within
the world is needed Merlin appears in whatever guise is most
fitting, or perhaps in no particular guise at all being then simply
a symbol:

> Dem Kuckucksweibchen ist das Ei
> Im federleichten Schoss gediehn.
> Wer war der Vogelbräutigam?
> Der schwebende Merlin.[25]

In the natural world there is a time for procreation based on the rhythm of the seasons, which are therefore of great importance to Lehmann. Not surprisingly spring represents the awakening of creative urges. The magpie, which in the early book of poems *Antwort des Schweigens* seems to have some sort of significance and rôle approaching that of Merlin in the others (particularly in *Der Grüne Gott*), sits on her nest :

> Gelockt von der Elster, brüten die Lüfte
> Und schmeicheln
> Verstockten Eckern, gefrorenen Eicheln
> Wurzelhaare, Blättermund ab :
> Prospero entsinnt sich immer,
> Nie verliert er seinen Stab.
>
> (*Windiger Februar.*)[26]

Late spring and early summer see these urges brought to their climax and satisfied. The summer solstice plays a significant part here. The sun, an all-important factor, rises to its climax and causes fruition, as we saw in *Rosen im Mittagsbrande*. Thereafter its power decreases and the creative activity of the natural world declines. The poem *Sonnenwende* shows this climax. The climax of fruition has been reached and everything is resting after the great exertion required :

> Mir deucht die Wasserprimel blass
> Von langen Tages langem Kuss.

Likewise the late poem *Genüge* :

> Zwar glühen noch die Essen
> Der Kapuzinerkressen—
> Doch süchtig, auszuruhn
> Von langem Sommertun.[27]

This resting continues through late summer and into autumn, but as autumn comes everything dies down, apart from occasional late bursts of activity. Winter is the time of apparent lifelessness and is the time when the *Nichts* or the *Oede* gains the upper hand. Sometimes, particularly in early poems, it is too much for the poet who is plunged into the depths of despair :

> Stoppeln starren wie ein schlecht gerupfter Hühnerleib.
> Keine Stimme hör ich trösten : "Bleib !"

Schmatzend haben sich die Grabenlippen satt getrunken.
Da ihr letztes Wort verrann
Oben ist und unten nichts mehr, was mir helfen kann.
                              (*Verzweiflung im März.*)[28]

Usually there is some alleviating hope, however. Being is not
dead in winter but merely asleep waiting for the spring and
summer when existence will once more be gloriously renewed. It
is being stored up in *"weiser Ohnmacht"*[29] for another time, as
Lehmann puts it in the poem *Im Winter zu singen. Kanzone im
Januar* begins :

> Gebot der Träume :
> Leg an die Rinde das Ohr,
> Es zischt
> der Saft,
> Es lauben die Bäume
> Mit grünem Taft.[30]

A fine poem, *Ahnung im Januar*, is explicit :

> Münchhausens Horn ist aufgetaut,
> Zerbrochene Gefangenschaft!
> Erstarrter Ton wird leise laut,
> In Holz und Stengel treibt der Saft.
>
> Dem Anruf als ein Widerhall,
> Aus Lehmesklumpen, eisig, kahl,
> Steigt Ammernleib, ein Federball
> Schon viele Male, erstes Mal.
>
> Ob Juniluft den Stier umblaut,
> Den Winterstall ein Wald durchlaubt?
> Ist es Europa, die ihn kraut?
> Leicht richtet er das schwere Haupt.
>
> So warmen Fusses, Sommergeist,
> Dass unter dir das Eis zerreisst—
> Verheissung, und schon brenne ich,
> Erfüllung, wie ertrag ich dich?[31]

Just as the coachman's horn in one of Münchhausen's tales released all the melodies which had been stored up in the extreme
cold upon being warmed in front of the fire, so the sap is beginning to rise, even in January, in preparation for the summer's
task. The bunting rises into the air again as it has done since time

began. But each time it is like the first, and the bunting behaves with the same rapture. The approach of spring makes the bull restless. In a rather different slant on the myth Lehmann asks whether it is Europe who is scratching him. The promise of the spirit of summer causes all this warmth and stir. Already the poet can scarcely stand it. What will it be like when fulfilment replaces the promise?

As has often been pointed out, Lehmann's novels and stories are really poetic self-confessions. Almost all are to some extent autobiographical—some blatantly so—and all contain references to Lehmann's poetic ideas or put such ideas into practice. The hero, in some ways a sort of anti-hero, is usually a character who can be likened to Lehmann himself, like Nuch in *Der Überläufer*. He finds comfort and consolation in nature and is otherwise oppressed and beset by the *Nichts*. Sometimes a whole man in the Lehmann sense appears. Such a man is Felfer in *Der Provinzlärm*, written in the thirties but not published until 1953 under the title *Ruhm des Daseins*. Felfer does not have to make any effort to attain union with the *All*. He is at all times serene and content and not threatened by the *Nichts*. His strange serenity works on others, and not least on Asbahr, the Lehmann-like hero, who finds solace in nature, but is otherwise oppressed by the *Nichts*. Felfer is complete in himself. Of him we read :

> Er brauchte nicht kreuz und quer mit Kopfschmerzen und Schweiss nach der Tür zu suchen, die zur Welt führte, und bang an ihr zu rütteln, sondern die Welt kam zu ihm, suchte ihn wie der Vogel einen geeigneten Nistplatz.[32]

Felfer tolerates the petty, gossiping, provincial life both in the school and in the small town where the novel is set—without even trying. He is almost god-like. His female counterpart in the same novel is Regine Tümema. Significantly Felfer is too much for this world and he is often sinned against. Finally he is dismissed from his post at school and sent to a remote village—to a school for maladjusted children.

Der Überläufer, written in the years 1925–27 but first published in the *Sämtliche Werke* in 1962 and as a separate book in 1964, is a monumental work taking the form of a story within a framework. The story within the framework is of Nuch whose childhood corresponds strikingly to Lehmann's. Nuch's second marriage to Dina Heerbrandt is a great success until after the First World War in which he is finally forced to take part. The experience is shattering and after once running away only to be packed off to the front again, Nuch finally runs over to the enemy and gives himself up. On his return after the war Nuch finds great difficulty in settling down to normal life again. Even Dina cannot help him as she used to. Nature is his only solace. He leaves Dina and becomes accepted as a sort of eccentric by a small community whose life revolves round a large country house. Nuch forms a strange relationship with the retiring old Landgrave, reading to him. Soon these readings are made public and are usually given with great success. Finally, against his will, he gets involved in a "triangle" with his best friend Thiessen and Jutta Hoschander. In an ecstatic frenzy Nuch makes a fantastic journey, ending, as we must assume from the framework introduction, with his death.

Throughout the novel we find the poem *An meinen Sohn*, which appears in the poems as *An meinen ältesten Sohn*, introduced and discussed, a justification of the use of nature images and frequent excursions into the natural world and attempts by Nuch at communion with it. The origin and the content of the poem *Traumleib der Wärme* is given and Nuch explains "his" philosophy of the *Letzte* and the *Vorletzte* which is also contained in the poem *Das Vorletzte*. There are countless references to basic nature images and finally a first-rate description from a soldier's point of view of the First World War and particularly of its effect on the sensitive Nuch.

None of the other novels or stories quite rises to the heights of *Der Überläufer* but the basic thread of Lehmann's ideas can be traced in them all. His essays show an intense love of the natural world and of the poetic word, as well as his fascination for myth, which represents for him the *eternal present*. There are essays on Storm, Arnim and Brentano, Fouqué, Elisabeth Langgässer and above all his great friend Oskar Loerke. His *Bukolisches Tagebuch* records his thoughts on every aspect of the natural world and the daily happenings of nature as seen through the poet's eyes. And his *Mühe des Anfangs* movingly describes the first years, both idyllically pleasant and bitterly tragic, of his life.

At the end of *Der Überläufer* the narrator of Nuch's story is gratified to think that his one listener has been patient and concerned enough to listen to something which was really quite foreign to her :

> Er war es zufrieden, dass sie mit ihm zusammen sich über ein ihrer Welt fremdes, vielleicht doch nicht ganz fremdes Schicksal gebückt und in der Himmelshölle des ewigen Wagnisses gehangen hatte.[33]

Lehmann himself would be gratified if more people who think that his world is not theirs were to apply themselves to his work.

They would then find out that his poetry is not quite so foreign to their world as they at first thought.

TRANSLATIONS

1. Everything in nature is at the same time simple and complex.

2. The true poet can be singled out by his close connection with natural phenomena and his belief in the power of language.

3. Where do poems come from? From experiences in and at all times, from the many thousands of chambers and cells of what has been perceived. In my case from the feeling, which is both gripping and which grips one, of and for perceptible phenomena. A creative and fruitful change takes place through mere looking. My poems are "deeds" of my eyes.

4. My poem springs from ecstatic observation. It would vanish were it not for the directly visible. Art without substance is an impossible conception; an unthinking poet is unthinkable, but a poem which is merely thought out is not a poem at all.... I owe practically all my poems to my sight, to what I see with my corporeal eyes.

5. Abstraction and Utopia are the enemies of poetry.

6. Indeed it needs experience to realize that one can only share in the whole if one takes possession of a part of it, to realize that the *All* can only be conjured up as an *Etwas*, and that God and the world only appear to the summons of mysteriously definite, carefully planned syllables.

7. A literary historian thinks that generalizations do not interest the reader of the twentieth century as opposed to the reader of eighteenth. Rather is he hungry for the particular. This hunger, however, has less to do with centuries than with the essence of the poetic. The poet, no matter when or where, declines fruit; he desires cherries.... Here we have the paradox—always the mark of truth: the more specific, the more personal the poem, the more universal its effect.

8. We can only become aware of the full experience by means of the single experience.

9. Let this something be everything for me.

10. Since the words *All* and *Etwas*, *Nichts* and *Öde* in the way Lehmann uses them are impossible to translate into single words in English, no translation for these is given. Where *Alles* is used to mean simply "everything" there is also no translation given.

11. What one calls *Alles* is very near to the *Nichts*. The *Etwas* hovers in between, and the whole hovers in the *Etwas* just as the whole of nature is present in a single plant or a single animal. The *Etwas*, like that tortoise of the Indians, carries the *Weltall*. The name of such an *Etwas*, however, is according to very ancient belief its actual and essential existence. Whatever was not named could not possibly *be*. An old poem begins: "At a time when the heavens in the heights were not yet named."

• •

Allah is the essence of God. This essence is incomprehensible, and in order that it can be understood God must have other names. In ancient Egypt he had 99 of them—one, the hundredth was hidden. King Solomon knew it and was for this reason named the wise. . . . And for this reason I am greedy for names.

12. The person who christened the snipe "goat of the sky" had really listened hard.

13. Dumb in admiration for their form I cannot pay the fluttering butterflies the respect of addressing them by their names. I do not know them. And I cannot pride myself on the fact that I know and can admit that I do not know their names. No, I should like to know them all, to be able to *determine* them. For the right names *belong* to the being; they were not coined by an individual in a moment of inspiration but composed by the world.

14. So let us continue to flee with round shoulders just as the jay does.

The body of the spider swelled up as large as a grape and inside it, right in the middle of it, I wept.

The carp swim in a soft aura of blue as if they were veiled in the skin of a plum.

The tulips reach out with urns to preserve the remains of summer.

15. The day blew the shadows from the stones so that they lay young and raw like new born leverets.

The swallows line up on the telephone wires like notes on a stave.

The penetrating cry of the swifts which whirled round the towers of the manor house like iron coloured sickles. . . .

16. I wandered out into creation which tolerated me for the length of a dream. Then it nervously barred its house. The dream dries like cuckoo-spit—it lasts only in poetry.

Streaming light, as if run through a sieve, the white gleam of September. O Time, escape from time, and let the moment become Always.

The fly hums, and the water purls and the bunting whets its bill: tell me the saying which charms you. . . . Quiet! quiet, time is sleeping. Remain profound moment.

17. Twelve partridges flew by like clods of loamy earth—I rode on their necks.

18. I had to return to my old toilsome form with the holy music in my ears. From the clouds clustered round the sun, a feather fell down.

19. A male, covered with thick hair and with small wings as black as soot, slipped out into my warm hand and whirred about as if mad. So the creature of nature did not find the human hand wholly foreign to it.

20. Whoever stops to think that we men live on a sphere which is revolving in infinite space will not marvel that wind can pass over the earth's surface, as Lichtenberg did, but that complete calm can ever manage to exist.

21. All my works originate in the open air. . . . If writing means to compose, then the place where I write is outdoors, mostly under the North German sky, or more precisely the Schleswig-Holstein sky, but under the Italian, Southern French, Dalmatian and Irish sky as well.

22.   *Roses in the Midday Heat*
The body, centifoliate, blossoms towards the great hour, which, with airy mouth, lecherously grubs about amongst the fragrant limbs. The hot lover takes the beautiful ones, anxiously arched; the stigma shudders like a woman.
Withstand the power of the cruelly gentle thrust aimed at the golden brown centre of the lovely womb.
But lustfully they follow their sinking sisters—the colourful splendour of the corpses plays at my feet.

23. Transcience frightens you? Allow yourselves to be destroyed. Your sons will continue the poetry.

24. I see the wind rooting about in the foliage; I see his hand carefully lift the seeds of the ash tree and turn the green tassels.
It (i.e. the wind) gently passes through the *All* on nimble toes to look beauty in the face. It has plucked the last fragrance from the rose bush which is already depressed by autumn.

25. The egg is growing in the hen cuckoo's womb which is as light as a feather. Who was the mate? It was soaring Merlin.

26. Enticed by the magpie the breezes warm and coax the root hairs and buds from the hardened beech nuts and frozen acorns: Prospero always remembers and never loses his staff.

27. It seems to me that the water primula is pale from the long day's long kiss.
The fires of the nasturtium are indeed still glowing—but desirous of rest after the long summer performance.

28. The stubble bristles like the badly plucked body of a chicken. I hear no consoling voice: "Stay."
The smacking lips of death have sated their thirst. Since their last word persisted there is nothing more above or below that can help me.

29. In wise unconsciousness.

30. The command of dreams: put your ear to the bark, the sap is sizzling and the trees put on leaves of green taffeta.

31. Munchhausen's horn has thawed out and what was imprisoned has escaped. The frozen sound becomes softly louder and in trees and plant stems the sap begins to rise.
The bunting, a ball of feathers, soars up from icy clods of bare earth, an echo to the summons. Many times has it done so; each time was the first.
Does the blue sky of June surround the bull? Does a forest fill its winter stable with foliage? Is it Europe who is scratching it? Lightly it raises its heavy head.
The spirit of summer has such warm feet that, under them, the ice begins to crack—Mere promise, and already I am burning. How will I be able to bear fulfilment?

32. He did not need to sweat and get headaches looking all over the place for the door which led to the world and anxiously to rattle it, for the world came to him and sought him out, like the bird a suitable nesting place.

33. He was content that, in his company, she had submitted to a fate

foreign to her world—though perhaps not quite as foreign as all that. He was content that she had whiled in the heaven-hell of the eternal venture.

SELECT BIBLIOGRAPHY

Published works

All the poems and practically all the essays and other prose works are in the *Sämtliche Werke* (Three volumes). Sigbert Mohn Verlag, Gütersloh 1962.
All the poems with the exception of the book *Abschiedslust* (1962) are contained in *Meine Gedichtbücher*, Suhrkamp Verlag, Frankfurt am Main 1957. The essays are available in the following separate volumes:
Bewegliche Ordnung. Suhrkamp Verlag, Berlin and Frankfurt am Main 1956.
Dichtung als Dasein. Hermann Luchterhand Verlag, Darmstadt 1960.
Kunst des Gedichts. Insel Verlag, Frankfurt am Main 1961.
Dauer des Staunens. Sigbert Mohn Verlag, Gütersloh 1963.
Der Uberläufer is available as a single volume in the Sigbert Mohn Verlag, Gütersloh 1964.

Secondary literature

Bienek H. In: *Werkstattgespräche mit Schriftstellern.* Carl Hanser Vlg., Munich 1962.
Blöcker G. In: *Kritisches Lesebuch.* Leibniz Vlg., Hamburg 1962.
Bruns H. Wilhelm Lehmann. Sein Leben und Dichten, Eine Chronik. Mühlau, Kiel 1962.
Conrady K. O. Zu einem Gedicht Wilhelm Lehmanns (*Augusttag.*) In: Wirkendes Wort, Heft 5. Düsseldorf 1955.
Härtling P. Fabelzeit. In: *In Zeilen zuhaus.* Neske, Pfullingen 1957.
Hohoff C. Poeta Magus. In: *Geist und Ursprung.* Ehrenwirth, Munich 1954.
Kraft W. Wort und Gedanke. Francke Vlg., Berne 1959.
Krolow K. Dichtung als Tat eines Einzelnen. Zum Werk Wilhelm Lehmanns. In. *Merkur.* Stuttgart 1963 (17) (5).
Loerke O. In: *Gedichte und Prosa.* Vol 2. Suhrkamp Vlg., Frankfurt am Main 1958.
Prawer S. S. The Poetry of Wilhelm Lehmann: In: German Life and Letters. New Series. Vol. XV July 1962, No. 4.
Weber W. Zeit ohne Zeit. Suite zur Gegenwart. Manesse Vlg., Zürich 1959.

Hermann Kasack

Hermann Kasack

by WILLIAM F. MAINLAND
(University of Sheffield)

The son of a physician, Hermann Kasack was born in Potsdam on July 24th, 1896. From 1915 he studied German and Political Economy at the universities of Berlin and Munich. From 1920 to 1925 he was publisher's reader and eventually a director of the firm of Kiepenheuer, and from 1926 to 1927 he worked with the publisher S. Fischer. Subsequently he devoted himself to writing and broadcasting. The seizure of power by the National Socialists put a strict limitation upon his activities. From 1940 to 1949 he was reader for the publisher Suhrkamp. After the end of World War II he visited Belgium, England, Italy, Finland and the Soviets. In 1948 he helped to found the German PEN Club, and in 1953 was elected President of the German Academy of Language and Literature in Darmstadt. In 1960 he was awarded the Leo Tolstoy Medal of the Maxim Gorky Institute for World Literature in Moscow.

Proofs of this chapter reached me after the sad news of Hermann Kasack's death on January 10th, 1966.—W.F.M.

> Die Zeit verweht. Was uns geschah,
> Erhellen Worte. Ihre Grenzen
> Mag nun der Lesende ergänzen.
> (Kasack, *Wasserzeichen*)

IF it is true, as some assert, that a man's style of living takes its deepest imprint from his twenties, we may learn much about a writer by looking at works of others much discussed at this stage of his life. A German born in 1896, destined to write the most eagerly debated novel of the years immediately after World War II, could not escape the remarkable analysis of history which began to appear before the break-up of the German Empire in 1918 : *Der Untergang des Abendlandes*. Since darkness fell on the genius of Friedrich Nietzsche the German imagination had not been more seriously provoked than it was by this two-volume treatise, the work of an obscure teacher who laboured by candle-light in a wretched room in Munich to stir his contemporaries from their suicidal optimism. As some of us in England, under German tutorship, struggled to comprehend the "Faustian man" in his historical setting, Oswald Spengler's prophecies no doubt had more incisive effect on our contemporaries in Germany. Now we see late evidence of their persistence. Spengler wrote for example of the

"megalopolis" where people would live obediently on top of one
another, engaged in mechanical tasks. After the Second World
War in the series forecast by Spengler we found his vision brought
into sharp focus by a novelist who was young in those early days.
In Hermann Kasack's *Stadt hinter dem Strom* we read : "Nicht
nur die Seiten der einzelnen Räume des Geschäftshauses ... waren
durch verschiebbare Glaswände abgeteilt, sondern auch die Decken
und Fußböden bestanden aus durchsichtigem Glas ... Die Un-
sicherheit, keinen Halt zu sehen, verstärkte sich, als er nicht nur
neben, sondern über und unter sich Räume erblickte, in denen
Menschen und ihre Gegenstände wie Attrappen in der Luft
hingen." [1]

Der *Untergang des Abendlandes* was an epitaph on an epoch.
So also is *Die Stadt hinter dem Strom*. They were both composed,
as it were, by provident journalists, who anticipated the demise.
Like a famous character of English tradition, the epoch seems to
be an unconscionable time a-dying. But our experience of time is
determined only in part by calendar and clock. Kasack's novel is
a "Protokoll der Schrecksekunde" [2] of Robert Lindhoff's death.
Yet in it he records visual evidence of the present, and of the distant past; something of the cyclical conception of history, which
Spengler again helped to bring into focus, begins to emerge. In
Anna, with whom Robert is in love, and who has crossed the river
a short time before, recognition of resemblances between layers of
culture is already effective. She reveals to Robert at an early stage
repetitive patterns in the life of mankind—the "ewige Wiederkehr".

First clue to the setting is the title of the novel : the city beyond
the river. Ancient traditions have associated the crossing of water
with the onset of death. The reader is induced to think of this before Robert is aware of his state. Uncanny motifs are gently introduced into the pattern of an otherwise ordinary journey; and
Robert, as an archaeologist, has been especially interested in the
Babylonian story of Gilgamesh. There is no question of the
author's "taking the reader into his confidence" in the manner of
an old-style, comfortable, family story-teller. Kasack, like many
other writers of serious intent today, trusts the literary awareness
of his readers, even at the risk of being accused of copying a
technique. It may indeed help Kasack if, at an early stage, the
reader is induced to say : "This reminds me of Kafka."

Robert Lindhoff, on a train-journey, comes to the other side of
a river, and has to present his credentials at the Prefecture of the
town where he alights. The town seems like a place shattered by
earthquake or war. There are many underground dwellings, called
the catacombs—a reminder, perhaps a forecast, of air-raid shelters.

Certain activities puzzle Robert. A window with no panes is being cleaned by a woman as though the glass were still there. People are going through the movements of re-arranging their household possessions, yet no objects can be seen. A crowd gathers round two men engaged in barter; there is a brisk exchange of personal belongings, until finally everybody has regained his own. Such purposeless effort is Kasack's pre-figuration of what seems to be the ultimate futility of the city's twofold industry. One factory produces artificial stones, the other pulverizes them, and the powder is transported to the first factory to be made again into blocks. But this is only an apparent culmination. Drawn from the vicious circle of human industry, it is one of a series of symbols for the cyclic and compensatory activity of nature itself. Production and destruction are continuous, and some approach to balance is perceived. At times it is necessary to increase the rate of destruction, and the most impressive demonstration of this is the effect of war— the arrival of larger batches of young people, the pathetic procession of children, whose swift passage through the town contrasts with the static presence of soldiers of many generations, some wearing uniforms of long ago. When Robert asks an artist friend what sort of "world" this is, saying that it seems like Purgatory, Kastell, the artist, replies : "Je nun, es ist wohl ein Weg einer großen Reinigung—ein Zwischenreich, wie manche sagen, wo die Schlacken der Erde abfallen." [3]

In the bleakness of a Germany not yet addicted to the drug of economic miracles, Kasack presented the tragically familiar setting of a grey and broken city, where, with slow and steady resolve he faced the task of burning away the illusions by which the National Socialist régime had corroded the spirit of his fellow-countrymen. He needed all that his apprenticeship and later practice in writing could give. To appreciate his effort and achievement we must remember that Kasack is one of the many whom the fascist Ministry of Culture felt it necessary to suppress. But we must also remember that he had been subjected earlier to the rigorous training of a literary school propelled by bitter experience of change. Of this, the expressionist training, Gottfried Benn wrote in 1955 (see *Lyrik des expressionistischen Jahrzehnts,* DTV, Munich, 1962) : "Gerade der Expressionist erfuhr die sachliche Notwendigkeit, die die Handhabung der Kunst erfordert, ihr handwerkliches Ethos, die Moral der Form. Zucht will er, da er der Zersprengteste war." [4] From the lucid and mellow assurance of the later prose-works and the recently published lyrics it is not easy for us to go back and recognise known features in the younger Kasack who wrote *Der Abschied* :

Das Grauen Nacht erschlägt den Abendgang.
Die Leerheit des Gesprächs verschluchzt Gebärde.
Das dunkle Loch des Mundes hält den Schrei.
—so nimm mich hin!

Zerreiß die Straße, schatten Menschen um.

Ich stürze, schwert Geröll auf meinem Kopf.
Entflattern Hände mit dem Hut, der grüßt,
und noch im Traum versäumt sich dieses Schweben—
verstöhnt vor Maske; Haar zersträhnt Gesicht :
entsetzt, gejagt peitscht Körper irren Raum.[5]

Yet this was the fibre from which grew the admired economy of
Kasack's style; here he found the significance of gesture, discovered
the motif of the mask which was to recur with deeper significance
in his post-war novels. "Aufsprung ins Firmament" he wrote in
praise of Georg Heym : the dynamic of such a phrase remained
when Kasack found a quieter discipline. Beside the lines just quoted
we may set these, from the collection *Wasserzeichen* (1964) :

Die Flaggen gehn von Bord,
Der Atem schleift.
Der Kompaß zeigt nach Nord.
Das Herz begreift :

Mit dieser letzten Fahrt
Endet die Welt.
Der Tod wird Gegenwart.
Die Maske fällt.[6]

Der Tod wird Gegenwart—this is the experience of the pilgrim
Robert. Now death as present experience is also the content of
Hofmannsthal's first great dramatic poem *Der Tor und der Tod*
of 1893, which had brought its persuasive music into the formative years of Kasack's generation. Between the individualism of
the Austrian poet and that of the early Kasack of *Der Mensch*
(1918) there is great contrast :

. . .   Und dieses wußt ich,
Obgleich ich's nicht begreife, doch ich wußt es :
Das ist der Tod. Der ist Musik geworden,
Gewaltig sehnend, süß und dunkelglühend,
Verwandt der tiefsten Schwermut. Aber seltsam!
Ein namenloses Heimweh weinte lautlos
In meiner Seele nach dem Leben. . . .[7]

(Hofmannsthal, *Erlebnis*)

... seine Sehnen strafften sich zum Mann.
Er wußte dieses : Ich allein bin *Ich*.
Erkannte seine Dreiheit, sein : Ich bin. Ich will. Ich kann.
Und goß das Meer in seine Hand. Und taufte sich.[8]

(Kasack, *Das Meer*).

In the first is what may now seem melancholy *"ichselige Lyrik"*, in the other defiant confidence in the limitless potentiality of the self. Both may, with taunting memories, embarrass any reader who has shared the two moods in literary experience. He will perhaps free himself more easily from the bravado of Kasack's lines because they evoke the breezy satire of Büchner whose chuckle-headed king in *Leonce und Lena* (written in 1836) cries out in ecstasy as he makes the startling discovery : *"Ich bin ein Ich."* With Hofmannsthal it is much more difficult, for we may in reverence seek to protect the golden phrases when strident voices, within and without, proclaim that these are "Zeugnisse, die gerade durch die Qualität der künstlerischen Darstellung ein um so gefährlicheres Instrument bildeten, weil sie überholten Anschauungen Raum gewährten".[9] (*Die Stadt hinter dem Strom*). The words quoted are an unmistakable mocking echo of the arrogant anti-decadent campaign of the Nazis (which is again inevitably finding brash support in the 1960s). That Death has "become" music. In Hofmannsthal's poem contrasts strongly with the representation of it in Kasack's city. The musician who comes to Robert begging that one of his compositions may be performed finds that he can no longer give expression to the music in his head. The power has left him, for music does not belong here. The Prefecture concedes that there *is* a kind of music, but it is the mathematics of the universe; human construct of tones belong among the *"Schlacken des Lebens"*.

But now we must ask how Kasack, moving from early expressionism to his later modes of writing, has overcome the vainglory and retained the vigour. His later works suggest a threefold answer : by tenacious interest in a great variety of detail; by trained observance of the demands of artistic structure; by resisting all encroachment upon that spiritual enclave of the individual artist's life which is the domain of creative thinking. Kasack's evolution has brought progressive understanding of a world so cruelly changed in the span of his life that to many of his generation it appears almost entirely loathsome. Terror, technocracy, and the epidemic of statistical formalism have demanded his comprehension and received it. It seems that he has actively recognised the paradox which Karl Jaspers formulated in *Die geistige Situation der Gegenwart* (1931): "Das Dasein des Menschen ist an den Apparat gebunden, der den Menschen durch seine Vollendung wie durch sein Zusammenbrechen gleicherweise ruiniert." [10] The sojourn of Dr Robert Lindhoff symbolizes that mode of contemplation which Jaspers sees threatened by the 20th century in its scornful distrust of the creative activity of the human spirit in solitude : "Ein Einzelner tritt hinaus aus der Welt, um zu finden, was er ihr dann zurückbringt." [11]

The document which Robert brings back from the *"Zwischen-reich"*—his *"Protokoll der Schrecksekunde"*—is edited into existence. The only entry made by Robert himself states that he has taken over the duties of Keeper of the Archives. But the book is commended by the Commissar of the Prefecture, and Robert's responses to particular situations receive generous mention. "Für uns steht alles da—für andere Leser brauchte es nur mit Tinte nachgezogen zu werden." [12] Kasack, as it were, carries out this operation. The whimsical author's trick may have been derived from E. T. A. Hoffmann's *Goldener Topf* : to Anselmus it seems that the words are there on the page before him, requiring only that he trace them to make them visible, as he sits in the library of the Archivarius Lindhorst. However this may be, Kasack has established some measure of aesthetic distance, and the complex document becomes the story of a man's struggle with habits of thought, a tract for the times, and an expanding satire.

Jaspers' metaphor—*"tritt hinaus aus der Welt"* is familiar in a variety of references to withdrawal from society—the hermit, the monk, the castaway, Hans Castorp in the sanatorium, the scholar in his study. It is so familiar that its substance and contour fade and lose force. From time to time the creative writer restores its significance in a fable presenting it as literal truth. By specific reference Kasack has revealed a source or prototype for his version of the fable. Dante is obvious. But long before Dante the story was told of a man who brought back news from beyond the bourne of birth and death : "And so, Glaucon, the tale was saved from perishing; and if we will listen, it may save us, and all will be well when we cross the river of Lethe. Also we shall not defile our souls; but if you will believe with me that the soul is immortal and able to endure all good and ill, we shall keep always to the upward way and in all things pursue justice with the help of wisdom." This final passage from Plato's *Republic* (cit. transl. Cornford, 1941) may or may not have been clearly in Kasack's mind when he recorded the spiritual adventures of his traveller; but in its setting —an essay on the pursuit of political wisdom—it may prove for some readers the proper focus for an analysis of Kasack's novel; for *Die Stadt hinter dem Strom,* in its most insistent, emphatic, and positive intention, seems to be a satire on man's stupidity.

Among the papers "recently deposited in the archives" is one in which the immortality of the soul is denied but man's stupidity is declared immortal : "Wenn einmal von unserer Erde nichts mehr übrig sein wird, dann wird an ihrer Statt noch lange ein Nebelfleck im Weltraum kreisen : der Dunst aller menschlichen Dummheit—von Adam an." [13]

Readers of Plato may find themselves led by his *Phaedo* to recognize a more profound and melancholy layer in the ethos of Kasack : *melete thanatou*—the practice of death as the purpose of life. The doctor whom Robert has known in life claims that he has penetrated the secret of Hippocrates and found Death as the law of Life. More incisively, with a force which seems to derive from Kasack's expressionist training, it is from Anna, who has begun to forget that she once called Robert Bob, Anna whose shadow has become fainter and who appears as "Frau Sorge" and as a sybil that we hear the denial of the Epicurean logic with its attempt to dismiss the thought of Death :

> Robert : Sage mir noch eins : warum lebt man?
> Anna : Damit man zu sterben lernt.[14]

As she takes a round stone into her hands the reader of Plato catches a glimpse of Necessity, in the myth of Er, revolving the cosmos on her lap. Then Anna speaks the last words which belong to a personal life, to her love which has linked her destiny with Robert's, and so brings to him the assurance that the dead serve the living : "Ich wiege ihn im Arm ... wie unser Kind." [15] But as she departs, the phrase she utters is impersonal, spoken in a language evoking mysteries as remote as the uncanny myth of Er : *"Eko dharma param sreyah ..."* (Truth alone is the greatest good, and patience supreme blessedness). Kasack leads us towards the legends and philosophies of the East, as many of his contemporaries were led in the great revival of Oriental interest of the 1920s in Germany and elsewhere. As we have noted, Robert Lindhoff is shown to have studied the Babylonian story of Gilgamesh (who visited Aralu, the abode of the Dead). Much influenced by the translations and notes on Chinese poetry by the German Sinologist Richard Wilhelm (1924), Kasack found himself strengthened in an anti-subjective approach to his art and saw an ideal in the Chinese artist, who "is used by the Spirit as its vessel" (see *Das Chinesische in der Kunst* in *Mosaiksteine* 1956, and the lyrics of *Chinesisches Bilderbuch*, 1955). In *Wasserzeichen* (1964) a dialogue between two Zen Buddhists points the meaning and origin of occasional aphorisms in *Die Stadt*, such as "Die Zeit bedarf der Worte, die Zeitlosigkeit bedient sich des Schweigens" ;[16] in *Wasserzeichen* we read :

Hier ist Dort und Dort ist Hier
Das Verlöschende von Dir.
Gibst du dich im Schweigen kund,
Hast du teil am alten Bund.[17]

So we may perhaps trace some of the literary processes in the construction of Kasack's novel, which at times takes on the semblance of a "westöstlicher Divan" of sombre hue.

Trying to arrive at a balanced view of Kasack's pre-occupation with the motif *"aus der Welt hinaustreten"*, we do well to turn from the elaborate literary pattern of *Die Stadt* to a dream fantasy of much simpler structure which he composed during World War II. *Totentraum* is the experience, in first-person narrative, of a man beheaded for a political crime. For a time he is aware of his divided condition and of his surroundings. Others lose sight of him, and after some show of concern for his death they begin to pick up the routine of life in apparent forgetfulness. He is anxious to remind them of death as an experience, to correct false ideas which the living entertain. He contrives to write notes on a scrap of paper, but he cannot control his hand, and the signs are meaningless even to him. The "writing" in fact disappears, as though washed away, and the paper is carried away by a gust of wind. Much even of this simple story is obviously derived from tradition. We note the old and persistent association of death with a passing into sleep (expressed in *Wasserzeichen* as "der Schlaf, des Todes milde Macht").[18] There is some evidence of more recent mode of analysis of the dream-state (of Romantic and Freudian contriving). But there is also a good share of common experience of the sensations in sleep and the moments immediately preceding sleep : the sense of separation (the head divided from the body) with a residual individual consciousness of what has happened. This may have been expanded in the harrowing mirror episode of the *Stadt*, where literary influence in a wide sense was possibly again at work —Werfel's *Spiegelmensch* (1920) or the expressionistic film *Dr. Mabuse* in its early form. More broadly significant is the feeling of ineffectiveness, especially in relation to the author's craft. In *Totentraum* the writing is meaningless and evanescent; in the *Stadt* Robert gets no further than the first entry of his *compte rendu*, and much of what comes into the archives is obliterated because it is not a contribution to "Geist". Reference has already been made to Hoffmann's Lindhorst, who obliterates the uninspired script of Anselmus; at a later stage, it will be recalled, Anselmus sees a jumble of untidy signs on the page, when his mind is not in tune with nature. In the early catechism of Robert Lindhoff in Kasack's *Stadt*, he ventures to say : "Nature is the language of the gods" and the response from the Presidium is: "Natur ist Geist." [19] This romantically tinged synthesis may perhaps have taken shape for Kasack in congenial association with Hoffmann's symbolism of calligraphy. Most important in *Totentraum* and *Stadt* is the reflection of familiar social organization. The little world of prison-warders in the short story gives place in the novel to the hierarchy of officials, clerks, and factory workers. The elementary attempt to "get a message through from beyond" is woven into a much larger human pattern in the presentation of an inverted Utopia. In attempting to convey wisdom derived from a contemplation of that realm Kasack has no doubt created difficulties for himself and his readers.

Criticism has been directed against Kasack's later novel *Das große Netz* because its satire is so pervasive as to leave the satirist no ground to stand on (see e.g. K. A. Horst, *Kritischer Führer durch die Literatur der Gegenwart*, 1962, pp. 124–25). This might equally unfairly be made to fall back upon *Die Stadt*. Excessive also is any association of Kasack's *Stadt* with a "Wiederumwertung aller Werte"[20] (see W. Kohlschmidt, *Dichter, Tradition und Zeitgeist*, 1965). Nor does Marxist comment on this novel seem adequate, when it presents Kasack's targets as war and national socialism and sees his weakness in a failure to recognize and portray the fundamental phenomena and relationships in society (see e.g. *Deutsches Literatur-Lexikon*, Weimar, 1963). There is, I think, an incongruity in Kasack's pattern of thought, which we must try to analyse and explain. Features of contemporary life which threaten the spiritual welfare of man and add to the dimensions of his stupidity are presented in *Die Stadt* in an intensified form. Such are the complex and unproductive machinery of communal life ("*Apparat*" and "*Leerlauf*"), the dwindling of friendly contact in casual encounter, the arrogant admission: "Für die Masse bleibt natürlich das Zwecklose ihres Treibens ein Geheimnis",[21] the inaccessibility and impersonal nature of the highest authorities. Erich Kahler (*The Tower and the Abyss*, 1958) sees in modern society "the concrete human particularity of the unique individual displaced by the abstract particularity of the collectively specialized function", and Kasack's Robert Lindhoff perceives around him "die Mechanik des Unpersönlichen".[22] Yet the yielding of personal identity is here presented as the aim and mark of wisdom drawn from many sources. "I have no will-power left" were the dying words of Robert's poet-friend, and he repeats them now, as a serene and sombre triumph of Schopenhauer's doctrine. A Professor of Catholic philosophy sees the "*Zwischenreich*" as a place where we learn at last not to be angry with ourselves. This may be a mingling of Christian self-denial and of Buddhist relinquishing of self-hatred, and Kasack appropriately introduces oracular ambiguity: "einige glauben, daß die Wanderung jeden zu sich bringt, andere, daß sie ihn von sich wegführt." [23] Now we may grant that it is good to assemble an anthology presenting the message of renunciation of the individual's hold on life. But when contribution to this message is made by officials of a state which is again and again made the object of satire, both the message and the satire lose force. The incongruity may be associated with a reluctance of the western mind, more deeply engrained than the two political systems of our time, to relinquish the crypto-fascism of the Platonic heritage.

As an artist Kasack is deeply concerned with the nature of art and its function in society, and keenly aware of the dangers which threaten it in modern society. These emerge from the new collectivism and technocracy, and whether the form of control is capitalist or communist makes no definable difference. The book *Der Webstuhl* (1949) was greeted by Hermann Broch as an innovation in modern allegory. The opening of the story will doubtless recall the collection of disused machinery in Butler's *Erewhon*, and it would be difficult to imagine the invention of such a story without some prompting from the last part of *Die Abderiten* by the great master of German satire, Wieland. In marginalia on the novel *Das große Netz* (during the composition of which the *Webstuhl* was written) Kasack had a good deal to say about different modes of satire, Cervantes, Wieland etc. With the skilfully assumed zeal of the archaeologist, distrusting the inevitably biased accounts of other historians, and resisting the temptation to trick out his record with fictional devices of anecdote and dialogue, Kasack pretends to trace in the ruins of an old settlement the cult and civilization of its former inhabitants. The cult had its centre in a legendary golden weaving loom, which produced the sacred carpet, patterned chronicle of the city's faith and traditions, revered possession of all the citizens. A few fragments and a book of patterns reveal varied and conflicting tastes of the epochs—realistic, formalistic, romantic, symbolist. But even these valuable museum specimens are not direct evidence of the original craft, for they date from a time when corruption had already set in, and over-organization of the carpet industry had led to a proliferation of offices. Mention of Joseph-Maria Jacquard, the silk-merchant of Lyons (who died in 1834) places the story of the city's troubles and eclipse in the very recent past. What has happened may be interpreted, once more by reference to Spengler: the original state of consciousness, which is of a religious nature, has given way to a tragic orgy of unbridled thinking. (Anna, in the *Stadt hinter dem Strom*, regards the hazardous escalation of thought as a male propensity, and calls it "spirales Denken".) Not the primitive cult, but the augmentation of apparatus enslaves the people. Papers left by a woodcarver of the city reveal details of the ludicrous and crippling taxation. The most pointed satire on the twentieth century mode of life is the profusion of abbreviations : this "*Blocksprache*" of mystagogic initials is the language of a new priesthood, the bureaucracy. Over-production, cheap imitation, and the expenses of administration undermine the economy of the country. Political parties wrangle. Only the administrative buildings are kept in good repair; private householders must cover delapidation with strips of carpet which they are permitted to hire, and carpets lie like lava over the neglected gardens. Because of the carpets the inhabitants of the carpet-state become a "Volk ohne Raum".[24] Before the war which is being contrived can be declared, explosion and a great fire reduce almost everything to ashes. Accident or design (perhaps on the part of some women's organization)?—the question remains unanswered : "das Faktum genügt, weil es einen organischen Vollzug sichtbar macht. Es bildet das folgerichtig gewaltsame Ende eines Unternehmens, das im Laufe der Geschichte die Maße seiner Struktur sprengte." [25]

This is an artist's view, and an artist's contrivance. The excess which destroys the fair proportion of structure is the denial of "Geist" and "Natur" (which, as we have seen, are equated in the *Stadt hinter dem Strom*). Where "die Beamten der toten Hand" [26] (*Webstuhl*) sit at their adding-machines, human nature is treated as an automaton, dominated by "*Ungeist*", "*Unnatur*". From the fetters of organization man is freed by a return to the organic, by reconciliation with nature's laws. His proper sphere and kinship is expressed in lines of familiar simplicity in the poem *Zeitengruß* (*Wasserzeichen*) :

> Der Tag hat seinen Morgen, seinen Abend,
> Und auch den Stunden unseres Lebens ist
> Das gleiche Maß an Licht und Nacht gegeben.[27]

But it is also an artist's contrivance to *show* the defeat of unnatural excess by natural forces and to force the issue and represent the process as violent explosion. In *Die Stadt hinter dem Strom* the expressionistic passage of Robert's diatribe against war, totalitarian terror, and gas-chambers precedes the final outburst of outraged human nature. The laughter which greets this, shaking the instruments and furniture of the Prefecture, may be the incalculable liberation of human mirth, or the self-confidence of the Establishment which absorbs the shock of individual scorn. The explosion at the end of *Der Webstuhl* is a devastating *"Faktum"*. So it is also in *Das große Netz*.

It is well to preface a consideration of this novel of 1952 by quoting from a poem of the same title in *Wasserzeichen* :

> Wo die Sterne schweigen, wo das Himmelsrund
> Seine Schwärze sammelt, mitten im Unsichtbaren
> Wacht, Jahrtausende alt, reglos lauernd,
> Gierig auf Menschenblut, die Weltenspinne.
> . . .
>
> Wir alle hängen, wehrlos gefangen,
> Beute im großen Netz . . .[28]

With this larger conception of the "net" in mind we may see more clearly the contours of the novel and recognize the intensity of its satirical aim. The specific theme of *Das große Netz* is oppressively familiar to the mid-twentieth century. We know that power which, in many guises, distorts our tastes and our mode of living, corrupts good manners by excess of communication, conjures up disaster by publishing elaborate fantasy, and creates news by spreading it. ("Common truth is today a product of the press. What the press dictates is true ... The newspapers must keep the minds of their readers under constant pressure" Spengler wrote in 1922.) Involved in this activity, perhaps at the centre of it, is the mass observer in a variety of forms—sometimes a vague, anonymous, identikit sort of figure, sometimes recognisable in instant interviews on sound radio and television screen. Kasack contrives a blend of anonymity and personality. His travelling salesman in the story of the net is called Herr Icks, and so he can sign the hotel register with an X. Like Dr. Lindhoff he becomes engaged in an occupation for which his own profession has given him some training, but the full nature and purpose is not explained to him. He is shown round a museum in process of development. Like Lindhoff he imagines a panopticum, but his guide tells him he is about to see the first "hominine Garten" where living people are on view. The notion has been exploited before in fiction : *Man in the Zoo* is an early twentieth century example. The living human exhibit goes far back in literature of widely differing inspiration—Bunyan, Dante etc. The particular significance of the device in *Das große Netz* is this : instead of using exhibits to point some lesson to society, Kasack introduces them to show the folly and tragic impertinence of society itself as it goes in more and more eagerly for organized Peeping-Tomfoolery. Unlike the people in the temple of *Die Stadt* who pose in historical costume and then go back to their work, those on show in the *Netz* represent themselves in their daily occupations. An elderly gentleman, busy with pen and foolscap sheets, is asked what he is doing, and replies : "ich beschrei hensle seniskennter im manro, an demje geta bensie tensei in surklauglas . . ." On the printed page this is easy to decipher : "ich schreibe Lebenserkenntnisse im Roman, an jedem Tage sieben Seiten in Glasklausur . . ."[29] But Herr Icks, merely listening, conceals his ignorance by the usual trick of non-committal approval and laughingly agreeing with the one syllable he can grasp : "ich bera gesa zuda dumm!"[30] We may roughly summarize Kasack's argument : "There you have 'Geheimsprache', schoolboy stuff, amusing, and if literary men have a fancy for it, you don't need to read it. But when the mystification spreads in the devices of worldly organization, it's not funny any more." In the Netz it becomes sinister, when a vast concern, the so-called IFE, in which Herr Icks finds himself employed, takes possession of the town. Measurements are taken of the muscular and mental energy expended in everyday activities, and the data set forth in algebraic formulae. Herr Icks' comment : "Da kann der Laie nur staunen" [31] is ambiguous, perhaps ironical; the widespread respect for statistical statement is the layman's weakness; Hitler, in his numerical hysteria, knew how to exploit this to the full. Observation and recording in Kasack's story become more and more oppressive as the ubiquitous authority asserts itself under the mysterious initials IFE. The town becomes a laboratory, cordoned off from the outside world. Its pathological state is intense, like that of Camus' plague-ridden town. A similar system in Kasack's style provides detailed documentation—snatches of speculative dialogue, and voices of patients relayed from hospital. These latter have eaten bread which has caused fever and mental unbalance. A teacher raves in impotent loathing against the incessant propaganda. Another patient announces in prophetic frenzy the imminence of the "bomb", and in a familiar mixture of fear and megalomania identifies himself with the instrument of destruction (cf. Das unbekannte Ziel, 1951, repr. Mosaiksteine). Destruction does come, in the form of a bomb devised by the directors of IFE, and the meaning of the initials is revealed : "Internationaler Film-Export." In order to show a world heading for disaster, and the disaster itself, a studio has been created and actors trained without being told of the intention. The core of their training has been to subject them to persistent observation in an isolated community, a culture-bed for the neuroses of a sick society. All appears to have been well planned, but in one technological detail the calculations go wrong. The reputedly weak Magnetic Bomb, specified in the internationally checked Disarmament List, and vouched for by leading physicists, does its work too well. Subsequent reports point out that only 30,000 people have lost their lives and that this is fewer than the death-toll on the roads of Europe for a single year.

What has Kasack sought to demonstrate in this narrative of devised catastrophe? First, that persistent observation of human beings tends to create data for observation; and then, that by expensive organization and the expertise of applied science consistent realism in art, whatever its alleged ethical aim may be, tends to produce a result far removed from anything we can call "a fair semblance" and is therefore a destructive usurper in the domain of art. This interpretation of Kasack's aim implies an austere view of the nature of art. I believe that Kasack's works show this austerity and are evidence of his concern for propriety in art, for the ethics which belong to artistic practice. We may make the transition from *Das große Netz* to the last novel I wish to consider by noting the farewell of a victim of the IFE disaster. The explosion has caused a flood, and the baker Zinnert and his wife have clambered to the roof of their house for safety. As it collapses, he is confronted by the thought that his sacrifice, caught by the cameras, will bring a salutary message to the cinema audiences. What he cannot know is that the episode of his death is to be cut in the editing.

The question of honesty in art, of the genuine and the nongenuine, is considered in subtle detail in Kasack's story of a collector, Clemens Sandberg, whose hobby asserts itself above his business interests, plays its part in alienating him from his wife, and destroys an affection for which it was responsible : Viola, a younger woman employed to look after the collection and prepare the catalogue, has becomes his mistress. *Fälschungen* (1953) may come to be regarded as the most skilful of Kasack's works in the structural mastery of episode. In his lecture *Deutsche Literatur seit 1945* he recognized that the relativist response to experience and individual character is accompanied in the modern novel by reduced significance of plot. It seems that in *Fälschungen*, more adroitly than in the *Stadt* and the *Netz*, Kasack has united an older novelistic treatment of plot and character with a present-day projection of ideas on the central, aesthetic theme. The title—"Forgeries"—has much the same simple, satisfying ambivalence as, say, Graham Greene's "Heart of the Matter". It refers not only to questions of art-history, the forgery of *objets d'art* and the uncertainties of the market in antiques, but also to mis-representation of human values in the most intense of human relationships. Early in the story of Sandberg's association with Viola there is a sadly impressive incident. The collector suggests frequent visits to villages in search of pieces to add to the collection : " 'Du weißt, unserer Sammlung fehlt noch mancherlei, ein altes Spinnard zum

Beispiel, geschnitzte Holzpantinen, eine alte Wiege. Nun, wir werden ja sehen.' Daß Viola damals weniger an der Ehe als an einem
Kind lag, begriff Clemens immer noch nicht." [32] This is recalled
some time later, when the divorce petition is lodged by Sandberg's
wife. Viola is indifferent to the news. Her love for Sandberg which
had grown with the discovery of order and peace in a rural setting, had been repelled and injured when she found, as Sandberg's wife had found, that the *objets d'art*, as perfection of work-
manship and record of the past, demanded from him a reverence
which was exclusive. Viola sees herself as the cataloguer, whose
work will soon be finished; even the thought of a likeness which
Sandberg has happily discovered between her and one of his
treasured figures stifles her. Words of affection which Sandberg
now uses bring only melancholy disturbing echoes of the love
which formerly united them. The words themselves are counter-
feit. Kasack's style is such that he does not need to make this comment; the reader derives it from incident and dialogue. These
common components of the story-structure are so controlled as
to produce semblance of life and at the same time progressively
serve the theme. Kasack's technique in *Fälschungen* has much in
common with the analytic form of drama. The imminent crisis in
Sandberg's affairs is apparent in the early part of the story, and
what has led to it is revealed in passages of retrospect. This is
entirely appropriate in a story which is to reach its climax in the
ultimate fate of a collection of antiques, and details from the history
of the collection have to be presented in order to explain that fate.
Very early in the composition two subjects are announced—the
weakening relation between Sandberg and Viola, and an article
published by Sandberg on "genuine or non-genuine" in the world
of antiques. The balance of these two subjects, the pursuit of them
in a kind of fugue, is the form which Kasack puts upon his story.
Viola recognizes that her love for Sandberg belongs to the past.
To this corresponds Sandberg's discovery that doubts which he
expressed in his essay are not only a scholar's anxious theorising,
but are also painfully relevant to his own collection. Notwithstand-
ing the assurance of experts, some of the most treasured items are
shown to be fakes. A young Dutchman, the mean and renegade
son of a dealer and restorer with whom Sandberg was friendly
before the war, produces evidence to prove that these "antiques"
were made by his father. The historical source of this *dénouement*
may have been the melancholy Van Meegeren scandal, which is in
fact mentioned in Kasack's narrative.

Sandberg's frank disclosure and decisive action are a ruthless
twentieth century contribution to the "*querelle des anciens et des
modernes*". Possessing the evidence of "genuine or fake", he puts

the judgement of the experts to a final test and reveals their fallibility. "Es ist also ganz natürlich," he says, "wenn unser Gefühl uns vor den alten Werken im Stich läßt. Sie sind uns allmählich so fremd geworden, daß wir den Unterschied zwischen Echt und Falsch nicht mehr empfinden, sondern nur durch technische Analysen ermitteln können—was für ein Armutszeugnis!" [33] Standing by an open fire, to the consternation of all the guests, he throws the reproductions, *and* the genuine antiques, into the flames. An observer of this aesthetic *auto-da-fé* exclaims: "Ein Mann verbrennt den Inhalt seines Lebens—das tut man nicht im Zeitalter der Kompromisse." [34] Sandberg replies: "Der berühmte Phönix kann nur aus der Asche steigen, wenn man das Alte bis zum Wurzelgrund verbrannt hat. Da gibt es keine Kompromisse. Mit Restaurieren und Renovieren und Aufpolieren machen wir aus dem Gestern ein falsches Heute." [35] To him, as to Viola and his wife Inge a *ménage à trois* has proved unmanageable. The third party, uncertain, indecipherable, is the dead wood, and it must go. Outside are the living trees, and tending them will bring no threat to matrimony.

Once again Kasack has summoned the destructive element as *deus ex machina* to establish a *"Faktum"* or, to use another of his chosen phrases, to create *tabula rasa*. But *"Flammenschrift"* is only one mode of Kasack's artistry. For the other we must look once more to *Wasserzeichen*:

> Vom heiteren Spiel der Farben
> Die Buchstaben ausgemalt,
> In deren dunkeln Silben
> Noch das Geheimnis strahlt,
> Erleben Schreiber und Leser
> Jahrhundertefern getrennt
> Das Glück des sich Vereinens
> Auf altem Pergament.[36]

and

> Ich suchte die Toten, zu fragen, was mit ihnen sei.
> Sie lächelten zögernd, ohne eine Antwort zu geben.
> Aber sie lockten mir, wie es schien, ein Echo herbei.
> Aus seinem Raunen vernahm ich, sie seien in meinem Leben.[37]

Encounters with the past, cherished moments when the departed seem close at hand ("Jenseits in das Diesseits dringend"[38] is the phrase in *Chinesisches Bilderbuch*) appear in Kasack as actual experience. But they also represent the constant humanitarian function which he acknowledges as that of the poet. He proclaims the source of poetry to be "Glaube an die Möglichkeit einer

gereinigten Welt" [39] (*Deutsche Literatur seit 1945*); he perceives
the strength of man's spiritual nature and its persistence beyond
the "Schicksalszugur. [40] With Gottfried Benn he finds evidence of
this in the revival of interest in the expressionists.

The urge of human charity, the origin of much day-to-day
letter-writing, may be intensified when the poet's aim is explicitly
humanitarian and he tries to convey a message of assurance,
patience and courage to those separated from him by divergence
of personality or by accidents of experience which do not belong
to his own life. In Kasack's short story *Das Birkenwäldchen*, a
travelling-companion during the war shows a profound interest in
flowers and trees, and particularly in a birchgrove seen on the daily
journey from Berlin to Potsdam. The acquaintance has begun to
turn to friendship when the encounters suddenly cease. The narrator learns only after weeks that his companion has been injured
in an air-raid and lost his sight. There is no certainty that he will
ever see his beloved birchgrove again, although the specialists offer
some shred of hope. The writer has not visited him. This would
have been contrary to Kasack's purpose. Generally the untidiness of
experience has to be disciplined by art; the composition of *Birkenwäldchen* on the other hand had to accommodate an incomplete
and disturbing experience in the author's life. His friend, a publisher, fell into the hands of the Gestapo and was held as a "political prisoner." Letters were for a time stopped. The only means
of communication Kasack could devise was to write a story, with
recognizable allusions, for a magazine which found its way into the
prison. In the *Birkenwäldchen* the measure of hope that the travelling companion would emerge from darkness was accompanied by
a message of fortitude, counsel of restraint, and solidarity. The
two men in the story meet for the last time in the narrator's house in
Potsdam and listen to a record of early seventeenth century choral
music—Heinrich Schutz' *Saul*. As the visitor leaves he sings softly
to himself : "Saul! Saul! Was verfolgst du mich !" [41] In the account
of their listening Kasack singles out the dramatic passage : "Es
wird dir schwer werden, wider den Stachel zu löcken." [42] Both
phrases could be interpreted as denunciation of the anti-Christian
behaviour of the Nazis, and the second also as counsel of forbear-
ance to the actual recipient of the story, the publisher Peter
Suhrkamp. But the message perhaps most potent for the particular
occasion, a message which retains its power for a growing range
of readers, is conveyed in two sentences. The first is : "Jeder sah
das seine." [43] In the restful community of silence the birch grove
has for each of the travellers its own meaning. Both have felt the
sanctity and wholesomeness of fields and trees in contrast to the
evils of the time. Then they are separated by no longer sharing

that mode of perception which brought them together. The man who retains his sight feels the need to convey what he now sees to the other who can only remember the spectacle of nature's myriad transformation. "Hier ging es um den Spiegel der Wirklichkeit, um einen Eindruck der Realität, nicht um die objektive Gültigkeit in der Darstellung—hier ging es um konkrete, greifbare Dinge." [44] Exercising his mind upon a long series of details which he might put into precise, descriptive words, Kasack returns to the question : "Wie steht es um die Kraft des Worts ... vermag es den Glauben an eine Wirklichkeit zu erwecken, der die sichtbare Bestätigung fehlt?" [45] Thus gently in passing he touches upon the nature of faith. The search for an answer to his poet's question is futile. But just as his friend has discovered the unique birch grove for him, so now the absorption in detail is evidence that the other's habit of absorption and observation, its directness, intensity, and utter lack of fanciful embroidery, has taken possession of him. This is probably the experience of many who learn the craft of writing; it is the experience in schools of art where the tenacious enthusiasm of true observation passes from teacher to student. But Kasack's sudden solution is both an acknowledgement of the teaching and a gracious gift in return. "Jeder sah das seine" is now superseded by "Ich sehe es beinahe täglich mit deinen Augen". [46] Those eyes can no longer see, but their vision is not lost. Through the dimming process of the years, the ravages of "entfesseltes Denken", [47] organic disaster, incarceration, even death, *one* will lose his perception. But by some sort of metempsychosis its survival in another is assured.

TRANSLATIONS

1. Not only the sides of the separate rooms of the business-block were divided by sliding glass walls. The ceilings and floors were also made of transparent glass ... The sense of insecurity, of having no foothold, was increased when he saw rooms not only abreast of him but also above and below him, where men and the things they were using hung like puppets in mid air.

2. Records of the moment of fear.

3. Well yes, I suppose it is a sort of way of purification; an interim realm some call it, where the dross of earth falls away.

4. The expressionist in particular was aware of the objective necessity which involves the manipulation of art, an observance of the ethics of the craft, the moral demands of form. The expressionist seeks discipline because he was the one most torn asunder.

5. *Parting.*—The horror, Night, destroys the evening walk. Emptiness of talk engulfs gesture with a sob. Mouth's dark chasm holds the cry—

so take me. Street tears apart, men silhouette. I fall, rubble weighs on my head. Hands flutter apart with the hat raised in greeting, and still in dream this hovering lingers; its moan dies away at sight of mask; hair makes strands of face. Horrified, hunted, body lashes drifting space.

6. Flags are hauled and breath comes slow, compass points north and the heart must know: the end of this trip is the end of the world. Death enters the present; the mask of life falls.

7. And this I knew, though comprehending not: This then is Death—death turned to music, with strong yearning, sweet and darkly glowing, akin to deepest sadness. And yet 'tis strange! With longing indefinable and mute my soul did weep....

8. His sinews tautened, in sudden sense of manhood. And this he knew: I am I, and I alone. Acknowledging his threefold self—I am, I will, I can—he cupped his hand in the sea, baptised himself.

9. Documents which, by their very style, were all the more dangerous because they afforded opportunity of expressing obsolete ideas.

10. Man's existence is bound up with apparatus, which ruins him both in its perfection and in its collapse.

11. The individual leaves the world in order to find something, which he then brings back with him.

12. To us it is quite clear. For other readers the only thing needed is to go over it in ink.

13. When there is nothing of our earth left, it will still leave in orbit for a long time a patch of mist—the haze of man's stupidity, right down from the time of Adam.

14. R: Tell me, why do we live? A: So we may learn to die.

15. I cradle it in my arms, like our child.

16. Time needs words. Timelessness is content with silence.

17. Here is There, and There is Here—that part of you which fades. Make yourself known with silence, and you shall share in the old covenant.

18. Sleep, Death's gentle power.

19. Nature is Spirit.

20. Another transvaluation of all values. (Derived from the sub-title of Nietzsche's *Wille zur Macht*—The Will to Power—fragment publ. 1895).

21. For the mass of the people the futility of what they are doing remains of course a secret.

22. The mechanism of the impersonal.

23. Some think the journey brings everyone back to himself, others that it takes him away from himself.

24. A people without living space. (Title of Hans Grimm's novel of 1926, which was widely popular in the National Socialist time.)

25. The fact in itself is sufficient, for it marks the completion of an organic process. It is the logical, violent end of an enterprise which, in the course of events, has broken the bonds of its structure.

26. Officials of mortmain.

27. Day has its morning and its evening, and to the hours of our life is given like measure of daylight and of darkness.

28. Where the stars are silent and the firmament gathers its darkness, in the midst of the unseen, the spider of the cosmos, millennia old, lies waiting. . . . Caught, defenceless, we all hang, a prey in the great net.

29. I am writing notes on life, in a novel, seven pages a day in a glass enclosure.

30. But I say it's daft.

31. As a mere outsider, all I can say is—it's astonishing.

32. You know, our collection still lacks a number of items—an old spinning-wheel, a pair of pattens, an old cradle. Well, we'll see.— Clemens still could not realize that marriage meant less to Anna than having a child.

33. So it's quite natural that our intuition should let us down when we are confronted by old works of art. They have gradually become so alien that we can no longer see the difference between genuine and fake, and we have to fall back on technical analysis. What a sign of our impoverished state!

34. A man goes and burns the content of his life—and he does it in this age of compromise!

35. The celebrated Phoenix can arise from its ashes only if the old things are burned right down to the roots. There's no compromise. With our restorations and our polishings and our renovations we are making our yesterday into a false today.

36. From the bright play of colours, illuminated letters in whose dark syllables the mystery still gleams, scribe and reader, centuries apart, find the joy of meeting in old parchment.

37. I sought out the dead, to see how they were faring. Hesitant they smiled, and gave no answer. But as it seemed, they drew from me an echo, and by its murmur I heard that they were in my life.

38. Into the present comes the hereafter.

39. Belief in the possibility of a world purified.

40. Caesura of destiny. (Kasack's word, in the work quoted, for the spiritual halt in Germany caused by the Nazi rule.)

41. Why persecutest thou me?

42. It will be hard for thee to kick against the pricks.

43. Each had his own particular view of it.

44. What was needed now was a mirror of reality, an impression of what was actually there; it was not a question of objective validity in presentation, but of concrete, palpable things.

45. What about the power of the word? Can it awaken faith in a reality for which there is no visible confirmation?

46. I see it almost every day with your eyes.

47. Unbridled thinking.

SELECT BIBLIOGRAPHY

Fiction

Tull der Meisterspringer, 1935 (Text ed. with English notes by K. H. Vignoles, London, Arnold, n.d.—Kasack adapted from Hugh Lofting's *Doctor Doolittle*).

Das Birkenwäldchen (in *Die Neue Rundschau* 1944).
Die Stadt hinter dem Strom, 1947.
Der Webstuhl, 1949.
Das große Netz, 1952.
Fälschungen, 1953.

Lyric

Der Mensch, 1918.
Der Gesang des Jahres, 1921.
Der Strom der Welt, 1940.
Das ewige Dasein, 1943 (selection of poems 1919–43; 2nd ed. 1949).
Aus dem chinesischen Bilderbuch, 1955.
Wasserzeichen, 1964.

Essays

Oskar Loerke/Charakterbild eines Dichters (Akad. d Wissensch. u.d.Lit., Abh. d. Kl. Lit.), 1951.
Mosaiksteine/Beiträge zu Literatur und Kunst, 1956.
Die deutsche Literatur nach 1945 (in *Duitse Kroniek* XIV, 1962).

For critical material see

W. Duwe, *Deutsche Dichtung des 20. Jahrhunderts, I,* 1962.
H. Friedmann, O. Mann, *Deutsche Literatur im 20. Jahrhundert,* 1954.
K. Hamburger, "Nachwort" to collection *Das unbekannte Ziel/Ausgewählte Proben und Arbeiten,* 1963.
K. A. Horst, *Die deutsche Literatur der Gegenwart,* 1957.
K. A. Horst, *Kurzer Führer durch die deutsche Literatur der Gegenwart,* 1962.
W. Jens, *Deutsche Literatur der Gegenwart/Themen, Stile, Tendenzen,* 4. Aufl. 1962.
W. Kohlschmidt, *Dichter, Tradition und Zeitgeist,* 1965.
R. Pascal, *The German Novel,* 1956 (University Paperbacks, 1965).
W. Waidson, *The Modern German Novel.* Oxford University Press, 1959.
Review notes in *Etudes germaniques,* IV, 1949, p. 428; VIII, 1953, p. 149.

Hans Erich Nossack

Hans Erich Nossack

by BRIAN KEITH-SMITH

(University of Bristol)

Hans Erich Nossack was born at Hamburg in 1901 son of a coffee-importer. In 1922, in revolt against the upper-middle class attitudes of his environment, he gave up his studies in philosophy and law at Jena to become a factory worker. After frequently changing employment as salesman, clerk and journalist, and having experience of unemployment, he sought to avoid the closer attention of the Nazis who banned his activities as a writer in 1933, and reluctantly joined his Father's firm to become an import merchant. He married in 1925 and remained politically inactive during the 20s and 30s, though his unfinished Lenin drama *Elnin* suggests the direction of his interests at the time. The most formative experience of his life was to be the destruction of Hamburg in the air-raids of July 1943 which he watched from the country outside. In this catastrophe he lost all his manuscripts and personal belongings. Jean-Paul Sartre drew attention to his published reactions to these events, and since 1947 his works have been read fervently by a small number of admirers, though not until 1956 was he able to live solely as an independent writer. He has now retreated from the public demands of living in a modern city and has made a home in the remote village of Aystetten near Augsburg. He is a member of the Akademie der Wissenschaften und der Literatur in Mainz, of the Freie Akademie der Künste in Hamburg, and of the Deutsche Akademie für Sprache und Dichtung in Darmstadt. In 1957 he was awarded the prize of the Kulturkreis im Bundesverband der Deutschen Industrie, in 1961 the Georg Büchner prize, and in 1963 the Wilhelm Raabe prize.

NOSSACK'S published work begins with destruction. *Der Untergang* written in November 1943 narrates the destruction of Hamburg four months earlier, and explains Nossack's awareness of a completely new personal position, starting with the timeless holiday idyll of a few days on the heath outside the town, and plunging into a vivid apocalyptical account of man's hatred and bestiality. Nossack felt the fate of Hamburg to be his fate, the guilt of its citizens to be his—the lurid descriptions of the heath on fire under the ghostly light of the searchlights quickly leading into soul-searching questions as to his and man's attitudes when faced with annihilation. The masked attitudes of the past behind which man had played out his bourgeois existence, and now as when a refugee demanding charity he feels unfairly deprived of all his belongings, stand out starkly in the harsh new light of Nossack's questioning, throw into relief the relativity of the different realities by which man lived before in the city. Nossack feels obliged to bear witness to these his experiences that include factual description of the raids seen from a distance, his new understanding of his fellowmen, and his reactions when he returns to the ruined city. To sum this up needs more than a report, more than a closed literary form can give, and so he asks :—

"Ob es wohl besser verstanden würde, wenn man es im Zwielicht als Märchen erzählt? Es war einmal ein Mensch, den hatte keine Mutter geboren. Ein Faust stieß ihn nackt in die Welt hinein, und eine Stimme rief : Sieh zu, wie du weiterkommst. Da öffnete er die Augen und wußte nichts anzufangen mit dem, was ihn umgab. Und er wagte nicht, hinter sich zu blicken, denn hinter ihm war nichts als Feuer."[1]

The situation and the style suggested in *Der Untergang* are more than a starting point for Nossack's works. They are at once the justification and the curse of his existence as a writer, for however dreamlike Nossack's literary phantasies may appear to be, once analysed—and more often than not Nossack hints at their exemplary character—in fact they are based on a sober, honest and bitterly independent facing up to the facts of contemporary life. Coming in mid-life the formative experience of Hamburg's destruction has moulded Nossack's attitude beyond the possible healing effects of time. The scars of his memory are open, and every new turn by man towards self-delusion, every attempt to pretend that the past bears no lessons for the present and the future must bring him further suffering.

He turns a ruthless eye on his own feelings after becoming a refugee, at first avoids returning to the city, then is greedy to see it again. On the way he experiences a surge of new life and hope suggesting the forlorn emptiness of his previous life, against which we can understand his disappointment in retrospect with the regrowth of post-war Germany. Even in the shattering experience of finding all his belongings destroyed, Nossack learns to face up to the truths found in the ruins—the physical horrors of flies and filth of course, the obliteration of his past held in 25 years of diary notes, the inconsequence of land ownership, the temptation of saying "if only we had done this or that", and the impossibility of playing out life as before.

Reality is not only no longer "absolute", nor is it made, nor predictable, nor timebound :—

"Denn was wir gewonnen haben und was anders wurde, das ist : Wir sind gegenwärtig geworden. Wir haben uns aus der

Zeit gelöst ... Der Verstand sagt, wie klingt das traurig. Aber es ist nicht traurig, es ist nur einfach so. Traurig ist nur der Verstand, weil er Flügel zu haben glaubt, und stürzt doch immer wieder." [2]

By renouncing passive acceptance of the past (a theme already expressed apparently in his pre-war Büchner drama *Der Hessische Landsbote*, less about Büchner's person than "the resistance of youth against dictatorship and restoration"), Nossack actively seeks a possible human way of life that overcomes man's instinctual responses to his neighbours. He analyses, spotlights and accuses the premises by which we live or are made to live, and sees change as a necessary tonic to a self-throttling humanity. No longer can he trust the reports of others, but will write to find his own self and values, hoping to find an echoing listener. Thus we read in *Nekyia, Bericht Eines Überlebenden* :

"Ich spreche zu einem Wesen, von dem ich glaube, daß es einmal da sein wird. Ich habe die Gewißheit, daß dies nicht nur ein kranker Wunsch ist, meiner Einsamkeit unter den hilflosen Schläfern zu entfliehen. Manchmal steht die Gestalt dieses Wesens schon ganz deutlich vor mir, und ich nenne es : Du. Ja, ich will es mit Du anreden, dann wird es am sichtbarsten." [3]

The basic uncertainty of man's condition and his awareness of the relativity of all experience, especially after living through a major catastrophe, encourages Nossack to examine human life often through the eyes of a complete stranger to human life—thus we find the first part of *Interview mit dem Tode* is the *Bericht eines fremden Wesens über die Menschen*. Even love he finds is too often man's attempt to escape from the truths of himself. This is given exemplary form in the story *Dorothea* (the title under which the whole collection appeared in its second edition). Here again the setting is Hamburg July 1943. Here again Nossack writes commemoratively, reproducing the turmoil caused by the city's destruction and erasing the barriers of time and place which have allowed us to forget what man can inflict on himself. The story overcomes such barriers by intertwining three strands—a young woman's experiences, her mysterious resemblance to a Carl Hofer portrait, and her rereading an early Nossack poem first after being helped out of the burning city by a young soldier and three years later when the narrator visits her and she recognizes him as the soldier's elder brother. The narrator and she find that something in the past seems to link them together, but cannot give this any certain expression, so to recapture as much as possible from her memory, Dorothea narrates

her story dispassionately and in great detail. This brings into focus
the function of the narrator's earlier dreams in which his mind
turns over in no logical manner possible connections with Dorothea
in empty landscapes, always searching, caught in moments of extreme need, faced with nothingness. It is important to consider
Nossack's own comments on this story, to realize that his concern
for man in such situations demands from him a certain honesty of
reportage, a refusal to judge by any reasoned categories :—

> "Es ist nicht gut, Dinge erklären zu wollen, die sich mit dem
> Verstande nicht erklären lassen. Es ist aber ebenso falsch, ihre
> Wirklichkeit nur deshalb zu verneinen, weil sie sich mit dem
> Verstande erklären lassen. Denn da sie eine Wirkung haben und
> Spuren hinterlassen, müssen sie auch eine Wirklichkeit haben.
> Am besten ist, man läßt diese Dinge mit schweigenden Staunen
> besehen."[4]

Of the other stories in this collection, in which we see silent
astonishment at the relevance for today of the Cassandra theme in
Kassandra, surrealist devices to portray the conflicting levels
of consciousness afflicting those who survive disaster in *Appas-
sionata*, and the subjection of death to ridicule by transferring
it into the figure of a black marketeer in *Interview mit dem
Tode*, *Klonz* is the most important. It is also Nossack's *De
Profundis*. After the catastrophe he is disgusted that the innocent
and the good die whereas the boasters and opportunists remain.
To now meet Klonz—one of his previously created characters—
is the worst he has had to suffer, leading him to contemplate
suicide and throw away his previous values for new expedient ones.
He finds now that he has a duty to the other person to overcome
the demands of self, to suppress his anxiety lest it affect others,
a moral duty to write, to describe things as they are rather than
as he thinks they should be, leading him in an unexpected and
certainly excusable way to base his actions and sense of priorities
on the demands of the moment—like Klonz!—for it is he and not
God that compels him to write. This leads him to experiment with
reality, to check what is being and what image. His existential
gymnastics in front of the barber's mirror allow him to look back
on the everyday world through the eyes of a man in another
world—not from a dreamworld, as he is quick to point out, but
from one which draws on facts from the past (not values of the
present) to describe the ruined landscape of today :—

> "Selbst die Trümmer heben dort nicht die Arme hilflos in den
> Himmel und klagen um ihren zerstörten Wert, sondern ver-
> künden sicher und bewußt von sich : Siehe, ich war ein Haus."

Nossack reflects on how he created Klonz, an innkeeper playing the part of the respectable citizen, married him to a Frau Habekost, and thought they had died in the catastrophe. He is now not sure if he talks about Klonz so as to grin and suppress his despair, but finds him waiting for him in his room. For the first time he becomes aware of the independence of creatures from their creator. The image lives on past the world catastrophe, and so by extension does the model on which it was formed. In spite of Klonz's rudeness, Nossack decides he will be sympathetic to him should he meet him again. He has come through the strongest temptation Klonz could throw at him—to hate his fellow creature because his fellow creature turned against him. *Klonz* is crisis and parable in one, an examination for man Nossack wishes him never to forget.

Nossack's vision of Klonz the opportunist, inhuman in his self-sufficiency, continues to torment his artistic sensibility. Thus we find a thinly-veiled attack on the self-satisfaction of a certain unnamed party in the short wireless talk *Nationalhymne der Opportunisten* in which we hear the anthem:

> *"Die Fenster zu!* Und Feuer in den Herd!
> Setzt euch zu Tisch und laßt die Pfropfen knallen!
> Die alte gute Kost hat sich bewährt:
> Wir leben noch und sind noch nicht gefallen.
>
> Zwar mußten wir vorübergehend kuschen
> Und sprachen so und taten so als ob,
> Versuchten unser Bäuchlein zu vertuschen
> Und dutzten uns mit jedem Hungermob.
>
> Die Fenster zu, damit uns niemand hört!
> Geist und Gewissen enden im Exil.
> *Wir* halten durch, denn wir sind gut genährt.
> O welche Lust, dies Ewigkeitsgefühl![6]

This is again sung in *Die Hauptprobe*, a tragic burlesque, by Klonz mine host of the "Paradise". As in Nossack's second play *Die Rotte Kain*, man's basic motives are here laid bare— sexual appetites, the lust for power, the childish belief in the power of money or goods to barter. *Die Rotte Kain* develops much of its rather obvious dramatic impact from the directness of langauge used on the most elemental and elementary level. *Die Hauptprobe* presents the staging by Klonz and his associates of the parable of the prodigal son, done partly to advertise the inn (though at a time when food is scarce and the visitors come to take part only for the reward of a hot meal), partly to support Klonz's own sense of ownership, and partly to defend himself from the mercenary attempts of Frau Habekost to improve her position by marrying him with the offer of her savings. The inter-change of characters from their rôles in the play to the play within the play and back again is but sketchily worked out, but this was only partly the reason for the complete refusal of public and critics alike to accept it on the stage. Nossack is guilty here of punctuat-ing the social façade too obviously—this being the reason for the effect of ridiculing the public that was caused. Hans Henny Jahnn in a speech on Nossack summed up what estranges Nossack from a wide public, and at the same time points out his characteristic quality as a writer :

> "Wenn Hans Erich Nossack eine Gabe hat, dann ist es diese, diese gepriesene Fähigkeit, das sonderbar Einfache, Unbeachtete zum Natürlichen und Wesentlichen zu entkleiden. Schlechte Worte mit guter Bedeutung zu versehen, unauffälligen Neben-sächlichkeiten schreiendes Leben zu geben."[7]

This is borne out by his latest play *Ein Sonderfall* (written also as a short story) about a man who wins a vast sum of money on a football pool, and who suddenly becomes aware of the false-ness of the lives of his family and acquaintances. Countless trivial turns of phrase, leitmotifs and relationships between the various characters that make up the interplay of this society ring false and cry out for condemnation. It comes in Paul's tirade near the end :

> "Glauben Sie noch an Dinge, die nichts mit Geld, nichts mit Erfolg, nichts mit Statistik zu tun haben und wofür es den Radioapparaten, die jetzt abgestellt sind, an einem Organ fehlt? Glauben Sie so daran, daß es sie gibt, auch wenn es uns nicht gibt? Der Pfirsichbaum zum Beispiel und der Mond, der durch die Schneise geht. Entschuldigen Sie die späte Frage, die man im Theater nicht stellen darf. Das ist ganz unerlaubt. Ich stelle sie auch nur, weil wir hier an der Rampe stehen. Einen Schritt weiter, und wir brechen uns den Hals. Wir haben mit einer Hochzeit begonnen und gespielt, was daraus wird. Bin ich ein Sonderfall? Dann braucht sich niemand nach mir zu richten. Ich sage Nein zu einer Welt, von der behauptet wird, ich sei in ihr nichts als ein Sonderfall. Sie geht mir nichts mehr an." [8]

Paul's words sum up Nossack's disgust, with the difference that Nossack remains intensely concerned. His concern with the sup-pression of human values in modern society shows particularly strongly in his first two novels.

Spätestens im November, his first published novel is a dead woman's story of her attempt to break away from her posi-tion as the beautiful but not too intelligent wife of a thrusting confident industrialist. For all her material comforts, she is just a

status symbol, an advertisement for her husband's firm. Even her
little boy who is meant to be bringing up so as to inherit his Father's
business realm, which he has inherited from her own Father on
their marriage. Her dissatisfaction with the boring round of social
platitudes and artificial veneer of the *Wirtschaftswunder* society
of a provincial industrial town turns into a fatally rational if at
first semi-conscious search for a way out. Marianne meets Berthold Möncken, a young writer honoured with the firm's prize—
another form of publicity—and is impelled to go away as if after
a great shock with this unknown man, leaving husband, child and
a luxurious home to find an unknown freedom. By describing what
we might normally find an over-emotional episode in the sober,
at times harsh language of the woman who deliberately breaks
away from her way of life so as to find some meaning to her
existence, Nossack cuts deep into the façade of the functionalized
purpose of the *Wirtschaftswunder*, but also deromanticizes the
break for freedom, and with it the modern writer's life. Both industrialist and writer are too preoccupied with their own struggles
for self-expression to care for the spiritual welfare of Marianne.
Love is seen free from traditional taboos, but also from any illusions of its overwhelming power to set right the ruthless self-
centredness of people with specific aims in life. Thus what begins
as a fairytale escape from deary reality, ends not as a tragedy when
the lovers die in Möncken's newly acquired secondhand Volks-
wagen, but as a parody of the Francesca and Paolo theme from
Dante. When Marianne returns to her home after finding life
impossibly lonely with Möncken, she has to live almost a double
existence—that of the faithful wife, who has been away con-
valescing after a breakdown (this being the only possible respectable
explanation for the disappearance for several months of the firm's
most glittering local social advertisement), and that of a woman
who cannot tell whether her husband's tolerant attitude is genuine
or patronizing, and who is equally uncertain of the direction of her
own emotions. Where her first experiment at flight was an act of
escape from her own environment, her second is one of flight from
her newly discovered and disintegrating personality.

Like Marianne in *Spätestens im November*, Stefan Schneider,
the engineer who returns to Hamburg after the Second
World War from Brazil, seeks in *Der Jüngere Bruder* a
reorientation of his existence. He looks for one Carlos Heller who
appears in the police report on Schneider's wife's death from a fall
from her balcony, leaving his notes to a writer Arno Breckwaldt to
write into a novel when he finally decides to return to Brazil. Carlos
Heller, the "younger brother", the idealized almost mythical em-
bodiment of the contemporary man, is only realized in the reader's

and in Schneider's minds by contrast with the highly efficient company secretary Stolling, Schneider's own narrow-minded dreamy academic brother Heinrich living in the detached world of Apolda in East Germany as if the war and the twentieth century had never taken place, the grotesque portrait of the self-made businessman Bruno Breckwaldt, and the purposeful slightly nervous young wife of Bruno's writer brother; all of whom live more or less as rôles or functions in utterly different ways of life, and on falsely developed values—yet how much at first Schneider would like to be like them. Carlos Heller he is convinced has managed to live a Bohemian life and retain the camouflage of modern man, has walked in Hamburg as an integral part of its life and yet has been loved and worshipped as an angel figure wherever he has gone. Revenge he has taken on Schneider's wife—symbol of false bourgeois security and the mushy morality of the "happy end". Where no one is certain of their identity, self-camouflage is necessary— all these characters seek for "truth" in life and try to live by it, yet Nossack condemns them :

> "Die sogenannte Wahrheit, die wir in die Welt hinauszuschreien versuchen, ist für euch nur ein Vitamin, ein Abführmittel oder Luxusartikel, den ihr euch nach Feierabend leistet."[9]

This image of man as a consumer of truth is the one that leads Nossack to attack the whole basis of post-war Western capitalist society, replacing man as a builder of truth, and it is along such themes that Marxist critics find Nossack's works useful propaganda. Schneider rakes over his past, going through varying stages of delight and disgust with the attitudes of the people he meets, and finally significantly succumbs in the night club Aporée (an incomplete anagram for Europe, taken from a book by Arno Breckwaldt) the name of a land now arid and waste after a great catastrophe. Schneider is judged and condemned against the ideal that he seeks, failing to act a part and keep sight of his true self—a central theme in many of Nossack's works.

> "Nossack rühmt sich, der bestgetarnte Schriftsteller zu sein"[10]

are words written in an article by a writer Berthold Möncken, a form of autobiographical examination of creator by his creature. He is eager that is to camouflage himself from misinterpretation, and knows full well how easy it is to be misrepresented. At a personally more intimate level he is concerned that man should keep control of the existential validity of his responses to his environment. This is particularly serious today as that environment is largely hostile to man in this respect. This may be said to be the central problem underlying the five loosely joined tales that make up Nossack's novel *Spirale. Roman einer Schlaflosen Nacht.* Thus he comments in the introduction :

"Ein Ereignis hat einen Mann schlaflos gemacht. Er müht sich, sein Leben zurück und zuende zu denken; mit verteilten Rollen hält er über sich Gericht, klagt sich an, verteidigt sich und versucht, sich zu begnadigen, um endlich Ruhe zu finden. Doch immer, wenn die Spirale seiner Gedanken in den Schlaf absinken will, stößt sie an andere Bruchstücke seines Lebens und wird von neuem in das unerbittliche Zwielicht der Schlaflosigkeit hochgerissen. Vielleicht wird der Mann schließlich den Kampf aufgeben müssen und frierend am Fenster stehen. Draußen dämmert es bereits, und die Vögel beginnen zu zwitschern." [11]

Each of these cautionary tales shows man faced with the possibility of completely changing course and going against the apparently natural laws of his environment. He is full of nausea for the normal everydayness of his life and blind to the other life close to hand. In both *Der Neugierige* (not in this novel) and *Unmögliche Beweisaufnahme* in particular man explicitly states his need to make tracks in life, to leave behind a trace of his individual existence, a proof of his worth and permanence. In many of Nossack's stories the individual feels he can only do this by breaking out of what he normally does, taking in *Spätestens im November* the form of adultery (which is here not in itself an immoral act in the traditional sense, for such self-conscious immorality shows up as too bourgeois a way out and hence self-defeating). In *Unmögliche Beweisaufnahme* there is a more essential break with a situation in which an insurance agent becomes obsessed with the normality he has wilfully created in his no-risks-lower-premiums-marriage. So featureless does his life become, that the hero in his trial at which he is defendant in an inquest on his wife's disappearance, has the greatest difficulty to explain away his apparently unmotivated actions. Man for him only begins where psychiatry or any other explanatory system leaves off, and he vigorously defends the inexplicability of love. Where the metaphysical impinges on the rationally definable or the tangible experience, he finds all common methods of communication and expression invalid. Thus he has to explain his confrontation with the "Aufbruch ins Unversicherbare" [12] in the fairytale form. He follows his wife out, so he tells the court, into a snowstorm where the necessities of individuality and physical limitations are blotted out. Like both Thomas Mann and Kafka before him, Nossack here questions the validity of our means of distinguishing between inner and outer worlds, and breaks down the notion of the individual as a separate entity. One cannot help recalling Kafka's remark—"Die Dinge versinken um mich wie ein Schneefall".[13] The same happens to Nossack's hero, but for him words ("mostly tablets for headaches") replace Kafka's things. There are many instances in this work where words in context can "prove" entirely contrary results. Thus on a direct level, the display in court of the wife's fur-coat seems to prove she is still alive, but the prosecutor takes this as proof of the defendant's complicity in his wife's disappearance.

Freedom from the past, Nossack's recurrent theme, can reinstate the primacy of the self, allowing for unimpeded inner monologue, an easy breakdown of time categories, and independence from the restrictions of local environment. It can also isolate the individual and lead to his disintegration—Thus Marianne in *Spätestens im November*, where a claustrophobic nausea with life as a functionalized routine completely cuts off her thinking self from the part which she first accepts, later has to play. In most of Nossack's stories the narrative Ich is fictitious and not autobiographical—with the obvious exception of *Der Untergang*—yet we are for ever reminded of his personal point of view, especially if we spot similar ideas in book after book : for instance the distrust that amounts at times to hatred for the Mother figure, and the dread of empty afternoons. In *Der Neugierige* Nossack recasts himself in the guise of a fish who swims away from his fellows so as to savour the fullness of knowledge of his existence. The Cartesian *cogito ergo sum* is replaced by an experience that is far more typical of the anguished twentieth century intellectual :

"Doch wenn jetzt einer fragte : Hast du das Glück kennengelernt? . . . dann werde ich bis ans Ende meines Lebens nur antworten können : Diese seligen Nächte waren es, als ich mit meinem einzigen Freunde ins Nichts sprang. Denn nur damals fühlten wir uns ganz. . . . Sicher aber ist eines : Diese Sprünge haben mich in der Fähigkeit das Nichts zu bestehen geübt." [14]

We remember that Nossack only started publishing in his midforties, and that his attitudes and use of formal literary device are set in a decidedly personal mould. All his Ich narrators bear the stamp of the unflagging, sometimes frenzied curiosity of late youth or early middle age. They all remember the rashness of their youth with the glazed eye of the experienced sufferer, and none more so than the fish in this story. Escaping being swallowed up like his friend by a luridly described monster at the bottom of the sea, and remembering that he is supposed to have developed as a fish from such an earlier natural form, he is full of disgust for his past. He slips away to the freedom of self-realization and the know-

ledge that he has overcome his passive, fish-like reactions to his
environment. Cast up on a beach he struggles from pool to pool
with each incoming wave and is granted a backward view over the
traces in the sand made by his progress. Resisting the sea's tempting whispers to turn back, he leaps up from the pool to look forward into the unknown and calls to his body :

> "Richte dich hoch, damit ich sehen kann, was vor mir ist!
> Mache dich leicht, indem du das Nichts schwerer machst!
> Stoße die Last aus, um die Leere zu füllen! Versuch es, zu
> rufen, damit es leiser in dir und die Stille um dich lauter wird!
> Ob auch keiner da ist, dich zu hören, es hilft dir. Und wer
> weiß, vielleicht ist doch einer da, und es hilft ihm." [15]

Finally, having comprehended his fish-like form as a hindrance to
his newly acquired vision, and his spirit having overcome the re-
trictions and temptations of its normal environment the sea, he
reflects on the innermost proof of his being :

> "Woher kommt mir eigentlich diese Neugierde, die mich
> immer von neuem aus den Tümpeln hochjagt? Und auf was
> denn richtet sie sich?" [16]

Nossack's fish has an understanding of his habitat parallel to that
of his creator. His calling out to someone who may be there to
hear him is also Nossack's justification for literature. This finds
theoretical expression in the speech *Die Dichterische Substanz im
Menschen*, taking as a starting point basic human curiosity about
the purpose of life. The writer lives out this question—*wozu?*—
to its bitterest consequences so as to break through the
façades and abstractions of modern life. Aware of the dangers
of becoming a misfit in society, he sees this rather as the purpose
of his existence. His books are the by-product of his experience, not
written for a public, but as witnesses to struggles in his past. Thus
he comments :

> "Ein Apfelbaum bringt seine Früchte nicht hervor, um den
> Gartenbesitzer eine gute Ernte zu verschaffen. Er blüht und die
> Äpfel entstehen, weil es seine Aufgabe ist, die Möglichkeiten
> eines Apfelbaums zu erfüllen; weil er gar nicht anders kann.
> Und der selbst hat auch nichts von seinen Äpfeln; ob jemand
> sie erntet und ihren Geschmack lobt, oder ob sie ins Gras fallen
> und verfaulen, was geht ihn das an! Seiner Natur nach denkt
> er schon ans nächste Blühen." [17]

Nor is the apple tree perverse because he brings forth bitter fruit,
for :

> "Dann wäre die Bitterkeit der Früchte eher ein Zeichen für

die Aufrichtigkeit des Apfelbaums; er täuscht nichts vor, was nicht da ist; literarisch gesprochen, er ist kein Romantiker." [18]

Life is only saved and reborn for him where a creative tension is produced such as in the recognition of an object or person as beautiful. But to do this, the individual must act as an individual self, full of human substance and in conscious control of his potential. This is what Nossack terms the poetic force in man, and his purpose in writing is to call forth that sleeping potential. It is easy to see how the fairytale of the sleeping beauty lurks in his mind as a fertile expression of this idea. Freedom from collectivization of the individual's potential, whether by political or other means, and a firm distance from one's environment as achieved in *Der Neugierige* is needed :

"Wo aber ein Mensch sich zu sich selbst bekennt, wird er für alle Dinge seiner Umwelt zum Gegenpol. Die Spannung ist hergestellt, und was uns noch eben als tote und abstrakte Mächte bedrängte, verliert seinen Schrecken, da wir uns unabhängig entscheidend verhalten." [19]

The façade becomes a positive factor, modified by the detached individual. This gives the tone to his ideas on a united Europe, the European being one who has the ability to grow out beyond his own being. Imploringly, yet tinged with a note of disappointment, he asks of his audience to lay on one side its mask of collectivity and show again its human face. This disappointment turns at times to bitter despair, for instance in the essay *Das Alltagsdasein von Büchern*, but cannot staunch the automatic flow of his writing, seen almost as a biological function, but not as a sub-human process :

"In den seltenen, rein menschlichen, oder noch genauer gesagt, rein kreatürlichen Augenblicken wird die Sprache wieder eins, ganz schlicht und selbstverständlich." [20]

He continues with an attack on religious practices and in particular the Christian acceptance of the New Testament as a detached and complete expression of truth. Nossack sees this as a thoroughly edited series of documents, carefully prepared for propaganda purposes. By way of contrast with its anaemic presentation of events which he does not deny, he finds the Old Testament, although also perhaps edited, resounds with the pulse of the world and hence man's own. He writes this not to cast doubts on the validity of the central events, but to point out the suicidal aloofness of the Christian church's appeal to the individual. He objects to the application of public performance to the most

intimate religious practice : private prayer, and forecasts the
Church turning more and more to appease mass instincts, despairing of the power of self-discipline and asceticism in the mass.
The result will be ritualistic observance for the many and with-
drawal into silence by the few. Behind this one can sense many
startling similarities with the lines of thought expressed in Ortega
y Gasset's *Le Rebelión de las Masas*—for instance in his comparison of the mass with the attitudes of a spoilt child (Marianne's son
in *Spätestens im November*, and Hermann Schneider's in *Der
Jüngere Bruder* are but two of several examples in Nossack's works),
or in his conviction that life today is a period of change from one
in which duties were accepted as the natural concomitant of
existence into one in which rights are the aim of life.

It is tempting to call Nossack a nihilist, but he shows too deep
a love for humanity to deserve this. He carefully describes his
position in his *Rede zur Verleihung des Georg Büchner Preises*
in which he defines the spirit of protest.

> "Das eigentlich Revolutionäre besteht doch wohl für alle
> Zeiten darin, daß der Einzelne sich genau der Grenze bewußt
> ist, wo das Unrecht beginnt, und an dieser Grenze haltmacht und
> Nein sagt. Wenn junge Menschen sich auf dies positive Nein
> nicht mehr verlassen können, gerät die Welt ins Taumeln."[21]

For Nossack the most despicable thing one can say of anyone
is that he is incapable of guilt, and he praises Georg Büchner
especially in the last section of his *Lenz* as particularly anxious to
feel responsible for and fight against a situation where nihilism
is seen as a final stage in mankind's downfall. Of Woyzeck he
writes :

> "*Woyzeck* ist aber eine höchst lästige Anklage gegen das
> Nützlichkeitdenken, gegen das Gesellschaftliche als Endziel,
> gegen die Diktatur der Norm und des als praktisch propagierten
> Modells. *Woyzeck* ist die Tragödie der Kreatur, die an der
> Abstraktion zugrunde geht, die Tragödie des Menschen, dem es
> nicht gelingt, 'alles zu tun, wie es die anderen tun'."[22]

Büchner foresaw a spiritual revolution against abstraction, and
Nossack sees this revolution by silent withdrawal, for example in
the refusal of the bait of depth advertizing and in independently
minded literature, as a positive way of human redemption. He sees
in the monologue nature of contemporary literature an attempt to
rehumanize and repersonalize the language in which it is written.
This refers partly to the double-edged play of jargon and cliché
and any device that is concerned with the image it presents, the
effect it produces. Monologue for Nossack is the only form of

literature by which the individual can find the way to his own
truth, and other peoples' monologues stand as exemplary semantic
models. Thus he favours the *Erlebnisbericht* as described in the
lecture *Über den Einsatz*, and of which his most complex and
powerful example is *Nach dem letzten Aufstand*.

Nach dem letzten Aufstand clearly fulfils Nossack's nature as a
writer—it speaks in a language that deliberately makes no concessions to the interpreter, yet its style is for the most part simple
and informative. It both invites and destroys all attempts to relate
the figures and events to actual historical categories of time and
place. The story is the reminiscences of a Munich hotel night-
porter, told to an ageing film-star and a mysterious young man
(Nossack's angel figure). In an era before the *"letzten Aufstand"* the
narrator has been selected from a circus troupe to be the right-
hand man of the current God, a youth appointed for nine months
as a puppet figurehead by those that hold the real power, and then
transferred (by murder) to immortality. He is intelligent enough to
appreciate and assist in his particular God's patient humanity and
refusal to be used as a function in many amusingly down-to-earth
incidents, spurred on by the God's chosen *"Gespielin"* who is different from all others because she can laugh at and fall in love
with her God. The authorities, anxious to conclude treaties or at
least avoid war with the Christian countries from which the narrator has come, cross-examine him about his past, and eventually
send him back to Germany just in time to have missed the last
uprising. According to the film-star he comes back as a refugee,
taking a new name from a dead man's passport which he exchanges
with his own, and eventually becomes the highly respected Alois
Mörtl, night-porter of the Schwarzen Lamm. The totalitarian
state from which he has returned, and the hocus pocus by which it
is ruled seem at times to be oriental, at times communist, at times
a parody of democratic processes. The individual events are previous fragments worked into the story to give it considerable
symbolic force. Or so it seems, for there is only one reality that
is true in this work—that of the narrator's experiences—all others
are elements of propaganda, pseudo-astronomical, semi-dogmatic.
Time and again the individuals who count in this—the narrator,
the God and his *"Gespielin"* Achuni—break through their functions to reveal natural human responses. Thus the God playfully
describes to Achuni the possible embarrassment of meeting another
God :

> "Es wäre wie ein Spiegel, und wir wüßten nicht, wer von uns
> Bild und wer Gestalt ist. Man würde den Spiegel zerbrechen
> müssen. Denn der Gott darf sich nicht spiegeln, das wäre das

Ende. Er ist doch selber nichts als ein Spiegel für alle, die ihres Bildes bedürfen."[23]

Man as "Ebenbild der Gottheit"[24] has to have clear in his mind who is *Bild* and who *Gestalt*. Taking this as a starting-point to interpret this work, the various figures elicit different responses—the tragic narrator, who only in narrating his discarded past can overcome the routine of his present; the despicable Oberst der Diener whose double-sidedness also controls the façade of power he exercises through the God; the saintly Achuni who sacrifices herself to a situation she knows to be false so as to save her God's individuality; and the sympathetic film-star, who has never managed to find herself in her various rôles. In doing so we are dangerously close to judging these figures against their functions, which is precisely the trap that Nossack hopes to lay bare. The narrator reflects this astutely when he comments of Achuni and God one cannot fall in love with a person's job. Even the narrator is tempted to interpret, but is honest enough to disclaim words he thinks the God might have said from what he actually did say. He realizes for the God (who is fallible enough not to have realized this) that all Gods have to be sacrificed so as to satisfy the people's sense of order—no one God can contravene this law, because it is necessary. He even is truthful enough to confess that the customs to which he alludes are now dead since the last uprising—nevertheless they stand for any customs, the Gods for any idols. The temptation to turn the individual into a symbol and allow this to be reincarnated as a restrictive myth that sets up various taboos and restrictions is the hidden theme of this work. This leads to the possible abuse of power to deny people any basic individuality. Thus Nossack defines the last uprising as :

> "Der letzte Aufstand, wenn das zu sagen erlaubt ist, muß eine Periode völliger Entmenschlichung gewesen sein, darum vermutlich liegt sie wie eine 'Lücke', über die, wenn wir ehrlich sind, zurückzudenken uns unmöglich ist, zwischen dem, was vorher war, und unserm heutigen Zustand."[25]

We cannot understand and live after a catastrophe unless we try to describe what we experienced or listen to what others experienced before and during that time. If this work does nothing else, it will sharpen the reader's awareness to the kind of double-think, propaganda and pressure brought to bear at all times on the individual. Narration, sober and truthful to an at times nauseatingly self-denying degree, is shown to be Alois Mörtl's only real way of retaining his humanity. As is pointed out in the introduction, the reading of these notes is not necessary, only the writing of them was essential.

If Nossack fulfils himself as a writer in *Nach dem letzten Aufstand*, the clearest and most revealing essay he has written is *Der Mensch in der heutigen Literatur* in which the cross-currents of ideas, convictions and reactions behind the complex structure of his imaginative works are charted in detail. He sees the writer's task to explain and counteract man's condition today. Against this then we must finally judge Nossack's works—firstly how clearly and tellingly does he portray himself and this central task behind and through each successive work, secondly how effectively do his works achieve their human significance? How does Nossack define man? A being he says "dem die einzigartige Gabe verliehen ist, Zwiesprache mit sich selber zu halten".[26] The author or artist, as opposed to the scientist, is intimately connected to his theme; and paradoxically, the closer this relationship is, the more authentic and objective the theme becomes. The theme enables the writer to examine and converse with himself—a relationship that is wholly personal and convinces him of his loneliness and individuality; whereas the scientist by the very nature of his calling loses his individuality in collective self-suppression by all those faced with the restrictive categories and laws of their special field. The special field demands a language tempered by reason to create fixed patterns, the individual relationship opens up endless possibilities of self-exploration and self-expression. Nossack openly condemns not only the restrictive demands of the welfare and free-enterprise state in which for instance everyone is held to persuasion that they need a washing-machine, but also the Marxist habit of explaining away all religious awe and personal desire to withdraw from agreement from everyone else. He sees the mere attempt to define or lay down laws for religion as a sign of religious decay, for religion is a personal way of life, not a formula for living. Today he finds man afflicted by conformism and taking refuge in its false utopia—refuge that is from the hurricane that surrounds him, as was shown in Stifter's works, a refuge whose views out into the hurricane are the theme of modern literature. Like a child in a fairytale man is subject to the forces around him which he can call up but not control.

He finds T. E. Lawrence, Cesare Pavese and Albert Camus typical representatives of this, and in particular in their realization of the loneliness of the natural landscape, where objects in it are not romantically in dialogue with one another, but at the most speakers of monologues. Thus in Pavese we find that

"Vergleich und Bild werden bei ihm nicht wie bisher zur

Umschreibung des Nicht-Aussprechbaren benutzt, sondern das Bild gehört zum Wesen des Dinges oder ist das Ding selber."[27]

Both Pavese and Camus see behind the man-made façade of relationships between things into their hidden reality. In this sense Nossack writes against what is normally called realism, but which he sees as abstraction. As he puts it in his interview with Horst Bienek :

> "Mich interessiert brennend, was die Dinge wohl sein mögen, wenn sie nicht nur unser Objekt sind. Oder deutlicher ausgedrückt : was sind sie in ihrer Einsamkeit, was sind sie, bevor sie Mythos geworden sind, denn der Mythos ist doch nur eine Vorderseite, die sie uns zukehren, und die wir verbrauchen."[28]

He finds that in the complexity of themes in most modern novels man is seen struggling out of social and communal commitments into anonymity, so as to refind himself. Nossack himself fled the city in an experiment to refind himself, but now acknowledges a deep desire to return to the city, to the utopia of having a room there but remaining unnoticed and alone. His self-appointed task then is to preserve the *homo religiosus* over an age of abstract rationalization, and Nossack explains :

> "Verstehen wir unter dem *homo religiosus* ganz schlicht den Menschen, der sich seiner einzigartigen Stellung in der Welt bewußt zu bleiben bemüht und die Verantwortung für diese Einzigartigkeit auf sich nehmen möchte."[29]

Not an idealist then, nor necessarily an angel (though Nossack's angel figures have many of these characteristics), but an independently living man, free but responsible. It is interesting to note who he considers in this category—the sober-minded Stendhal, to whom he acknowledges a debt in his speech accepting the Wilhelm Raabe prize, and Wilhelm Raabe for his way of tearing the reader away from any illusory effects created by his descriptive style. Nossack himself shows he has reached such independence in his new formulation of *"proligio"*, seeing in *"religio"* a verbal construct denoting man's museum-like existence in the past instead of a hopeful richness of possibilities for the future.

Nossack's recent work *Das kennt man* shows us the tragic acceptance of individual responsibility on the part of a street-woman, now telling her tale to a young medical student as she lies dying in hospital after a traffic accident. It is hardly surprising, but alarmingly true to life, that she misinterprets the whole set-up of society, men, police, employers, doctors and nurses as part of one infinitely complex plot scheming to do her out of her life and right to withdraw into her own self-satisfied secretiveness about common knowledge. We are given a clinical analysis by means of traumatic monologue of the gradual breakdown of a simple mind that can less and less distinguish between reality and its image, and one that is more and more dependent on people it believes to be hostile, when they are mostly sympathetic. Failure to communicate and helpless loneliness are the themes of the *Sechs Etüden*, which are noteworthy for their technical mastery in throwing open perspectives out of a single limited episode on to a background of natural laws fraught with possibilities and threateningly different from what the face of the episode might lead us to expect its character to be.

In his latest work *Das Testament des Lucius Eurinus*, Nossack writes the explanation of a Roman patrician of about A.D. 200 for his suicide following his wife telling him she has become a Christian. In doing so he opens up the gulf that has arisen between Christian custom and political reality, and the development of Christianity into a minority with traditions and a rôle already fixed and accepted. The old Bishop explains that he reveals his fears to Eurinus so as to hear his own true voice more clearly and then to follow it. One may take this as a further example of Nossack searching for an answer to and clarification of a personal problem, which at the same time he knows to be one shared by many of his contemporaries and ancestors who lived in regions reached by Christianity.

It is perhaps wrong to ever attempt to sum up the achievements of a living writer, still less to evaluate what he has written. Nossack would be one of the first to find such an approach irrelevant. His works are hard to read because they refuse to accept face values as true ones. They are essentially voyages of exploration by Nossack into himself and the social situations in which he finds post-war Germans to be. They do not set out to preach, but rather to spotlight and by insistence on straight thinking about experience, to remind man he can make himself free from his environment if he does not set out to shackle himself with its temptations. His is not the withdrawal of the aesthete, nor of the snob, but rather of the monk believing in values that are choked in the rush of modern life. Possibly the best summing-up of Nossack is given by himself in the poem *Der Angeklagte hat das Wort* where he speaks not as a writer but as a person :

> Mein Anfang war, ich wurde ausgespien.
> Man hat mich zwar—sonst hätt ich ganz geschwiegen—
> Verlornen Sohn genannt; doch das sind Lügen.
> Ich stelle fest : Mein Anfang war kein Fliehn.

Was vor mir geschah, dafür bin ich nicht schuldig.
Sie waren wohl nicht glücklich, und man wollte
Vielleicht, daß ich es besser machen sollte.
Aber mein Anfang machte mich ungeduldig.

Denn die Bewegung dieses Von-sich-Speins
Wie ätzendes Gift ward meines ganzen Seins
Bewegung, meine Schwäche—meine Kraft.

Denn ausgespien—ich spreche nicht als Dichter—,
Spei ich mich aus. Versteht es, meine Richter :
Ich rechne nicht, ich gebe Rechenschaft.[30]

TRANSLATIONS

1. Whether it would be better understood if it was narrated in the
twilight as a fairytale? Once upon a time there was a man to whom no
Mother had given birth. A fist thrust him naked into the world, and a
voice called out: Mind how you go. Then he opened his eyes and did
not know how to begin with all that he saw around him. And he did
not dare to look back, for behind him there was nothing but fire.

2. For what we have won and has become different is that we have
become part of the present. We have freed ourself from time . . . Reason
says, how sad that sounds. But it is not sad, merely so. Reason alone is
sad, because it thinks it has wings, but is for ever falling down.

3. I speak to a being, of whom I believe it will one day be there. I
am certain this is not just a weak wish of my loneliness to flee away
among the helpless sleepers. Often the figure of this being already stands
clearly before me, and I call it: Thou. Yes, I like to call it Thou, for
then it is most visible to me.

4. It is not good to wish to explain things which cannot be explained
by reason. But it is just as false to deny their reality only because they
can be explained by reason. For as they have an effect and leave a trace
behind them, they must also have a reality. Best of all would be to
confirm their existence by silent astonishment.

5. Even the ruins there do not raise their arms helplessly to the sky and
lament their destroyed worth, but announce with full assurance: Look,
I was a house.

6.   Close now the windows! Light fire in the hearth!
     Sit down to table and let the corks pop free!
     Our daily food has lasted to the aftermath;
     And we are still alive, among the dead not we.

     Of course we had at times to lick the other's shoes,
     And did and said for us the best to do,
     And tried to hide our stomachs obvious ooze,
     Politely rubbing shoulders with every hungry crew.

Close now the windows! so no one hears our rout!
Mind and our conscience will end up in exile.
We are alright, for we are well blown out.
And O what a treat, to feel eternal style!

7. If Hans Erich Nossack has a gift, then it is this, a praised ability to strip the strangely simple and unnoticed down to the natural and elemental. He endows bad words with good meanings, and makes inconspicuous details cry out with life.

8. Do you believe in things that have nothing to do with money, success or statistics, and which cannot be explained by wireless sets now turned off? Do you believe there are such things, even if we do not have them? The peach tree and the moon peeping down a forest glade? Excuse this late question, which should not be asked in the theatre. That is quite inexcusable. And I only ask it as we are standing on the edge of the stage. One step farther and we break our necks. We began with a marriage and played what came out of it. Am I a special case? If so, no one need conform with me. I say no to a world, of which it is said I may be nothing in it but a special case. I have no more time for it.

9. The so-called truth which we try to scream out into the world is for you only a vitamin, a laxative or article of luxury that you take after your work is over.

10. Nossack prides himself on being the best-disguised writer.

11. An event has given a man insomnia. He tries hard to think back over his life and forward to its end. Taking different rôles he holds judgement over, accuses, defends, and tries to pardon himself so as to find peace at last. But always when the spiral of his thoughts wants to sink into sleep, it knocks up against bits of his life and is wrenched up again into the merciless twilight of sleeplessness. Perhaps the man will have to give up the struggle in the end and stand shivering at the window. Outside it is already dawn and the birds begin to twitter.

12. Departure into the unassurable.

13. Things are sinking away around me like a fall of snow.

14. Yet if anyone were to ask you: have you experienced happiness? ...then I shall not be able to answer to the end of my life: Those blessed nights when I sprang with my friend into nothingness. For only then did we fully feel ourselves....But one thing is certain: Those leaps have practiced me in the art of outlasting nothingness.

15. Raise yourself high so I can see what is in front of me! Lighten yourself in making nothingness around you heavier! Cast off from you the burden so as to feel the emptiness! Try to call out, so that it is quieter in you and louder in the calm around you! Even if no one is there to hear you, it will help you. And who knows, perhaps there is someone there, and it will help him.

16. Where in fact does this inquisitiveness come from, which for ever drives me on out of the pools? And what is its direction?

17. An apple tree does not bring forth its fruits to give the owner of the garden a good harvest. It blossoms and the apples grow because it has the task of fulfilling the possibilities of an apple tree, because it cannot do otherwise. Nor does it gain anything from its apples; for what

does it matter to it if someone harvests them and praises their taste, or if they fall into the grass and rot away! Its nature makes it already think about next season.

18. Then the bitterness of the fruit would be rather a sign of the tree's sincerity. It does not deceive by producing what is not there. In literary terms, it is no romantic.

19. But where a man emphasizes his individuality, he becomes an opposite pole to everything around him. Tension is set up, and whatever oppressed us as dead and abstract forces, loses its horror as soon as we act decidedly and independently from it.

20. In the rare, purely human, or, more accurately, purely creaturely moments, language becomes unified again, quite simple and self-explanatory.

21. The actual spirit of revolution always consists of the individual being exactly aware of that frontier where injustice begins, and of halting at that frontier and saying no. When young people can no longer rely on using this positive no, then the world will begin to totter.

22. But *Woyzeck* is an extremely burdensome accusation against utilitarian thought, against all social activity as a final aim, against dictatorship of the norm and of any model set up for its practicality. *Woyzeck* is the tragedy of the creature who goes to grief on abstraction, the tragedy of a man who cannot succeed in "doing everything as others do".

23. It would be like a mirror, and we should not know which of us was reflection and which person. We should have to break the mirror. For God may not mirror himself, that would be the end. Yet he is nothing but a mirror for all those that need an image of themselves.

24. Mirror image of God. (Goethe.)

25. The last uprising, if I may say so, must have been a time of complete dehumanization, hence I suppose it lies like a void over which, if we are honest, it is impossible to think back, a void between what was before and our situation today.

26. To whom the single gift is given to hold dialogue with himself.

27. Comparison and image are not as formerly used by him to describe the inexpressible, but the image belongs to the essence of the thing, or is the thing itself.

28. I am intensely interested in what things might be if they were not just objects to us. Or more clearly expressed: what are they in their loneliness, what are they before they became myth, for myth is but the front side which they turn towards us, and which we wear out.

29. Let us understand the *homo religiosus* quite simply as the man who strives to remain conscious of his unique position in the world, and who would like to take on himself the responsibility of being so unique.

30. At the beginning I was spat out. Indeed they called me prodigal son —otherwise I should have remained silent—yet that is not the truth. I insist: my beginning was no flight. What happened before me, for that I bear no guilt. They were maybe not happy, and it was hoped perhaps that I should make up for it. But my beginning made me impatient. For the movement of this spitting away from one as if a corrosive poison,

became the movement of my whole being, my weakness and my strength. For spat out I now spit myself out—I do not speak here as a writer. Please understand, my judges: I do not dispute, I merely render an account.

SELECT BIBLIOGRAPHY

Published works

Apart from his *Gedichte* (Hamburg 1947), three plays (*Die Rotte Kain* Hamburg 1949 Uraufführung Wiesbaden 1951, *Die Hauptprobe* Hamburg 1956 written 1943 Uraufführung Wiesbaden 1953, and *Ein Sonderfall* Darmstadt 1963) and translations of Joyce Carey's *The Horse's Mouth,* Gerald Hanley's *Drinkers of Darkness,* Harold Nicolson's *The English Sense of Humour* and Sherwood Anderson's *Winesburg Ohio,* Nossack's works fall into two main categories:

1. Imaginative prose works

Nekyia. Bericht eines Uberlebenden. 1947 Bibliothek Suhrkamp 1961.
Interview mit dem Tode. Berichte. 1948 Bibliothek Suhrkamp 1963.
Spätestens im November. Roman. 1955 DTV paperback 1963.
Spirale. Roman einer schlaflosen Nacht. Suhrkamp Vlg. Frankfurt 1956.
Der jüngere Bruder. Roman. 1958 Knaur paperback 1964.
Nach dem letzten Aufstand. Ein Bericht. Suhrkamp Vlg, Frankfurt 1961.
Begegnung im Vorraum. Erzählungen. Bücher der 19 1963.
Der Untergang. 1948 written 1943 Edition Suhrkamp 1963.
Das kennt man. Erzählung. Suhrkamp Vlg, Frankfurt 1964.
Sechs Etüden. Inselbücherei 1964.
Das Testament des Lucius Eurinus. Edition Suhrkamp 1965 written 1963.

2. Essays, speeches, etc.

Publikum und Dichter. Neues Hamburg 1949–50.
Die dichterische Substanz im Menschen. Jahrbuch der Akademie Mainz 1954.
Vorwort zu H. H. Jahnn *Thomas Chatterton.* Akzente 1955(2).
Uber den Einsatz. Abhandlungen der Akademie Mainz 1956.
Nossack von Berthold Möncken. Jahrbuch der Akademie Hamburg 1957.
Der Weg ins Verschweigen. In *Was halten sie vom Christentum.* List Vlg, München 1957.
Nationalhymne der Opportunisten. Jahrbuch der Akademie Hamburg 1959.
Freizeitliteratur. Ein Fastenpredigt. Abhandlungen der Akademie Mainz 1959.
Das Alltagsdasein von Büchern. Jahrbuch der Akademie Mainz 1960.
Rede zum Georg Büchner Preis. Jahrbuch der Akademie Darmstadt 1961, also in Merkur 1961.
Der Mensch in der heutigen Literatur. Jahresring Stuttgart 1962–63.

Strickwaren für Neger. Ist unsere Literatur arbeiterfremd? Merkur 1962.
Ansprache zum Wilhelm-Raabe-Preis. Jahrbuch der Raabe Gesellschaft 1963, also in Jahresring, Stuttgart 1964–65.
Proligio. Ein Traktat über die Zukunft des Menschen. Merkur 1965.
Die schwache Position der Literatur. Edition Suhrkamp 1966.

Secondary literature

Horst Bienek. Interview mit Nossack in *Werkstattgespräche mit Schriftstellern*. Hanser Vlg, München 1962.
Walter Boehlich. Am Rand des unsichtbaren Abgrunds. Die Zeit 3.2.1961.
Walter Boehlich. Nachwort zu *Der Untergang*. Edition Suhrkamp 1963.
Hans Henny Jahnn. Kleine Rede auf Hans Erich Nossack. Sinn und Form 1955(2).
Hermann Kasack. Rede auf den Preisträger. Jahrbuch der Deutschen Akademie für Sprache und Dichtung, Darmstadt 1961.
Marcel Reich-Ranicki. Hans Erich Nossack, der nüchterne Visionär. In *Deutsche Literatur in West und Ost*. Piper Vlg, München 1963.
Heinz Schöffler. Hans Erich Nossack. In *Schriftsteller der Gegenwart* hsg. K. Nonnemann. Walter Vlg, Olten 1963.
Hans Schwab-Felisch. Die falschen Gefühle. Zum neuesten Roman Hans Erich Nossacks. *Der Jüngere Bruder*. Der Monat 1958 (11) (122).
Hans Schwab-Felisch. In *Handbuch der Deutschen Gegenwartsliteratur* hsg. H. Kunisch. Nymphenburger Vlg, München 1965.
Christa Wolf. "Freiheit" oder Auflösung der Persönlichkeit? (*Spätestens im November* und *Spirale*). Neue Deutsche Literatur 1957(4).

Günter Eich

Günter Eich

by F. M. FOWLER
(University of Kent)

Günter Eich was born in the little town of Lebus on the Oder in 1907 and was brought up in Brandenburg. At university, first in Leipzig, then in Paris and Berlin, he studied law and also Chinese. From 1932 he earned his living by writing, especially for radio. In 1930 he published his first *Gedichte*, in 1933 a dramatization of Eichendorff's *Die Glücksritter*, and in 1936 a short story, *Katharina*. During the war Eich served in the armed forces and was finally taken prisoner by the Americans, who released him in 1946. Further volumes of poetry appearing in 1948 and 1949 and radio plays broadcast and published in the early fifties established Eich as an important contemporary writer, and it is in lyric poetry and the radio play that he has since specialized. One of the founder members of the influential post-war literary circle, the Gruppe 47, Eich became in 1950 the first to receive its coveted annual award. His other prizes include the *Literaturpreis der Bayerischen Akademie der schönen Künste* (1951), the *Hörspielpreis der Kriegsblinden* (1952), the *Literaturpreis des Kulturkreises im Bundesverband der Deutschen Industrie* (1954), and the *Georg-Büchner-Preis* (1959). In 1953 Eich married Ilse Aichinger; they now live in Upper Bavaria.

"Dichter, die niemanden erschrecken, sind zu nichts anderem wert, als daß man sich über sie unterhält."[1]

—Eich : *Die Brandung vor Setúbal*

ALTHOUGH Günter Eich was born in 1907 and published a first slim volume of verse at the age of twenty-three, it was only after the end of the Second World War that he emerged as an important lyric poet and a leading writer of radio plays. In 1948 the collection *Abgelegene Gehöfte* firmly established his reputation as a poet, but it was the first broadcast of *Träume* in 1951 ("the birth of the German radio play") that really made an impact on a wider public and finally showed that Eich did not fall into the category of writers who "alarming no one, can serve only as topics for polite conversation". Like Borchert's *Draußen vor der Tür*, broadcast four years earlier, *Träume* was a sensation, but while Borchert's play met with almost universal acclaim, Eich's raised an immediate storm of protest. An explanation for the different reactions is not hard to find : whereas *Draußen vor der Tür* ran on a comparatively realistic level, the symbolic character of *Träume* made a far greater demand on the listener; and secondly, whereas Borchert summed up the feelings of thousands if not millions in Germany at the time, Eich was obviously telling his listeners something that they did not want to hear.

Since the war, Eich has published three volumes of *Hörspiele* and three major collections of poems (the volume entitled *Untergrundbahn* contains only fifteen pieces, more than half of which are re-printed—some in a revised version—in *Botschaften des Regens*). Given his acknowledged success in both fields, it may at first seem difficult to decide whether Eich is primarily poet or playwright. But no real dichotomy exists at all, for Eich is not torn between poetry and the theatre : it is a striking fact that he has never written a single play for the theatre, and that despite the example of *Draußen vor der Tür* and Max Frisch's *Herr Biedermann und die Brandstifter* none of his *Hörspiele* has ever become a stage success. Eich has created not so much a theatre of the air as a poetry of the air, a "spirit-world of voices", a medium in which, as in lyric poetry, the word or word-complex is dominant. Dispensing with the visual dimension (and limitation) of the stage as well as the communal reaction of a mass audience, Eich's *Hörspiele* demand the total engagement of the listener's imagination so that they may subtly or violently awaken the individual conscience.

The play entitled *Träume*, though somewhat uneven in quality, is indisputably a key work; no one hearing or reading it could possibly be left in doubt as to the nature or extent of Eich's commitment as a writer. From a formal point of view, too, though not typical, it is significant : the five dreams acted out as separate scenes are framed by verse passages increasing the involvement of the listener, and finally—in a near-Brechtian manner—making a direct appeal to his sense of duty as a human being. Eich begins by voicing distrust of the clear conscience and with the reminder that no man is an island, that no one can opt out of his share of responsibility for human suffering—

Alles, was geschieht, geht dich an[2]—

a theme memorably brought home in the lines following the first dream :

Denke daran :
Nirgendwo auf der Landkarte liegt Korea und Bikini,
aber in deinem Herzen.[3]

The writer concludes with the warning that we cannot afford to lie sleeping, dreaming our time away while the world is being run by others for their own (sinister) purposes. Every single lapse

from the values of true humanity is seen as another step on the
road to universal disaster, and so Eich advises his listeners:

> Tut das Unnütze, singt die Lieder, die man aus
> eurem Mund nicht erwartet!
> Seid unbequem, seid Sand, nicht das Öl im
> Getriebe der Welt![4]

Thus on the one hand the dream is seen as an escape, a potentially dangerous flight from a reality that should command all our
attention:

> Im Grunde aber meine ich, daß auch das gute
> Gewissen nicht ausreicht,
> und ich zweifle an der Güte des Schlafs, in dem
> wir uns alle wiegen.[5]

But at the same time the dreams reveal, through the five scenes,
the fundamental insecurity of twentieth-century man, uncovering
a reality far below the surface of everyday life. Significantly
enough, the dreams are not all those of one person, or even of a
few people living in similar circumstances: the fictitious dreamers
are spread over four continents, and their dreams give a clue not
to the peculiar psychological state of any one set of individuals
but rather to the condition of a whole diseased society.

Each of the dreams in *Träume* is prefaced by a brief sober introduction giving the date, place, and identity of the dreamer,
providing a counterpoint to the verse intermezzos; the contrast is
further heightened by ironic suggestions that the dreams should
not be taken too seriously. But whereas the introduction to the
first scene blandly states that bad dreams are the result of indigestion, the preface to the third (and no less horrible) nightmare contains the "re-assuring" information that the dreamer was in the
best of health at the time he had his dream and has long since
forgotten it.

The first dream deals with the dehumanised victims of a totalitarian régime: a closed goods-waggon containing a few miserable
people has been travelling on for so many years that only the two
oldest dimly remember the outside world—and even they begin to
wonder if their memories are only an hallucination. For the others,
the claustrophobic life in the goods-wagon is the norm, indeed the
only possibility they can imagine: they cannot conceive of the
alternation of day and night or of bread not mouldy like that which
is pushed in to them through a flap. Eventually they receive proof
of the existence of an outside world when a hole appears in the
wall—through which they see a world changed, in which those
outside (the people in power) have meanwhile grown to gigantic

stature; the reaction of the victims is fear, and they seal up the hole. At this point the train, which has hitherto been travelling slowly, gathers speed, the sound of the wheels increases to deafening volume and then dies away in the distance, suggesting that the victims are being rushed off to an unknown doom.

Whereas in the first dream explicit brutality is entirely avoided, the second emphasises the horrific or thoroughly nightmarish aspect. With complete *sang-froid* a six-year-old boy is sold for slaughter by his own parents, who, having previously got rid of their other children in the same way, treat the transaction as an everyday event. Human values are completely extinguished—indeed the very mention of them, purely as a means of increasing the price, calls forth only ridicule. The invalid who buys the boy so as to drink his blood ("the new therapy, a blessing for humanity") happily laughs over his pretence that the child is going into the kitchen to play with a toy train. But, ironically, the buyers are not without feelings—of a sort : the wife does not want to do the "dirty job" of slaughter herself and the husband is annoyed at having to listen to the shrieks of the dying child.

The third dream on the other hand shows the family relationship still inviolate. A happy family (possibly, like the first, Jewish) is reduced to terror and driven from home at the arrival of a sinister and potentially violent nocturnal visitor, "the enemy", whose irregular steps suggest a monster and who appears to be blind. The theme of inhumanity recurs when first their neighbour, then the whole town turns against them—all acting out of fear for themselves, but by their action in fact aiding and abetting the dreaded "enemy" and increasing his power. At the end of the scene the members of the family console themselves with the thought that they still have each other and are thus richer than the collaborating townspeople. But despite the symbolic coming of daylight the scene does not end on a note of hope, for they have nowhere to go.

The last two dreams are concerned with the aimlessness and emptiness of modern civilization. In the fourth dream, two Europeans exploring the African jungle lose their memories as a result of eating herbs given to them on the instructions of the witch-doctors. As a result one goes off aimlessly into the jungle "looking for happiness", while the other thinks he will find happiness in sleep, especially if he is lulled by the sound of drums, the very symbol of their destruction. Destruction is also the subject of the final dream : the hollowness and superficiality of twentieth-century life are presented through the fate of a young couple who have moved into a splendid modern apartment in New York. On the surface all seems to be going well for them; yet there is a strange

sound in the house which the young wife at first pretends is the
lift but which, as she well knows, is really the sound of termites
gnawing at the building till only an empty shell is left, ready to
fall in the first storm. The termites are everywhere, even hollow-
ing out the people themselves, so that there is no escape. The scene
ends with approaching thunder heralding the collapse of the
building.

Thus in *Träume* Eich conjures up a picture of a society insecure
and unstable, haunted by anxious dreams and liable to lose the
values of humanity. If the images themselves are Kafkaesque in
quality, the appeal to the social conscience is Brechtian : the individual dare not be deaf to the unceasing cries of pain in the world,
he must give up his dreaming and be ever on his guard to ensure
that those in authority, acting in his name, use their power not to
inflict but rather to alleviate suffering. In no other *Hörspiel* by
Eich is the social message so strongly and directly expressed; but
the recurrence of themes from *Träume* in his latest lyric poetry
shows this concern to be no mere passing phase in his thought.

If the first broadcast of *Träume* deserves Gerhard Prager's
designation "the birth of the German radio-play", it is not because
of technical or formal innovations in the play but rather owing
to the masterful verbal economy. Far more impressive than the
appropriate use of sound effects—the train accelerating, the steps
in the night, the tribal drums, the sound of the termites—is the
suggestive character of the language, particularly in the first scene,
in which a few lines reveal the insecurity of man's relation to
reality and his need of language to command it.

Although it may be said that formally *Träume* is unique in
Eich's *oeuvre*, the dream motif at least recurs regularly throughout the plays. In several cases the motif is combined with a typically Eich pattern : the individual awakens from a state of torpor
or sterile self-satisfaction, a kind of death in life, to a new acceptance of reality; mysteriously, he is driven to seek his true destiny,
the finding of which frequently involves his own actual death. We
find dream and awakening juxtaposed in this manner as early as
1951 in *Geh nicht nach El Kuwehd*, first of four plays in the collection entitled *Träume* : at the opening the hero, an eastern
merchant, lives only to excite the envy of others; then suddenly
filled with an inexplicable disquiet he sees in a dream how he is
led to his death and how at the moment of his execution he recognizes his "mistake", vowing that if he could have the choice a
second time he would act differently; on awakening, however, he
is faced with the choice in reality and knowingly follows the fatal
path, for at all costs he must find an escape from his previous
mode of existence. The development of the individual in a kind of

growth towards death or real life forms the central theme of at
least four of the seven plays in *Stimmen*, Eich's second collection :
Die Andere und Ich, Das Jahr Lazertis, Die Mädchen aus Viterbo,
and the last piece, a play suffused with a tender lyrical mysticism,
Die Brandung vor Setúbal.

In *Die Andere und Ich*, one of the author's most impressive
achievements, Eich uses a variation on the dream-motif—the hallucination experienced by a woman on the point of drowning. The
form of the play is a first-person narrative interrupted by dialogues complete with realistic sound-effects. The play opens in a
world of respectability and security with fixed values which are
accepted without thought : the well-to-do Harland family (father,
mother, and two children) from Cleveland are touring Italy by car
viewing the sights that merit two stars in the guide-book. At the
age of 41 the narrator, Ellen Harland, is entirely satisfied with
herself and the world in which she feels completely at home : she
has read her Hemingway and her Gide, she gives talks to the
Ladies' Club, and corresponds on theological problems with the
Methodist Bishop of Baltimore. But in a few moments she is to
undergo an experience which will radically alter her whole outlook
on life. Deciding to go bathing on what is an exceptionally hot
day, the family drives to the coast, passing on the way a miserable
little fishing-village, the sight and stench of which Ellen finds
appalling. To her the notion of human beings living and loving
here is almost inconceivable; little does she know that she is soon
to experience their way of life at first hand. When they arrive at
the beach, Ellen first goes swimming with her family, then, remembering the old woman who seemed to look at her strangely as
they drove by the village, she feels an urge to leave the others and
walk back to the place. She sees no-one in the streets, but enters
one of the houses, where she finds the woman, who unaccountably
looks far younger and greets Ellen as her daughter Camilla. To
her horror Ellen finds that she has taken on the appearance of an
Italian fisher-girl, and that her poverty-stricken "parents" are trying to persuade her—without much hope of success—to marry one
of the "richest" men in the village, Giovanni Foscolo, who is
however old and unattractive. Recovering from the initial shock
Ellen proceeds to treat the situation as a game, seeing a chance to
play God in the fortunes of the fisher people. Thus she decides to
accept Giovanni's proposal before returning to her own family. On
the way back she feels some twinges of conscience at the high-
handedness of her action, but on balance thinks that she has done
Camilla and her people a good turn. Only on her return to the
beach does Eich permit Ellen to discover the whole truth—the
date is now not 1951 but 1910 and, conscious though she still is of

her "real" identity as Ellen Harland, she can find no way back into
the world of security and respectability. Ironically, Ellen has acted
according to the material standards to which she was accustomed
and must now, quite unexpectedly, reap the fruits of her decision.
For forty years she has to live as Camilla, married first to Giovanni,
an old man whom she does not love, then to Carlo, who had been
her lover but grows away from her, taking to drink and finally
hanging himself, unable to bear the knowledge that he has murdered Giovanni for her. At first Ellen schemes to return to
America, but her plans are frustrated when Carlo squanders
Giovanni's money on wine and again when his son Antonio steals
all her savings. Reduced to direst poverty, she ekes out a bare
existence by gutting fish : having lived through the murder of her
first husband, the suicide of her second, and the death of her two
sons in the war, Camilla has by the time the Harland's car arrives
in the village lost all recollection of her former self : "Ellen Harland
fuhr dort vorüber—ich hatte sie vergessen".[6] It is at this point that
Ellen "returns to reality", when she is rescued from drowning : all
that she has experienced from the moment she decided to leave
the others has passed in a few seconds of "real" time. The next
day the rest of the family again go bathing, leaving Ellen in the
hotel. She walks back to the village to find herself unrecognized
by Camilla's family; when she asks for Camilla herself, she is
shown into a room where Camilla lies dead.

For Ellen, her life as Camilla is no mere bad dream : it is an
essential part of reality, for her little cosmos is shaken, her basic
scale of values shattered. But her experience is essentially incom-
municable : her family cannot possibly understand what has happened to her, and when they leave for the beach their departure
is seen to be symbolic : "Ich hätte sie gerne zurückgerufen, aber
sie waren schon zu weit. Mit jedem Schritt wurden sie mir frem-
der . . ."[7] We do not know the exact shape of Ellen's future life,
but it seems clear that she will no longer feel at home in a world
of talks at the Ladies' Club and dabblings in amateur theology.

In this respect Das Jahr Lazertis goes a step farther : here the
effect of the unique experience on the individual's life is explicit.
As in Die Andere und Ich, first person narration alternates with
dialogue scenes. The hero, Paul, is an artist who earns his living by
painting not what his artistic sensibility demands but what will sell
well—the same old sentimental subject over and over again. But
early one New Year's morning something happens which changes
the course of his entire life. Lying in bed, he is awakened from
his dream by the sound of a word spoken by someone passing outside his window, a word which seems to him to provide the "solution to all mysteries" : for a split second the world is transformed.

Yet try as he may, Paul discovers that he cannot quite recall the word in question, nor does he succeed in finding the person who used it so casually in passing; he knows only that it sounded "something like 'Lazertis' ". Now there begins a series of variations as Paul decides that his destiny is bound up with the finding of this word and, since it reminds him first of "Lazerten" (lizards), sets off for Brazil to paint lizards for a scientific expedition (the year is 1880). On arrival in Pernambuco Paul meets the second variation on Lazertis in the person of Bayard, a fashionable French doctor who sees himself in the role of Laertes, father of Odysseus, waiting for the return of his son. But there follows a more significant variation: once established in the Brazilian jungle the other members of the expedition send Paul to the aid of a sick white man, Richards, who turns out to be dying of leprosy and immediately reminds Paul of the traditional patron of lepers—Lazarus. At first repelled, Paul nonetheless resolves to stay behind to look after Richards until his death. After burying him, Paul discovers on his own body the red patches which Richards had described as the first symptom of leprosy, and in Pernambuco Bayard confirms his suspicions, providing him with another variation on Lazertis: *la certitude*. Even here, however, Eich has not reached the last of his series of assonances, for Paul is now taken to the Brazilian lepers' home, a former Italian monastery still known as *La Certosa*. For three years he shares the wretched existence of the inmates of the home, helping those worst afflicted in their daily lives. Only at the end of this period does he learn that Bayard has been declared insane. Having no further symptoms of leprosy (Bayard had suggested that he was a "slow case"), Paul, who has never been re-examined, persuades the resident doctor to give him a discharge. He is determined to go out again into the world of freedom, undaunted by the doctor's warning: "Sehen Sie sich um in der Welt: Wie schwer ist es für einen, der nicht aussätzig ist... Für den, der die Gewißheit hat, wird alles einfach." [8] But as he packs his suitcase Paul realizes that for him the liberty he dreams of no longer exists, happiness outside La Certosa is no more than a brief illusion: "blieb nicht die einzige Gewißheit die, daß ich die anderen verlassen hatte? ... Gewiß, sie konnten alle auch ohne mich sterben, aber ich konnte nicht ohne sie leben." [9] In the end there can be no doubt: Paul's decision to remain with the lepers represents his progress to a full self-realization. He has found a way out of his earlier suffocating, purposeless existence through a tangle of mysterious and inexplicable connexions to his true destiny—the solution to all mysteries, the point at which Lazarus and Laertes, *la certitude* and *La Certosa* coincide with a last, unspoken word: *caritas* or *la charité*.

The presentation of the individual's development through his search for a word is not peculiar to *Das Jahr Lazertis* : the play has its comic counterpart in one of Eich's favourite pieces, *Allah hut hundert Namen*. Hakim, whom the prophet miraculously rescues from death and turns into a prosperous merchant, decides to search for the hundredth name of Allah, for in him the secret of the world lies hidden. He finds the choice of people to whom the prophet sends him for illumination—a cobbler, a cook, a prostitute —extremely peculiar, until finally he realizes the truth : "... das nie Gehörte ist eine Dattelpalme." [10] Losing all his capital, and reduced to the status of an embassy servant, Hakim remains contented with his fate, for he has learnt that the hundredth name of Allah, far from being necessarily inaccessible and esoteric, is to be found in the full enjoyment of the things of everyday life, even the satisfaction to be gained from sweeping the embassy steps.

The comic element again appears as a notable feature of *Festianus, Märtyrer*, a play about a nervous little saint who feels ill at ease in heaven because he fails to find his friends and relations. The great saints appear singularly unhelpful on the subject, Laurence priggishly refusing to see any problem, and Peter, though clearly disturbed, unwilling to take action. Eventually Festianus descends to hell (a sophisticated concentration-camp) and chooses to remain there, for while he can in no way diminish the sufferings of the others, he prefers at least to share them. Although Eich here treats a real problem in traditional theology, the context of his other plays reveals that he is not primarily concerned with the Christian notion of the hereafter but rather with the problem of suffering and our attitude to it : through Festianus he again condemns complacency, indifference and rigidity—whether on the part of the individual or the institution. The theme of caring for others likewise predominates in the satire *Zinngeschrei*, in which, however, a cynical reversing of rôles takes place—the idealist's conversion to material self-interest balancing the progress of the other main character from self-interest to idealism.

Eich's best-known, perhaps most effective play, *Die Mädchen aus Viterbo*, is again concerned with the self-realization of the individual who is "on the way to becoming what he really is". Formally, the work is Eich's most elaborate to date : in contrast to the majority of his plays, *Die Mädchen aus Viterbo* has a well-outlined second principal character, and the scenes alternate between war-time Berlin, where a Jewish girl and her grandfather are hiding from the authorities, and the catacombs of Rome, where we encounter a second set of voices, imagined by the first but scarcely less real for the listener. In Berlin old Goldschmidt and his granddaughter Gabriele are awaiting the arrival of a postcard

from Switzerland as a signal that their friends have escaped from
Germany and that the way is safe for them too. Goldschmidt has
just awakened from a dream in which he was the teacher from
Viterbo about whom he had read in a picture paper : having
taken a class of girls to the Roman catacombs, he could not find
the way back. (According to the newspaper report they were never
discovered.) In order to distract Gabriele's attention from an air-
raid, Goldschmidt makes her imagine the situation of the girls
lost in the catacombs. At first Gabriele is determined to have a
thoroughly romantic happy ending but Goldschmidt, fearing that
their fate may have no relation to this, tries to show her that her
conclusion is purely arbitrary. When the expected postcard arrives,
Frau Winter, who has been sheltering them, reveals that their
friends have been seen in a Berlin police prison : clearly it can
be only a matter of time before the Gestapo arrive to arrest them
also. While Frau Winter desperately tries to arrange for an acquaintance to take them in, the Goldschmidts wait in the flat and
the old man insists that Gabriele finish the story. At this stage
the young girl still cannot face the thought of death. But gradually, by imagining the girls' situation, Gabriele comes to accept
her fate and finally awaits death with complete dignity and resignation : "Mir ist es, als liefe alles in meinem Leben darauf zu,
die Schulaufgaben und die Kinderlieder, auf diesen Augenblick,
in dem ich einverstanden bin." [11] With two natural and quiet allusions to Nicolai's chorale *Wachet auf, ruft uns die Stimme* with
its ecstatic vision of the heavenly Jerusalem, Eich both heightens
his effect and gives his play a rounded ending : from the opening
line "Wach auf ! Wach auf !" [12] we progress to Goldschmidt's last
word of advice, now no longer necessary—"Mach dich bereit,
Gabriele[13]."

Anyone already acquainted with Eich's plays will hardly be surprised to find in his verse an all-pervading sense of solitude, any
prominent I-thou relationship being absent. For just as in the plays
Eich presents a lonely protagonist, the object or objects of whose
love have become remote or finally inaccessible, so too in the poems
the (comparatively rare) introduction of a "thou" inevitably involves a remoteness either spacial or spiritual, temporal or emotional—

Wo bist du, wenn du neben mir gehst?[14]

The beloved remains at a distance, and only the impossibility of
communication remains. In this context it is interesting to note
that Karl Krolow describes Eich's use of the pronoun "I" as a kind
of substitute for the impersonal "one". In Eich's verse we find

the individual constantly alone with nature, his problems and his
fears—but these appear as the problems and fears of twentieth-
century man.

In Eich's first post-war collection, *Abgelegene Gehöfte*, where
most of the poems still have a traditional four-line rhymed stanza,
the most powerful pieces are those in which the poet deals with
his experiences as a soldier and particularly as a prisoner of war.
Quite the most stark in form and basic in content is the beauti-
fully controlled poem *Inventur*, in which, without a trace of self-
pity or false pathos, Eich conveys the atmosphere of life in a
prisoner-of-war camp at the same time raising the situation to a
symbolic plane.

Inventur

Dies ist mein Mütze,
dies ist mein Mantel,
hier mein Rasierzeug
im Beutel aus Leinen.

Konservenbüchse :
Mein Teller, mein Becher,
ich hab in das Weißblech
den Namen geritzt.

Geritzt hier mit diesem
kostbaren Nagel,
den vor begehrlichen
Augen ich berge.

Im Brotbeutel sind
ein Paar wollene Socken
und einiges, was ich
niemand verrate,

so dient es als Kissen
nachts meinem Kopf.
Die Pappe hier liegt
zwischen mir und der Erde.

Die Bleistiftmine
lieb ich am meisten :
Tags schreibt sie mir Verse,
die nachts ich erdacht.

> Dies ist mein Notizbuch,
> dies meine Zeltbahn,
> dies ist mein Handtuch,
> dies ist mein Zwirn.[15]

In this poem the marked sobriety of the utterance is suited to the "prosaic" nature of the subject : a man takes stock of the few miserable possesions left him as a prisoner, and the words, like the things themselves, are reduced to an absolute minimum. But for all its unsensational *parlando*, the poem is cunningly constructed with a moving climax. Stanza 2 shows the individual's intense desire for some rights even in his present situation. This leads to a more general consideration of his relations with the outside world : the prisoners are by no means united against a common oppressor, for among them envy and distrust predominate. The isolation of the individual is absolute, and the reader is led to share this experience through his perception of the unsuspected value assigned to simple everyday objects. Then the spiritual element is brought in with an emotional climax at the point where the poet quietly reveals his own feeling—"lieb ich" : with a propelling pencil refill (not even a proper pencil) he can write down the poems that he composes in the privacy and solitude of the night. The poem could, of course, have ended here, but it is typical of Eich that it does not, must not finish at this point. Instead the inventory continues—quite naturally, with the notebook in which he writes, and so on again to purely material things. Thus there is no romantic or emotional ending in which the poet puts forward a pretentious claim that even in adversity the mind triumphs gloriously over matter, creating beauty amid ugliness and need. Instead, quietly, he returns almost to the *point de départ*, to the thread which is necessary for mending the cap and the coat with which he began. The two things co-exist—the poverty and the poetry—and indeed the form of the poem represents exactly the relation of one to the other. Only one stanza out of the seven deals with the writing of verse—the second last, suggesting that this escape from material wretchedness, long looked forward to, is essentially transitory. The return to the physical environment, to the terrible monotony weighing on the spirit is inevitable. (It can hardly be mere coincidence that whereas the first stanza has only two lines beginning "dies ist", the last has four.) At the same time the process of taking stock, starting with the simplest material objects, the only things man can be sure of, applies to the situation of a whole civilization, in particular Germany after the Second World War, seeking to find a new way amid a chaos of lost values.

In another poem in the same collection, *Latrine*, Eich tries to present the paradoxical situation of man in a world in which beauty seems no longer to have a place, except as a near-mirage in a desert of horror. The traditional form of the poem serves only to underline the shocking character of the content.

Latrine

Über stinkendem Graben,
Papier voll Blut und Urin
umschwirrt von funkelnden Fliegen,
hocke ich in den Knien,

den Blick auf bewaldete Ufer,
Gärten, gestrandetes Boot.
In den Schlamm der Verwesung
klatscht der versteinte Kot.

Irr mir im Ohre schallen
Verse von Hölderlin.
In schneeiger Reinheit spiegeln
Wolken sich im Urin.

"Geh aber nun und grüße
die schöne Garonne—"
Unter den schwankenden Füßen
schwimmen die Wolken davon.[16]

To invoke the criterion of "good taste" in condemnation of this poem merely excludes from literature an intense and intensely human experience. Shocking though the content may be, *Latrine* is no mere undergraduate attempt at *épater le bourgeois* but a poem with a serious purpose and a ring of truth. The experience, unique as it stands, is in fact capable of application to the whole paradoxical human situation in all its tragedy and absurdity. On the one hand we have Hölderlin and the clouds, a symbol of the loftiest flights of the human spirit; on the other hand, and at the same time, blood, war, horror, represented by the most disgusting of man's bodily functions. How is it possible that the two should co-exist, and what can be the meaning and place of beauty in a world so hostile to it? Perhaps the answer lies in another poem, *Abends am Zaun* :

Am Abend duftet holder die Kamille
vom Feldrain her. Der Posten bläst ein Lied
auf seiner Okarina. Gottes Wille
im Glanz des Abendsternes sich vollzieht.

> Wie viele doch sind nun für immer stille,
> die gerne sich erfreut an Stern und Lied!
> Nun sind sie selbst darin und Gottes Wille
> in Glanz und Duft und solcher Abendstille
> geschieht.[17]

But only rarely do we find such a moment of harmony and acceptance; far more typical are the last lines of *An die Lerche*. From a series of baroque images of transitoriness and desolation, Eich turns his eyes upwards to the lark, the only source of joy left to the prisoners. But its song is not to lull them into a comfortable oblivion:

> Oh sing uns keinen falschen Schlummertrost,
> sei uns Prophet und sing die kalte Zukunft,
> die jubelnde![18]

In these poems we have the core of Eich's war experience. Other poems, too, in *Abgelegene Gehöfte* communicate a sense of desolation and disorientation through the individual's reaction to the natural scene. Just as the autumn and late summer poems convey a pervasive sadness and solitude, so even the spring is tinged with bitterness and associated with suffering and death. In fact, even after the war experiences had found full expression, a basic insecurity or existential *Angst* persists, together with a nagging doubt as to the purpose of life. An early poem entitled *Verse an vielen Abenden* is clearly permeated with the notion of man having lost his originally pure essence; through his very humanity he is excluded from the harmony and simple truth of the animals and plants. In Eich's later poetry the same fiction appears in more developed form: life has indeed a meaning but man is not permitted to know it except through death. The natural world around him provides strange signs and indications of a different set of values, but these are mysterious clues for which man possesses no key, incomprehensible fragments of an unknown language. At times the signs seem thoroughly hostile and threatening, as when a flight of crows causes a dark writing to appear in the sky:

> In den leeren Himmel starrend
> weiß ich ihn doch voll,
> regungslos des Grauens harrend,
> das ich lesen soll.
>
> (*Angst*)[19]

The symbol of the bird standing for another order or scale of values recurs regularly in Eich's work: the jay, the pigeon, and in the radio play *Sabeth* the huge black bird that brings happiness but cannot remain indefinitely on earth.

Moments of sudden and inexplicable uneasiness such as that in *Angst* are no less common in the poems than in the plays; thus in *Botschaften des Regens* the consciously idyllic picture of a worker returning from the fields at evening finally takes on an unmistakably menacing aspect :

> Der Mann in der blauen Jacke geht heimwärts.
> seine Hacke, die er geschultert hat,
> gleicht in der sinkenden Dämmerung einem Gewehr.[20]

Man is never safe in his own self-sufficiency; in the calm of natural surroundings or the silence of a deserted street the unexpected may at any time break in on his little world, instantly transforming his state of mind. Such moments, which provide a striking starting-point for many of Eich's plays, are caught and unsensationally retained in suggestive and memorable form in pieces such as *Februar* or *Weg zum Bahnhof*.

In another poem, *Im Sonnenlicht*, the background of cold and darkness is replaced by an emphasis on warmth and light, but these too can bring on a moment of dread as, in this contemporary equivalent of a baroque meditation on the Last Judgement, Eich considers the implications of our enjoyment of the gifts brought by the sun :

> Was üppig sie gab,
> was wir genommen ohne Besinnen,
> das unverlangte Geschenk,
> eines bestürzenden Tages
> wird es zurückverlangt.
>
> . . . .
>
> Aber wir werden leere Taschen haben
> und der Gläubiger ist unbarmherzig.
> Womit werden wir zahlen?
> O Brüder, daß ihr nicht bangt![21]

Ende eines Sommers, the opening poem in the collection *Botschaften des Regens*, is typical not only in its gentle melancholy and rhythmic subtlety but also in its concentration of recurrent themes : the notion of transitoriness, the bird symbol, the coin to pay the ferryman, the idea of enlightenment through death.

Ende eines Sommers

> Wer möchte leben ohne den Trost der Bäume!
>
> Wie gut, daß sie am Sterben teilhaben!
> Die Pfirsiche sind geerntet, die Pflaumen färben sich,
> Während unter dem Brückenbogen die Zeit rauscht.

Dem Vogelzug vertraue ich meine Verzweiflung an,
Er mißt seinen Teil von Ewigkeit gelassen ab.
Seine Strecken
werden sichtbar im Blattwerk als dunkler Zwang,
die Bewegung der Flügel färbt die Früchte.

Es heißt Geduld haben.
Bald wird die Vogelschrift entsiegelt,
unter der Zunge ist der Pfennig zu schmecken.[22]

From a formal point of view, *Botschaften des Regens* (1955) occupies a place midway between *Abgelegene Gehöfte* (1948) and Eich's most recent collection *Zu den Akten* (1964). Whereas in the early volume the four-line rhymed poem rather surprisingly predominates, it is in *Botschaften* the exception rather than the rule and in *Zu den Akten* has been entirely abandoned. In keeping with their freer form the newest poems tend to be more laconic and cryptic than the early ones, but they also avoid the occasional bathos bordering on the ludicrous, a danger to which Eich's everyday language left him open, as when he ended a poem with the line :

Gleich regnet es.   Hol die Wäsche herein.[23]

The romantic element and the singing quality found in some of Eich's earlier verse have been greatly reduced in his later work : the change in tone is indicated by the titles themselves, as the *Botschaften des Regens* are superseded by the more sober, brittle *Zu den Akten*. But nonetheless Eich shows no signs of abandoning his earlier themes : the opening lines of *Nachhut*, for instance,

Steh auf ! steh auf !
Wir werden nicht angenommen ![24]

promptly remind the reader of *Träume* and of *Die Mädchen aus Viterbo*. A certain surrealistic quality, evident throughout Eich's work, re-appears here in a nightmarish vision :

Unsere Worte werden von der Stille aufgezeichnet.
Die Kanaldeckel heben sich um einen Spalt.
Die Wegweiser haben sich gedreht.[25]

But perhaps the most striking feature of Eich's most recent poems —apart from the wry humour noticeable in several—is the recurring concern expressed for the suffering, the refusal of Festianus and Paul simply to turn their backs, to pass by on the other side (*Wildwechsel, Tauerntunnel*).

Now as in 1950 Eich is unrelenting in his indictment of a society that turns a deaf ear to the cries of the afflicted or meets them with a convenient sophistry,

In this context it is easy to understand why in a broadcast review of *Zu den Akten* Günter Bien remarked "Anderes mag interessant sein, Eichs Gedichte sind notwendig".[26] Constantly eschewing all rhetoric and false pathos Eich continues to translate, as he puts it, from an imperfectly known original, rousing his readers from their false slumber, reminding us of the ideals to which we all too readily pay mere lip-service. And yet Eich does not see himself cast in the exalted role of the high-priest ministering to an unworthy and ungrateful humanity but rather looks upon each new work as a means of orientation, another buoy in the uncharted and unknown sea that is reality. "Erst durch das Schreiben erlangen für mich die Dinge Wirklichkeit. Sie ist nicht meine Voraussetzung, sondern mein Ziel." [27]

TRANSLATIONS

1. Poets who frighten no-one are of use only as topics for conversation.

2. Everything that happens concerns you.

3. Remember—Korea and Bikini are to be found not on the map but in your heart.

4. Do what is useless, sing the songs that they don't expect to hear you sing! Be awkward, be sand, not oil, in the machinery of the world.

5. But at bottom I think that even a good conscience is not sufficient, and I doubt whether the sleep in which we lull ourselves is a good thing.

6. Ellen Harland was driving past—I had forgotten her.

7. I would have liked to call them back, but they were already too far off. They were becoming stranger to me with every step.

8. Look about you in the world: see how difficult it is for someone who's not a leper. . . . For the man who possesses certainty everything becomes simple.

9. . . . wasn't the only thing that was certain the fact that I had deserted the others? . . . Assuredly they could all die without me, but I could not live without them.

10. . . . the word that has never been heard is a date-palm.

11. I feel as though everything in my life, the homework and the children's songs, as though they all led up to this moment in which I have reached acceptance.

12. Wake up, wake up!

13. Get ready, Gabriele.

14. Where are you when you walk beside me?

15. Inventory. This is my cap, this is my coat, here are my shaving things in the linen bag. Preserve tin, my plate, my cup, I have scratched my name in the metal. Scratched it with this precious nail which I hide from covetous eyes. In the haversack are a pair of woollen socks and some things that I tell no-one about; thus at night it serves as a pillow for my head. The pasteboard here lies between me and the ground. The

pencil-lead is the thing I love most: by day it writes down the lines that I have composed at night. This is my note-book, this is my tarpaulin, this is my towel, this is my thread.

16. Latrine. Over a stinking ditch, paper saturated with blood and urine, surrounded by buzzing, glistening flies, I squat, looking towards wooded banks, gardens, a boat run aground. The hardened filth plops into the mud of putrefaction. Some lines of Hölderlin ring madly in my ears. In snowy purity the clouds are reflected in the urine. "But go now and greet the lovely Garonne—" beneath my unsteady feet the clouds swim away.

17. Evening by the Fence. In the evening the camomile sends out a lovelier scent from the edge of the field. The sentry plays a song on his ocarina. God's will is accomplished in the brightness of the evening's star. Yet how many are now for ever silent who would have enjoyed seeing the star and listening to the song! Now they are themselves in them, and in the brightness and the scent and such stillness of the evening God's will is done.

18. Oh sing to us no false consoling lullaby, be our prophet and sing the cold, exultant future.

19. Staring into the empty skies, I know them nonetheless to be filled, waiting motionless for the dread that I am to read. (*Fear*)

20. The man in the blue jacket goes homewards; his hoe, which he has shouldered, looks in the falling twilight like a rifle.

21. What it gave in abundance, what we took without thinking, the gift unasked-for—one day that will throw us into confusion we shall be asked to give it back. . . . But we shall have empty pockets and the creditor is pitiless. What shall we pay with? O brothers, I wonder that you are not afraid!

22. End of a Summer. Who would want to live without the consolation of the trees! How good it is that they partake of death! The peaches are gathered in, the plums are colouring, while time rushes beneath the arch of the bridge. I confide my despair to the flight of the birds. They calmly measure off their share of eternity. Their distances become visible in the foliage in the form of a dark compulsion, the movement of the wings colours the fruits. It is necessary to be patient. Soon the writing of the birds will be deciphered, under the tongue the coin can be tasted.

23. It's just going to rain. Get the washing in.

24. Get up, get up! We shall not be accepted.

25. Our words are noted down by silence. The covers of the sewers rise up a crack. The signposts have turned round.

26. Other things may be interesting, Eich's poems are necessary.

27. Only through writing do things become real for me. Reality is not my prerequisite but my goal.

SELECT BIBLIOGRAPHY

Principal Works

Gedichte, Dresden 1930.
Katharina, Erzählung, Leipzig 1936.
Abgelegene Gehöfte, Gedichte, Frankfurt am Main 1948.
Untergrundbahn, Gedichte, Hamburg 1949.
Träume, Vier Spiele, Frankfurt am Main 1953.
Botschaften des Regens, Gedichte, Frankfurt am Main 1955.
Stimmen, Sieben Hörspiele, Frankfurt am Main 1958.
Zu den Akten, Gedichte, Frankfurt am Main 1964.
In anderen Sprachen, Vier Hörspiele, Frankfurt am Main 1964.
Unter Wasser. Böhmische Schneider. Marionettenspiele, Frankfurt am Main 1964.

Articles on Eich

Herbert Ahl: "Günter Eich" in *Literarische Porträts*, Munich 1962.
Andreas Donath: "Hörspiel als Kunstform" in *Schriftsteller der Gegenwart*, ed. Klaus Nonnenmann, Olten 1963.
Walter Höllerer: Nachwort zu: Günter Eich, *Ausgewählte Gedichte*, Frankfurt am Main 1960.
A more detailed bibliography is to be found in the Suhrkamp Texte edition of *Die Mädchen aus Viterbo*, Frankfurt am Main 1964.

Gerd Gaiser

Gerd Gaiser

by IAN HILTON
(University College of North Wales, Bangor)

Gerd Gaiser was born on September 15th, 1908, in Würtemberg, the only son of a vicar. He entered the evangelical theological Training Colleges of Schöntal and Urach, but did not proceed to the Tübingen Stift, which would have been the next logical step. His interests had already turned him to art studies, in the pursuit of which he travelled extensively during the next few years—to the Baltic and Danube areas, Italy, France and Spain. His dissertation, in fact, was *Die Plastik der Renaissance und des Frühbarock in Neukastilien* (1934). His travels and art studies have left their indelible mark on Gaiser's writings. He was an art-teacher for a time until the outbreak of war, when he entered the German Air Force in the Flying Branch due to his old interest in gliding (this keenness for gliding is captured in his short-story, *Der Wind bringt die Zeit*). War service took Gaiser to the German Bight, Rumania and Italy where he finished up in a British P.O.W. camp. After the war he spent three or four years as an independent artist, before turning to teaching once more. He is now a "Professor" at the Pädagogische Hochschule in Reutlingen. The war has provided the material for his novel *Die Sterbende Jagd*; and, indeed, his concern with the figure of the "Heimkehrer" and his search for meaning in a world grown ever more complex provide the content of Gaiser's work. In 1951 he was awarded the Fontane-Prize of Berlin for his first published novel, *Eine Stimme hebt an*. In 1955 Gaiser received the Literary Prize of the Bavarian Academy of Fine Arts, four years later the Immerman Prize, and in 1960 the Wilhelm Raabe Prize of Brunswick. He has been a member of the Berlin Academy of Arts since 1956.

In addition to his own creative writings, Gaiser has also edited several books on modern art.

THE central themes of Gerd Gaiser are war and its effect on man, love and death. His creative output to date numbers four novels and six collections of short stories and anecdotes, and these works have, for one reason or another, succeeded in sharply dividing the literary critics as to their merits. Thus of his champions, Günter Blöcker, for example, commits himself to calling Gaiser the most talented prose-writer in postwar German literature. In the other camp his decriers, amongst them W. Jens and H. Kreuzer, are equally as outspoken on Gaiser's literary ability. Ironically Gaiser himself confesses to finding little pleasure in writing. "Freuden eines Schriftstellers kann ich mir

indessen durchaus nicht vorstellen... Schreiben verzehrt... Der
Schreibtisch ist nicht meine Welt."¹ Gaiser's primary interest had
been painting, which accounts for the comparatively late start in
creative writing when he had already turned thirty. However he
acknowledges the need to write, to give expression to, and thereby
came to some sort of terms with the shattering experiences of the
Second World War and its aftermath.

> "Das Vergangene sah er nackt und vergeblich, die Gegenwart
> feindselig, und wie viele seinesgleichen sah er die Zukunft für
> eine Vokabel an".²

> "Wir aber gingen herum und suchten den Anfang, kramten
> nach Überbleibseln und fürchteten uns." ³

> "Er sah all diese Welt des Aufstieges nur durch die Glasscheibe.
> Er hatte aufgehört, mitzuspielen." ⁴

These passages fairly reflect the mood and outlook of his typical
fictional hero—the ex-soldier, benumbed by war experiences,
returning to a land shattered physically and spiritually. It could
well be the mood of Gaiser himself and many thousands of other
former German soldiers. In his work Gaiser becomes the recorder
of the predicament facing so many men today in their search for
the purpose of life. "Wozu das alles?" ("for what purpose?") is a
familiar enough cry in his writings.

But the tone of resignation in the earlier quoted passages has
not always been apparent in his work, not, for example, in *Reiter
am Himmel*. On the strength of this one book of poems available
to the reader,⁵ Gaiser does not rate much success as a poet. Critics
tend to pass over these verses in silence and Gaiser himself prefers
to forget them. But *Reiter am Himmel* (1941) is interesting for
the light it sheds on Gaiser's attitude to his homeland up to that
time. The poems, all written in free verse in the ecstatic style of
an immature, groping poet, reflect the influence that youth movements, as part of the general scene of the Twenties, must have
exerted on an impressionable and idealistic youth. The vocabulary
is pregnant with *Heimat* and *Erde*, with *Ahnen* and *Volk*.

These are *Blut und Boden* poems expressive of the poet's whole-
some patriotism; whose spirit finds an echo in Frenssen, one of
the main fictional characters in Gaiser's *Die Sterbende Jagd*, considered by many to be the best German novel of the Second World
War. But by the time of Frenssen's creation the mood has changed,
disillusion is creeping in and Frenssen illustrates this new attitude.
Gaiser, himself an officer in the *Luftwaffe* during the war, here
transmits real experiences into art in the fictional account of the
"realization by fighter pilots stationed in Norway that the war was

already lost by 1942 and that, in any case, the cause for which
they were fighting was an unjust one". Gaiser's fighter pilots are
not flyers living for the sensation of flying or of dying, nor inspired
any longer by the image "vom blanken Schild und den goldenen
Sporen, von fliegenden Haaren und der Zügelfaust".[6] That image
is shattered; the chivalrous nature of fighting in the sky in the
First World War manner is no longer manifest; and the German
fighter pilot, aware of the shortage of planes on his own side,
comes to realize the hopelessness of the situation when facing
ever-increasing bomber attacks. And yet, still they fight. "Everyone likes to fight when he has the chance", declares one character.
Another asserts that "war merely brings out what was already
there". Yet, when directly faced with the question of why they
fight, no immediate satisfactory answer seems to be forthcoming
from them. Thus : "Schwersenz schwieg. Er schwieg erst über-
rascht, dann ratlos und dann plötzlich hartnäckig".[7] De Bruyn,
another pilot, likewise cannot give an answer. "Is it for honour?",
asks Waaga. But what is honour?—"an invention of man, a tool
with which a man destroys himself". And what if the cause for
which they are fighting is recognized as unjust, as Frenssen acknowledges in a key passage in the book, chapter forty-six? Frenssen
considers the whole business of war :

> "Man kann eine Sache wollen und für sie kämpfen, das ist
> ein herrliches Los. Man kann sie wollen und nicht für sie
> kämpfen : nicht der Rede wert. Man kann sie nicht wollen und
> sich deshalb weigern, zu kämpfen für sie, das kann sehr schwer
> werden; aber du hast deinen Frieden mit dir. Aber sie nicht
> wollen und doch kämpfen, weil da ganz bestimmte Umstände
> vorliegen, dabei musst du verlieren so oder so. Da gibt es keinen
> Ausweg." [8]

In short, the individual by this reckoning can not just cut himself off. Frenssen reminds himself and his flyers that they must
hold onto something, and fulfil their task. But this is rather an
ambivalent position if man is merely to do his job without question
and any deeper moral sense of combatting corruptness of power
and inhumanity. De Bruyn states that conscience is indivisible, it
belongs to us all, and Frenssen acknowledges that everyone is
guilty, whether he likes it or not. Yet neither of them does anything about this question of guilt. The moral possibility of freeing
oneself from the devil is here unthinkable in the way it is presented
in Zuckmayer's *Des Teufels General*. Despite a positive affirmation
that war must not happen again, Gaiser seems to treat the question
of the guilt of the individual rather superficially. The tone is one
of resignation, identifiable with pilots who go to their death with-

out hope and yet without bitterness, resignation which can be summed up in the words of the Commander to Waaga when the latter requests to be returned to active flying duties : "Bitte gehorsamst. Wille und schon kein Wille mehr".[9]

War changes reality in that it makes man do unreal and inhuman things; it leads to the tragic isolation of man, as symbolized in *Die Sterbende Jagd* in the figure of the fighter pilot, alone in his plane, often unable to see the ground because of cloud, his only contact with the ground and his fellow men being the radio which is often faulty. How man is to face up to this isolation after the war is shown in *Eine Stimme hebt an* (1950), Gaiser's first completed novel which brought its author public acclaim. The war is over and peace exists. But what *is* Peace? Vehlgast had already given a hint in *Die Sterbende Jagd*.

> "Worin besteht der Friede? Ranglisten und Beförderungen, verhinderter Ehrgeiz, Lügen, Warenhäuser, Zwischenhandel und organisierte Verdauung. Einer macht den andern fertig, damit er selbst besser lebt. Kann er es nicht, kauft er ihn, und das heisst dann Gemeinschaft. Der Alltag, von Hass und Gereiztheiten keuchend..."[10]

A bleak prospect would seem to await Oberstelehn, the *"Heimkehrer"* hero of *Eine Stimme hebt an* who returns to a Germany of the *Hungerjahre*, to discover his wife has been unfaithful to him. Back in the country town where he spent his childhood he is hurt by his wife's infidelity, is silent and unresponsive apart from indulging in half-hearted affairs with other women. He realises the need, however, to bring some order back to life, tries to help people, but without much success, and generally attempts to bring some sense into an age of senselessness and deliberate destruction of old values, as symbolized in the burning down of the *"Gartenhaus"* and its contents. Oberstelehn and his efforts are not appreciated by the mass of people who use their influence to machinate his downfall and force him to leave. The mass remains corrupt but the hopelessness of the situation is not total as far as Oberstelehn himself is concerned. He at least acknowledges that man is responsible for himself in every moment of life and that it is up to man to turn to and recognize the *"Ordnungsmacht"* :

> "Wir haben so viele Ordnung vergessen oder zuschanden gemacht, dass wir uns jetzt an das wenige halten müssen, was noch gilt".[11]

Oberstelehn's eventual return to his wife can be seen as the upholding of the *"Ordnungsmacht"*; and Gaiser's use of marriage as the recognition of the need for human sympathy, the need of man for his fellow beings as a means of overcoming the crisis of the age, is reminiscent of Böll's application of the sacrament in his novel, *Und sagte kein einziges Wort*.

The picture of post-war Germany is completed in the novel *Schlussball* (1958), which did much to establish Gaiser's standing as an international literary figure. The Germany depicted here is that of the *Wirtschaftswunder* seen through a glass screen, as if the author was no longer directly involved. The story, as the title suggests, centres on the last dance of the season of a school-class, whose teacher is Soldner, the hero of the book. Soldner is another Outsider like Oberstelehn; he objects to the insurgent materialism of the town of Neu-Spuhl, which symbolizes the growth of prosperity of the New Germany. But alongside this undoubted material improvement, is there any betterment in the spiritual crisis of the age? Is the improvement in man's lot deep and lasting, or is it merely a façade? Through Soldner, Gaiser shows his concern with what lies beneath the red dust that so effectively covers the town, emanating from Pansalva, the local factory which has brought wealth to Neu-Spuhl. Soldner attempts to find some meaning and sense to life, but his efforts to point out true values to his pupils only antagonize some of the children who imitate their parents in their concern for money. For such as the Drautzmann boy, education is merely functional, the means whereby one is taught to make money. Culture loses in the face of Materialism. Soldner, as Oberstelehn had done, raises his voice in the spiritual wilderness, but again it is not heard, or rather it is stifled. His attempts to help people are likewise unsuccessful. He is no more successful in trying to save Diemut from the lad Rakitsch, than he is in championing his pupils in the dog-episode in Chapter 8. Soldner's downfall is managed by the wealthy and influential who accuse him unjustly of subversive activities. Once again the individual is overwhelmed by the mass, here the thriving business men, the Klöpplers and the Blechers, to whom it is impossible to attribute any individual characters or characteristics; for, as Soldner indicates in the Fairground scene at the end of the book, they are *homines spulici*, mechanical mass-produced dolls strikingly resembling human figures. Half the trouble for Soldner's downfall lies in the fact that in an age that is status-conscious he is not suitably qualified, and has not the necessary paper qualifications for his job as teacher. Similarly, Oberstelehn regretted that he had held a variety of jobs, the result of which was that he remained a layman through and through. Again, the Pulverdinger priest in *Eine Stimme hebt an* is ironically also a layman. He has not the necessary papers and has to give up his post. All these figures remain social outsiders and spiritually isolated. It would seem that a sense of humanity in itself is insufficient for acceptance in the world of today.

The idea of marriage conveyed in *Eine Stimme hebt an* reappears in *Schlussball*. Like Oberstelehn, Soldner has had personal troubles in human contact being at fault in his marriage to Rosamund because he would not take his wife seriously. His interest in Herse Andernoth is ironically rejected as she wishes to remain true to the memory of her husband, missing, presumed killed in action. For Herse Andernoth it is the means of conscious association of solidarity with the past, the means of being able to bring up her daughter properly, as she thinks. This decision not to marry again she felt to be her duty; it is a "must", as important to her as it was, for example, for Frenssen to do his duty as he saw it in *Die Sterbernde Jagd*, however misguided such an action might be. On the other hand, the marriage of the Foerckhs serves to illustrate just how difficult communication is in the present day. Initially they were full of concern for each other in their greatest hour of need during the war, but with the beginnings of recovery and the establishment of his business after the war Foerckh gradually becomes estranged from his wife, an estrangement which increases in proportion to the expansion of his business interests. Their attendance at the dance is simply due to the prospect of doing business with the Klöpplers and the Blechers. Whilst he is able to give his wife all that money can buy, he is incapable of seeing that he is not providing for her real happiness. By this time they have grown so far apart that they do not even talk on the same wavelength. Communication, the means of explanation to bring about a betterment in relations, is not possible. Words are there, but beneath the surface, wishing to break through but unable to. The result is long periods of silence which produce the sense of isolation, and the distance between the two is heightened by the fact that they occupy separate rooms in a large house which is so emptily their home. If only self-renunciation were possible, the barrier could be broken, but Foerckh remains unconscious of his wife's unhappiness, which leads to her suicide.

Wolfe's dictum in *The Story of a Novel* that all serious writing must at bottom be autobiographical would seem to be observed by Gaiser in these novels. In each of the three works he has transmitted real experiences into literary form. And whilst one is obliged to form one's own judgement on a work or author, one is reminded in passing of Krämer-Badoni's verdict that there are no thoughts or works of lasting value at all apart from those that arise shrewdly from the present day, which exist in the present day, and which are there with a vigorous blow for the present day. Should one, however, apply this yardstick to Gaiser's work, one could accept

the validity of the first two-thirds of the statement with reference
to these novels. Where difficulty of agreement might arise would
be over the degree of vigour of the blow that Gaiser strikes for the
present day. Thus one may dislike his apparent lack of commitment already referred to in *Die Sterbende Jagd*, compared to
Zuckmayer's treatment of the question of moral guilt in war.
Again, whilst a sigh of relief may be heaved at not having a really
nihilistic picture of a post-war German town presented in *Eine
Stimme hebt an*, one is nevertheless entitled to ask : does Gaiser
really tackle the moral problems in that novel? Is it more social
description than social criticism? And, does Gaiser take a hard
enough look at Federal Republic prosperity after the war in
Schlussball?

The answer might well be no. In fact, the sense of isolation with
which Gaiser is so concerned has perhaps led him to lose sight in
the narrower sense of the political perspective, in the broader sense
the historical perspective in *Die Sterbende Jagd, Eine Stimme hebt
an* and *Schlussball*. In any case, what *is* history for Gaiser? *Das
Schiff im Berg* (1955) provides the clue. This traces the development of a mountainside from primitive times to the present day
when its poor community discovers forgotten caves tunnelled
through the mountain itself. The people plan to open these up,
hoping to catch the tourist trade, and thereby become rich. But
it becomes abundantly clear in the course of the novel that the
human element is pushed into the background, and that the soil
is the lasting thing or link binding the ages. And history...?

> "Die Geschichte sei ohnedies eine Art von Hochstapelei, vor
> allem dann, wenn wir versuchen, ein wenig Abwechslung in
> ihren Gang zu bringen. Die Versuchung des Menschen öffent-
> lich nachzuweisen, dass er mehr als Natur ist und sich nicht
> damit begnügt, zu erleiden." [12]

In other words, it is merely an attempt on man's part to show he
is superior to nature. But, we learn elsewhere, "Gras und Staub.
Der Mensch auch wie Gras, wie das niedrigste Leben, eine Beute
des Zufalls, Ursachen und Wirkungen unterworfen".[13] Man is part
of Nature, yet subordinate to it, and must inevitably return to the
soil, whatever happens. "Zur Erde muss der Mensch wieder kommen, auch wenn er sich in der Luft eine Weile hat halten können.
Er kann nicht droben bleiben."[14] In this context one is reminded
in *Die Sterbende Jagd* of Dumont plunging to the ground in his
plane and literally being swallowed up in the boggy ground; or
again, of De Bruyn returning in death to nature, as symbolized in
his huddled shape in the bottom of his dinghy, "er lag zusammen-
gekrümmt wie ein Kind im Mutterschosse";[15] and in *Das Schiff im*

Berg itself, of the student, who has even made a point of studying the laws of nature, engulfed in the yawning chasms of the earth. Gaiser asserts that man has been sent on earth originally by God ("Die Erde träumte; ihn riss Gott aus dem Traum, wählte ihn aus und entliess ihn. Aber er liess Zeichen nicht fehlen")[16] and set a task which he has to fulfil. The advice to man should be :

> "Nehmen die Dinge wie sie der liebe Gott Ihnen sendet, als Rohmaterial. Es kommt bloss darauf an, was Sie daraus machen. Er hat augenscheinlich die Absicht gehabt, Sie am Leben zu lassen, und jetzt müssen Sie bestehen".[17]

So it is up to man to make what he will out of the raw material provided, implying all will be well if man does not try so emphatically to prove his superiority to Nature and thus go against it. The Machine Age is acceptable so long as it benefits all mankind and the results are not applied to destructive or useless purposes. Gaiser shows his deep concern by constantly contrasting the natural and the unnatural or artificial; In *Die Sterbende Jagd* the picture of the lush meadow and fjord at Randvig is set off by the soulless airstrip from which the pilots take off in their planes on their missions of destruction; in *Eine Stimme hebt an* there's chaotic townlife, where the townsfolk are forced to go to the country to beg, steal or buy food to sustain them; in *Schlussball* one reads of the gradual encroachment of the landscape by houses and factories (shades of what has actually happened at Gaiser's hometown of Reutlingen, for example); in *Das Schiff im Berg* the mountain representing the constancy of the earth clashes with the sense of progress implied in the development of that mountain for tourist purposes; and in *Damals in Promischur* from the collection *Am Pass Nascondo*, the narrator makes it quite clear that he has no time for chlorinated water but prefers pure well-water, and further expresses his dislike of food that has come straight from the refrigerator, because, whilst it may have been hygenically (and by implication, artificially) kept, the food has tended to lose its natural aroma and taste. Time and again in Gaiser's stories the hero loves the (natural) smell of hay or wants to pick and eat straightaway the warm and dusty wild berries on the bushes in the countryside.

If man does go against Nature, life becomes senseless. This is indicated in the very title of *Kahle Weihnacht*, a short story which illustrates the conscious destruction of Nature in the chopping down of some trees in Upper Italy in 1944. Scientific and technological progress makes its contribution but also brings with it the means of its own destruction, and civilization can happily destroy all that is genuine and real as *Das Rad in Sghemboli* reveals. In

this short story an almost inaccessible mountain village finally
acquires a new road which connects it with the outside world. Yet
with the resulting advances that civilization brings, man is divided
and the final outcome is that the village, gradually abandoned
over the years by the villagers who have been lured away by the
prospect of even quicker personal advancement elsewhere once
they acquired the taste for it, becomes a target range for artillery
practice, thereby making a mockery of all that was once real and
genuine. Only if one does not strive against nature but trusts in
the soil, does contentment come and a sense and meaning in life
become apparent at least for a time. This the paralysed girl in
Schlussball discovered. Because of her condition she was unable to
participate fully in life and so did not strive to prove her superiority
to Nature but rather retained her trust in Nature and the splendour of Creation. De Bruyn in *Die Sterbende Jagd* had occasion to
seek comfort in the solace of nature when questioning the purpose
of war and fighting. And Ertinger in *Mittagsgesicht* did likewise,
when reflecting over the secret of life and death, matters beyond
his grasp and comprehension. Thereby it is perhaps possible to get
a little closer to God. In Gaiser's works there is not much direct
mention of God, but he himself is aware in his own mind of the
existence of God and has a personal belief in Him, that found its
first literary expression in his poetry in such poems as *Bekenntnis*
and *Das innere Gesetz*. Gaiser's conscious recognition of isolation
which he treats in his writings is however also an awareness of the
inapproachability of God. For, after all, we are not living in a
time of mystic closeness to God but rather in a time of hopeful
expectation. If God seems so distant, it is, Gaiser argues, because
man has so brought it about. "Es quälte sie, dass sie den Sinn nicht
entdecken konnten ... es kamen Tage, dass Gott ihnen tot oder
abgereist schien," [18] we read in *Das Schiff im Berg* but we also
remember the end of one passage elsewhere in that same novel,
quoted earlier : "... Aber er(God) liess Zeichen nicht fehlen." It
may just be that man is unable to understand God's advice and
decisions—something that is constantly hinted at in Gaiser's writings—and the destructive elements of nature, as seen, for example,
in *Das Schiff im Berg*, may be taken as a sign of God's warnings.
Until man can bring himself to make a response to God's signs
however obscure they are—for, after all, an effort is required on
the part of man—, life will continue to appear senseless.

Sometimes man can make the response. A specific instance is
given in *Gianna aus dem Schatten,* perhaps the best known of
Gaiser's short stories, in which the senselessness of revenge and the
subsequent realization of this on the part of an individual is illustrated. In the tale that is reminiscent of W. Pfeiffer's *Der Zwischen-*

fall, a German ex-soldier visits Italy again, this time as a tourist with his wife. He meets by chance a woman partisan who has an old score to settle and he is driven inexorably into an inescapable situation. The problem facing Raumer, the hero, is whether he could have done something to help the girl at the time of her betrayal in the war. The fact remained that he did not, although he loved her. He acknowledges he has no alibi—shades of *Die Sterbende Jagd* : "To each his guilt and responsibility." It is no good Raumer declaring that by the time of the betrayal it was too late to do anything in any case. The note of resignation is once more to be heard ! But just as Schwersenz in *Die Sterbende Jagd* hoped to purge himself of guilt by making out a report of his witnessing cruelties to civilians in a camp he visited during the war, so does Raumer now seek to salve his conscience of not wanting to *do* anything about the nastiness of war by relating the episode from the past to his wife. The actual threat of danger from Gianna enables Raumer and his wife to come properly together for the first time. Their marriage has been far from a happy union. He had not really cared for Enna, his second wife, and she, for her part, had had an affair with another man, whilst Raumer was away in the war. Communication between the two had remained strained and words did not break surface easily. So often it was a case of choked words, embarrassed silences. But in the crisis that develops and with the threat of death in the air, husband and wife draw nearer as each realizes the need for the other, and true communication is achieved, unlike the situation in the case of the Foerckhs in *Schlussball*. The validity of Enna's earlier statement : "Zum Rufen ist immer Zeit," [19] which runs like a *leitmotif* through the story, is now realized. Further, as soon as she has fired the shot, Gianna herself understands that "an eye for an eye, a tooth for a tooth" is not the answer, and she is the one, in fact, who runs to fetch the doctor. The feeling that out of this near tragedy something positive at least has emerged, some humanitarian instinct, is heightened symbolically at the end of the tale when Enna accepts a glass of wine from one of the villagers, who assures her : "There is no one here who won't help you !"

Probably in no other work of Gaiser is the question of love and his attitude towards woman formulated in such a clear-cut concise manner.

> "Viele der Ungelegenheiten jener Zeit rührten vielleicht daher, dass man sich unter Liebe nichts mehr vorstellte." [20]

was the view expressed in *Das Schiff im Berg*. Love for Gaiser is clearly no mere romantic notion but something fundamental and in his terminology comes to signify human sympathy, human understanding. Such a spirit can be displayed by man (thus by Waaga towards Frau Dumont in *Die Sterbende Jagd*, for instance), but so often he remains incapable of feeling it because it is not his nature to know of renunciation and self-denial. These are characteristics more readily associated with woman, so the women characters in Gaiser's stories tend to stand apart, such as Herse Andernoth for the reasons noted already in *Schlussball*, or Frau Waaga in *Eine Stimme hebt an*, or Ness Kämmerer (e.g. in *Hyazinthenfenster*, a story from the collection *Am Pass Nascondo*, where she readily helps an old teacher through hard times without there being any necessity for her to act whatsoever). So often the Gaiser hero will admire and love such a woman but generally it is a relationship which cannot be satisfactorily achieved, an unattainable relationship which is perhaps best symbolized in the tale from the collection *Einmal und oft* entitled *Ich warte auf Ness*, a tense account of a meeting that in fact does not materialize but always remains *"jenseits"*. The narrator thinks back on a childhood occurrence when he was saved from drowning by Ness which becomes the one meaningful central-experience in his life. As one might expect, it is at awkward moments as in *Gianna aus dem Schatten* or in the hardships of war as in *Die Sterbende Jagd* where there is the threat of death or death itself, that the role of woman is shown to the best advantage. Thus in *Die Sterbende Jagd* Frau Dumont and Mette de Bruyn show compassion through the very act of keeping watch over the dead man off the train—"it no longer mattered that he was dead or whose dead he was". In death itself fulfilment in the sense of some indefinable contact between beings is achieved—"der Tod und die Fülle kommen aus ein und demselben Dunkel",[21]—a communication which is so often impossible in life. It is given to but few to know the "status conferred by self-denial, the distinction that lies in renunciation" and the other fellow-travellers pass by the dead body without stopping: "alle waren unterwegs wie aufgescheucht, verloren und suchten einander und strengten ihre Augen an und fanden sich nicht." [22] Only the dead could find each other, the living stretched out their hands in vain and made no contact.

Why stir up old troubles? was the plaintive cry of *Gianna aus dem Schatten*. It is also the cry in *Der Hund von Scholm*, another short story from the collection *Einmal und oft* dealing with the senselessness of revenge. The hero has a dog which acted as a lucky mascot throughout the war. In peacetime he returns to Scholm, where he was based during the war, and his dog is savaged and killed by another, much bigger dog. He has in mind to revenge himself on the dog but comes to realize the futility of such an action. The irony of fate in the situation in both stories lies in the fact that the return to Scholm in the one instance, and the visit to Lostallo in the other occur at the harmless and innocent instigation of the respective wives; and in the former story the irony is further heightened in that the place that Raumer and his wife have been making for all day proves to be but fifteen minutes walk away. Fifteen minutes from safety and yet eternity! It may seem unbelievable that Raumer should happen to meet Gianna just on a chance visit to Lostallo, but one remembers Böll's words : "What is real, is fantastic." It emerges from such stories that events are not due to the guilty and explicable actions of man, but really the consequence of fate. The question that faces man is namely how he can defend himself against *that*. "Die Welt für harmlos ansehen, ist die schlimmste von allen Täuschungen," [23] Raumer had said, and indeed it would appear from Gaiser's stories that nothing is certain in life. Perhaps that, in fact, is the only sure thing!

The consequence of action independent of the will of the individual is seen to startling effect in *Motorradunfall*. An act which was performed with the best of intentions is shown to have very bad results in this short story from the collection *Gib acht in Domokosch*, in which an elderly lady, in an attempt to help following a motorbike accident, has aggravated one of the persons' injuries by moving the body. Life remains a puzzle in which reason is not dominant. One of man's basic troubles, Gaiser would imply, is his attempt to establish a logical connection in the pattern of events, something which is not always possible, as Fehleisen in the short story of that name came to appreciate. He lost a ring and then found it again many years later in unusual circumstances; he cannot recognize the connection and is forced to the conclusion that his intention to deal only with facts, having no faith in anything, cannot be rigidly maintained. Similarly, Spelder, the complete business-man from the Pansalva factory in Neu-Spuhl, has the whole tempo of his life thrown out of gear in *Die Vögel singen so laut* by birds singing. Only the approach of death makes him realize that there need not be any purpose for their singing. To always try to question the point and connection of things is not the answer or even always desirable, as the lady narrator of *Vorspiel* implies. She realizes the presence of evil in the world, both in man and in nature; she sees a cat toying with its prey and is unable to do anything about it even though she tries (one is reminded of the attempted though unsuccessful acts of service on the part of Oberstelehn, and of Soldner). But Gaiser's basic belief that there *is* nevertheless goodness in the world can be seen through the narrator's natural reaction to sympathize and attempt to help. That there is an order to life, even if but darkly recognized amidst the general chaos that is experienced, is indicated in his stories. Fate, for example, can restore order even when it has been disturbed. The humorous tale, *Du sollst nicht stehlen*, illustrates this. A poor artist is trying to raise sufficient money so that his daughter can receive medical treatment. The theft of a piece of sculpture of his on display provides the means through the high insurance cover which will now have to be paid out. In a fit of conscience the thief returns the stolen item, which the artist will never be able to sell at the necessary sum of money required. But fate takes a hand, as the piece is stolen for a second time, on this occasion by a lad for a dare, and is smashed. The artist will, after all, receive the insurance money and his daughter can be cured because of the theft. So, strangely enough, the health and happiness of the girl are closely bound up with the breaking of the Lord's Commandment, and it is due to the unconscious game of the children that the solution comes about. They do easily and without thinking things that their elders, and supposedly betters, cannot and will not dare to do. One recalls H. M. Enzensberger's comment in the Foreword to a collection of Children's Rhymes[24] that children are immune to every ideology; their anarchic sense of humour enables them to face up to the world and come to terms with its senselessness.

From these short stories it becomes clear that man is but the toy of fate, but that all will generally turn out well if he but trusts. "History" in Gaiser's sense is, in fact, seen as fate.

"Eine geordnete Geschichte? Eine sogenannte Entwicklung, oder wie man so etwas nennt? Was für ein Blödsinn. Alles Spiel. Und lauter Monstrositäten." [25]

The meaning of this passage from *Das Schiff im Berg* is well indicated in Gaiser's tales. And further, history as such has a way of repeating itself, which leads to a consideration of Gaiser's attitude towards Time. He sees Time more as a medium of repetition, not so much as a linear process of continuity. One of the mottos from *Das Schiff im Berg* runs: "Die Historie dieses Bergs besteht aus seinen Frühlingen, seinen Sommern, seinen Herbsten, und seinen Wintern." [26] Time and again in Gaiser's writings one comes across examples of this cyclic process. *Das Schiff im Berg* again: "Es war immer dasselbe. Das Ende fing wieder an, den Aufgang vorzubereiten." [27] Even the mountain itself will not last indefinitely as it stands. In *Die Sterbende Jagd*, following the death of De Bruyn, the last sentence in the book laconically runs: "The squadron got another captain." The whole process begins all over again. In *Mittagsgesicht* Ertinger reflects over the cyclic process of his father begetting him, how he himself had sons who in turn would beget children. It is the theme of *Schlussball* ("It begins with an end and ends with a beginning", so the preface runs) as symbolized in the image of "inexplicable dirty life stirring in the marsh", that materializes into a dragonfly emerging. Larva; chrysalis; *imago*. And the repetitive process is echoed in this story at a more mundane level when Ditta declares that, given the opportunity to live her life again, she would do the same things once more. The whole point of existence, therefore, would seem to be to go through the whole turgid act of creation once again, through all the joys, the grief, the tedium, the destruction as listed in *Das Schiff im Berg*.

The prospect would seem very bleak indeed if the process of repetition is to occur as shown. It is clear that as far as Gaiser is concerned, the world has of late become even more "ungraspable" and "opaque". As *Das Schiff im Berg* indicated, the more seemingly secure in life a man is, the more insecure he actually becomes. This mood is captured in the collection of stories *Am Pass Nascondo* (1960). The insecurity of life is shown to be even greater now. In *Eine Stimme hebt an* the voice was at least raised in the wilderness, even if it was not satisfactorily answered; In *Gianna aus dem Schatten*, "Zum Rufen ist immer Zeit" was the plea, and Raumer was able to do just that. But in the tale *In fahrenden Zügen*, one of the thirteen that make up *Am Pass Nascondo,* the narrator is not even able to bring himself to call out to his friend Lavinia. These stories show the narrator to be a *viator* like the previous Gaiser heroes but the journey is very much more one into the darkness of the mind and the soul. True, there is a background of semi-reality, a quasi-Alpine-Mediterranean landscape. In itself it has an ominous significance as it is border country—"a totalitarian state has converted a once-familiar land into a region now allien and fearsome". It could, therefore, be an allegory of different political and social phenomena, but the concentration throughout is on direct experience. Life for Gaiser is a mysterious adventure in which man is helpless. The war having made everything so unreal, man's problem is to determine what *is* real of all that is left. Because of this, Gaiser often seems to fight shy of rational depiction of events and their connections—something that can be traced right from the very start of his writings through to his latest work. Thus in *Schwesterlegende*, a tale from his first published collection of short stories *Zwischenland* (1949) (the very title is significant in itself!), a sister awaits her brother, a flyer, who is supposed to be coming for a wedding. He does not come, but when he does eventually turn up, he finds his sister dead. It is probably the first time Gaiser has delved into the various levels as hinted in the motto of the book: "Im Wachbewusstsein besitzen alle eine eindeutige gemeinsame Welt. Im Schlaf aber wendet sich jeder davon in die eigene." [28] The same is seen in *Revanche* and *Vorspiel* (from the collection *Einmal und oft*) and in the stories of *Am Pass Nascondo*. The matter is well summed up in a story from the collection *Gib acht in Domokosch*, entitled *Die weisse Amsel und der Neger*, in which the narrator is at a mysterious place which he takes to be a coffee-house. What it is in reality the reader never discovers and the narrator ends the tale : "Was für ein Abenteuer hast du damals versäumt, oder welchem bist du entgangen, wo bist du überhaupt gewesen? Aber das wissen wir ohnedies nur selten." [29]

In fact, Gaiser does not know the answer himself. For him as for his characters who seek to understand the pattern of events, the connection remains insoluble. He is still groping after the meaning and as the seminarist in *Lass dich doch einmal hinauf* (from *Das Schiff im Berg*) had discovered, everything remains "schattenhaft" (shadowy, a favourite Gaiser word!); as death approached, the seminarist had wanted to believe in God, for Him to show some sign, but at the end he "knew less of himself than ever before". Certainly his fear of death is not seen positively as a transitional stage to salvation in the sense presented, for example, in Gertrud von le Fort's *Die Letzte am Schafott*. It is rather the note of resignation creeping in again.

The world Gaiser sees as ungraspable and that is why he indulges so much in dreams, which are also fragmentary, *"ungreifbar"*. At the same time they are the means to greater reality. As it is put in the title-story of *Gib acht in Domokosch*, "im Halbschlaf wurde eine Weile alles durchsichtig".[30] Such a phrase or a variant is common in Gaiser's writings. And so frequently the hero will feel physically exhausted (by the time night falls following a strenuous day of dog-fights in the air; thus De Bruyn in *Die Sterbende Jagd* : but significantly, so often because of the heat at the height of the day, around midday or early afternoon, which encourages man to relax and when resistance is low; thus, for example, Raumer in *Gianna aus dem Schatten*) whereby is induced a trance-like state of imagining things already happened before, the recognition or re-recognition of something sunken, as was suggested in *Schwesterlegende* :

> "Es schien ihm, er habe bisher das Land gekannt und es gelernt aus Karten ... So glänzen Wälder in unseren Träumen, zu denen die Wege vergessen sind; sie steigen in unseren Blick, und obwohl wir wissen, dass wir sie nie gesehen haben, wissen wir unüberwindlich : wir kommen von dort." [31]

But in such a state too, characters tend to become projections of the imagination, and times and experiences crowd on one another and become interchangeable. *Kies nach Monastir* (from the collection *Am Pass Nascondo*) illustrates this very well. The narrator of the tale, stretched out in a small boat and (inevitably) "zwischen Wachen und Schlaf zu gelähmt, um zu wissen, wieviel die Uhr zeigt (though we know it is not long past midday) und um auf etwas zu warten",[32] is suddenly startled out of his day-dreaming by a large ship bearing slowly and silently down on him. He manages to save himself and actually boards this ship to find it supposedly deserted save for a woman on deck. He thinks he recognizes her, but her identity changes frequently until finally she merges into the shape of Ness Kämmerer. When he returns to the shore he makes his way to the house where Ness Kämmerer is staying, only to discover that she had left that very day. The logical step, of course, from that of re-recognition of something sunken is the state of death. One recalls the already quoted passage from *Der Hund von Scholm* : "Der Tod und die Fülle kommen aus ein und demselben Dunkel," and that for Gaiser death would seem to be the only reality amid the present senselessness of life which man has created for himself. Death allows no one to retreat or be protected from it. In fact, the threat of death helps man to find the way to himself, to face the world. Thus De Bruyn's vision of death in his dream in Chapter Fifteen of *Die Sterbende Jagd* enables him to meet bravely and realistically the future dangers in the sky and his subsequent death. A similar presentiment is experienced by the narrator of the title-story *Am Pass Nascondo* :

> "Ich schlief ein; wie lange, das weiss ich nicht, bis das Bewusstsein einer fremden Gegenwart langsam in mein Dämmern einsickerte und mich endlich weckte. Da sah ich an der Mauer den Adjutanten Herms lehnen, *den wir nicht hatten begraben können, weil er ostwärts Turnu Magurele mit seiner Maschine ein Loch, tiefer als einen Fahrstuhlschacht, in den lehmigen Grund geschlagen hatte, und die Hitze hatte den Schacht zu einer roten Röhre gebrannt.* Das fiel mit sogleich ein, als Hermes sich mir zuwandte, aber es war nichts Besonderes an ihm zu entdecken, er war wie immer, als er sagte : Steh auf, wenn du ausgeruht hast, aber wir haben Zeit. Ich begleite dich." [33]

". . . aber wir haben Zeit." Again that phrase, echoing the idea contained in *Gianna aus dem Schatten*. But, of course, there always is time enough, since time now becomes of no importance in the state described above. The ambivalence of time in *Am Pass Nascondo* matches the ambivalence of the individual, the isolated character on whom everything is centred, and the whole collection of stories really becomes the expression of the experience of life of which death is an intrinsic part.

The *Am Pass Nascondo* collection cannot be passed over without mention of the skilful use Gaiser makes of landscape, which provides a loose sense of unity to the work as the characters and style do. This is one of the outstanding features of Gaiser's writings, for he has always been a traveller, and his journeys before, during and after the Second World War have taken him to most European countries, including Spain, Italy, Rumania, Norway, France. His own home is in Swabia and he feels deeply attached to the soil. As will already have been noticed in his work, the soil is something real for him and has a hold on him. And so landscape comes to play a twofold rôle in his writings. On the one hand it serves as a medium of detail, descriptive background pure and simple. The Norwegian scene of fjords and thin coastal strips of land dividing vast areas of sea and sky of the same colour is well captured, for example, in *Die Sterbende Jagd*; Swabia provides the solid setting for *Eine Stimme hebt an* and *Das Schiff im Berg*; and this southern warmth permeates Domokosch. On the other hand, landscape can also be seen through impressionistic eyes, whereby it becomes something vague and, as it were, unreal, the private world of the individual, when mood is more important than anything else; the *Zwischenland* atmosphere once again, such as that in *Am Pass Nascondo*.

It may be that Gaiser will be remembered not so much for what he wrote, but rather how he wrote it. After all, the themes he selects are fundamental but not exclusively his. Other writers like Plievier, Heinrich, Borchert, Risse and Landgrebe have concerned themselves with the theme of war. The figure of the returning soldier has been created time and time again, occasionally with greater perception and depth than achieved by Gaiser. The German Revival has been treated in many a novel and sometimes seen (perhaps by Bender, or Schilling, for example) with a more critical eye than Gaiser's. It is how Gaiser writes, however, that catches one's attention so forcibly. It has been argued by Gaiser's critics that there are deficiencies in his style. In *Die Sterbende Jagd*, for example, too many characters diffuse interest in the story. They see *Eine Stimme hebt an* as being too long and laboured (though 450 pages is not long by, say, Doderer's standards, or many others for that matter!). *Schlussball* shows insufficient differentiation in character-drawing, they declare. With such criticism it is easy to get sidetracked into forgetting what *is* good in these works. His writing is good narrative and he clearly obeys E. M. Forster's dictum that the task of the novelist is to tell a story. Frank Morris's cry : "To hell with fine style. We don't want literature. We want life" would certainly not be echoed by Gaiser. He tries hard to present life, but in artistic terms. His war novel, *Die Sterbende*

Jagd, for example, is not reportage, a charge that might be levelled with more justification at Plievier.

It is clear, nevertheless, that whilst he does concern himself with the telling of a tale as such, Gaiser does want his readers' attention fixed on problems that he presents, even if his own reaction to these problems is opaque. This goes much of the way towards explaining Gaiser's turning to the short-story form. The short story has been a most popular post-war German literary means of expression. It does tend to have an economy of narrative, conciseness of mood and a suggestiveness that can be more than facile, and sometimes, indeed, Gaiser's short story form borders on the anecdote which is a concentrated form of the *Novelle.* It is not without significance that Gaiser should admire Cervantes' *Novelas ejemplares.* His short stories do not deal with basically new situations or treat basically new themes, as against his novels. It might be argued that the limitations of his subject-matter constitute a deficiency in Gaiser's art, but at the same time it can be construed as a source of his very strength. For since he is dealing with situations which he knows at first hand and because his experiences are common to so many, Gaiser can establish a contemporary realism with which the reader is able to identify himself, and a sense of immediacy. As on a canvas, Gaiser succeeds in his short-stories in capturing in a moment a mood or situation dealt with at greater length in the novels (though, conversely, on the odd occasion a minor episode in a novel is given fuller treatment in a short-story. For example, the episode in *Die Sterbende Jagd* of the airman Moell who had run off because permission to marry a Norwegian girl during the war had been refused, but who had subsequently returned voluntarily to camp, finds a more comprehensive counterpart in *Aniela*). Further, whilst dealing with the particular in one of his short-stories, Gaiser obviously intends it also to come to represent the general and universal. The *Wespennest* episode in *Medusa* from the collection *Gazelle, grün* illustrates this well. The narrator as a boy watches some young wasps emerging into life for the first time and beating helplessly against the glass of a window, for they are sealed in a room; "Wohin ich blickte, überall sah ich dieses Leben sich rühren, voll Qual, und sich wieder strecken und enden."[34] The same purpose is also observable in the novels. In *Schlussball,* for example, the particular state of affairs encountered in Neu-Spuhl can be seen as the state of affairs in life overall as symbolized in the image of the dragonfly emerging to live its life until death overtakes it.

Half of the reason for the criticism levelled at Gaiser may well stem from the fact that he is a conservative modernist. Post-war German writing in the hands of the young authors took on new

adventurous forms to match the content of their work. But Gaiser
is not properly one of the post-war generation, and he retains a
mixture of the old and the new, thereby creating a kind of ambivalence in form as much as he does in content through his seeming
unreadiness to wholesale commitment.

The thing, therefore, that marks Gaiser's writings is the variety,
the curious blending. Too many characters in *Die Sterbende Jagd*
is the cry. Perhaps, but one must remember that Gaiser is interested in the individual who undergoes an experience common to
many, so he employs these many characters to present, as it were,
different perspectives of one and the same problem facing man.
Similarly, time : chapter six of the war novel centres on one night
and the actions and thoughts of various people in different places
all facing up to the bleakness of war on one particular night.
Again, *Schlussball* comprises a series of monologues by various
people, all looking at the events of the Last Dance of the Season
from different viewpoints; here, in fact, the scene is observed by
both the living and the dead, from above and below. This viewing
from the different levels of space as well as of time is further well
illustrated in *Die Sterbende Jagd* in the dog-fight episodes which
are witnessed now from the ground, now from the air.

A common complaint raised at Gaiser is that nothing much ever
happens in his stories. That there is relatively little action is
basically true (though one does well to remember the carefully
controlled build-up of tension in *Die Sterbende Jagd* through the
periods of hectic battle-activity followed by the spells of inactive
waiting : again, in *Schlussball*, where it is categorically stated at the
start : "Little action, yet two murders towards morning," tension
is maintained through to the end), for Gaiser, in his concern for
the individual facing up to his problem, is not over-worried about
external action. As there has been occasion to say earlier, since
this problem is one common to many people, Gaiser's individual
can tend to become a type without necessarily any lessening of
credibility or resulting loss of interest on the readers' part, and this
helps to account for the repeated appearance of characters, of
places in different stories. Thus Ness Kämmerer keeps popping
up in *Eine Stimme hebt an*, *Am Pass Nascondo*, *Sizilianische
Notizen*, Hagmann in *Das Schiff im Berg*, *Am Pass Nascondo*,
Gazelle, grün, Gianna reappears in *Kahle Weihnacht*; Neu-Spuhl,
the setting of *Schlussball* is mentioned, for example, in *Die Vögel
singen so laut*, together with the factory of Pansalva, Muntmischur
and the landscape of *Am Pass Nascondo* in *Schlussball*. These
characters, for example, are not repeatedly appearing because
Gaiser is concerned with showing *progression* of events or *development* of character so much as because he is trying to present a

particular person in the *same* kind of situation at a *different* time against a different or even similar background in illustration of his belief in the cyclic process or history repeating itself. Repeated appearance of characters, therefore, is one of Gaiser's methods of drawing readers' attention to this very fact and making it register, as well as serving as a very loose means of unity to his work overall. Another method is the simple expedient of placing his short stories in collections. The very title of one of these collections, *Einmal und oft*, is a clear enough indication of what Gaiser has in mind. The series of episodes which constitute the novel *Das Schiff im Berg*, wherein the narrator Hagmann acts as the link binding the whole loosely together, continues this same idea and is really at the back of *Die Sterbende Jagd* and *Schlussball*.

His concern for the person faced with a problem that stems as often as not from the senselessness of modern life leads to Gaiser's use of interior monologue. *Schlussball* immediately springs to mind as a prime example of this, but really Gaiser makes considerable application of it throughout his writings. Interior monologue, of course, is nothing startlingly new but it has come back in vogue with the post-war revival of experimentation with the stream-of-consciousness technique due to pre-occupation with time and memory. It is noteworthy that Gaiser should employ this method that represents an inward turn towards a subjective, symbolic art which is at the other pole of realism. As Wellek says : "The use of the stream of consciousness technique actually achieves the most radical dissolution of ordinary reality."[35] The *Ich* in effect serves as a thread between the external and the inner world. Often the boundaries are virtually unrecognizable, especially when Gaiser dispenses in his writings with inverted commas, whereby figures and ideas fuse together.

Gaiser can, of course, be objective in his description of action, in his pure narrative, particularly in his novels, *Die Sterbende Jagd* and *Eine Stimme hebt an* or in a short-story like *Die schlesische Gräfin*, but more frequently there is a predominance of presentation of action by reflection, as in *Schlussball* or the short-stories *Der Mensch, den ich erlegt hatte, Vorspiel*, etc. Where inner monologue occurs (and it occurs everywhere, though *en passant* one might pin-point *Im leeren Zelt* as an example from Gaiser's latest publication, *Gazelle, grün*) a language is discovered that is fragmentary, evocative and lyrical to match the stream of inner experiences, conscious and unconscious thoughts. It might mean that the language becomes (and possibly remains) misunderstood, and the reader who likes a simple, straightforward tale may well complain that a work like *Am Pass Nascondo* does not come sufficiently into focus.

The variety in his choice of language is most marked. In *Die Sterbende Jagd* technical vocabulary and air-force jargon abound; in *Schlussball* there is teen-age slang; in *Das Schiff im Berg*, scientific language. Clearly Gaiser has the ear to capture sounds as he has the eye for colour and imagery. Through the very variety to fit the different situations Gaiser is able to create a living world, and Joyce's belief that words can produce a reality by themselves is affirmed by him :

"In die Luft kann einer dichten, und es ensteht eine Wirklichkeit."[36]

Laconic prose and the more poetic touches alternate in his work. To take one example from *Die Sterbende Jagd* : The cold, factual and casual announcement of death or the replacement for De Bruyn comes hard alongside the poetic diction of the description of some Focke-Wulf 190's taking off, or of the dog-fights themselves (say, in Chapters Twenty-two and Twenty-three), where a sense of distance and detachment in the sky is presented that is in such paradoxical contrast to the horrible actuality of war in the air. Eye and ear combine to good effect in *Eine Stimme hebt an*. Here Gaiser's employment of the Swabian landscape as the basis for background is matched by his use of South German for "local colour"—unusual forms, rare names traditional and very actual in one sense, yet unreal and strange-sounding in their unusualness. Indeed, Gaiser has a liking for the strange-sounding and the exotic that breathes of southern warmth. So often Swabian and quasi-Mediterranean landscapes serve as background for his stories; even more frequent in his work are foreign words and phrases from the Spanish, the Italian, semi-Rumanian, or a mixture that resembles the old Romance language. It may be argued that this is unnecessary and imparts to his work a "gimmicky" touch. But, generally speaking, where it does occur, it blends well with the particular situation presented and meets the purpose demanded of it; this is often to emphasise a sense of detachment or distance between persons with the resulting difficulties of communication. For the expressions, as often as not, are incorporated in interior monologues (as in the instance in *Schlussball* of Soldner being lost in reverie when dancing with Diemut Andernoth), where the detachment of the individual results in any case, or are uttered by foreigners who consequently detach themselves from the narrator or character concerned wherever a language barrier exists. Conversely, of course, language, be it one's mother tongue or a foreign one, can be the very means of breaking down barriers and establishing contact between people, *provided* they are prepared voluntarily to make the effort required. The earlier-quoted example of *Gianna aus dem Schatten* can serve to illustrate this point : the threat of danger lurking in the air enables Raumer and his wife to communicate properly for the first time since their marriage, and once the tragedy has occurred, with the need for human help and sympathy being understood, Enna is able to get through to the Italian villagers, and they to her. No language barrier is encountered now, no question of detachment. The colouring of the old Romance language in particular in his work may be seen, too, as indicative of Gaiser's interest in words, in language and its origin as a living thing, the so-called *Ursprache*, and this in turn can be linked with his basic faith in the soil seen *int. al.* in *Das Schiff im Berg*. The inclusion of such foreign words undeniably adds to the lyrical aspect of his writing.

Gaiser's attitude to sound and language in his stories is such that he seems to order his words whereby the reader has to let them work upon him as musical variations on a theme. It accounts for the repetition of phrases, be it for simple effect, as in the exclamation with reference to the dance of the paralysed girl in *Schlussball* : "Ball! schöner Klang" (which speaks for itself!); for the purpose of helping to identify a character, as with Ditta's "Nicht für einen Wald voll Affen" in the same novel; or for the building up of tension and the creating of the sense of inevitability, as in the sombre "In den Vorhöfen des Todes" from *Gib acht in Domokosch*. Though the taking of one further example from this last tale, for example, well illustrates the weakness that is dangerously inherent in repetition : "Wir gingen im warmen Schatten, wir gingen unter den hängenden Blumen durch über den Hof gegen das Dorf hin, und dann gingen wir durch das Dorf auf dem Mittelweg."[37] It accounts for the author's liking for *coincidentia oppositorum* like : "Sie floss nicht über, aber Mangel war nie bei ihr" (from *Gianna aus dem Schatten*) or : "Trockenes Land, trüb ohne Tränen, tränkend das trockene und alle Trübe scheuchend, selber sich sättigend an dem Rauchzeichen des Leids" (from *Eine Stimme hebt an*).[38] One can understand that poetic effusions in the descriptive sections of Gaiser's work are often there to act as a deliberate artistic counter to the contrived sense of sparseness in dialogue, where characters are often choked or at a loss for words. But sometimes the diction is overworked and the result is an unhappy sounding sentence like "Die Mittagsgöttin hob träge ein Lid"[39] (from *Eine Stimme hebt an*) standing uneasily in its paragraph.

A feature of his writings in the past has been the author's apparent liking for *Sprüche* (which, of course, if overplayed, could come to sound too much like moral tags to prove a point and thus become undesirable). Not infrequently Gaiser has drawn upon

classical writers for mottos for his books (e.g., Heraclitus for
Zwischenland, Eine Stimme hebt an Am Pass Nascondo Aristo-
phanes for *Schlussball*, etc.) and admittedly the very ambivalence
of the *Spruch* well serves Gaiser's ambiguous approach in his work.
Naturally, with such an approach, the value of the image cannot
be overlooked. The image for Gaiser comes to seem more real
than the fact in this present age of distorted values. Indeed, the
value lies in the very image itself. Two examples from his stories
help to illustrate this point : "Die Wirklichkeit war das Gleichnis
und das Gleichnis die Wirklichkeit. Diese Augenblicke kamen nicht
wieder, es wäre denn nach dem Tod. Wohnen in der Gewissheit
ohne Täuschungen, nicht mehr wir selbst, nicht mehr, wofür wir
uns gehalten hatten" (from *Gib acht in Domokosch*)[40]; and from
Die Sterbende Jagd : "Das Bild des Bootes stand in dem Spiegel
verkehrt, schwarz und scharf wie gestochen, das verkehrte Bild
viel wirklicher als der Gegenstand, lauter verwechselte Wirklich-
keiten."[41] The point Gaiser is at pains to make is namely : What
if phantasy is real and life with all its glitter is phantasy? It is very
significant that in his writings frequent use is made of glass as an
image. Glass is transparent, yet it can shatter and hurt people;
or, to put it another way : Seeing is believing. The question is,
believing in what? The whole problem of facing up to the horror
of life is symbolized in *Medusa* (from the collection *Gazelle, grün*).
The third part of this short story briefly outlines the well-known
classical tale of mythology. Perseus is to kill the terrifying figure
of Medusa, but, if he is to survive, he can only look indirectly at
her through a mirror given him by Athene.

The mention of Perseus and the wanderer-image brings us back
to Gaiser himself. Like his heroes, Gaiser is restless in a world that
is in a state of flux ("nirgends Stillstand noch Dauer"[42]), bemoan-
ing the loss of values and culture (the plaintive cry is particularly
loud in *Schlussball, Von den Farben der vergangenen Tage* and
Sizilianische Notizen) and seeking the meaning to life. "To want
to know the purpose you are serving is too large a claim to make
on ultimate enlightenment" was a parting shot in *Schlussball*, but
Gaiser is definitely not prepared to accept a defeatist attitude as
an answer, nor ultimately even necessarily that of resignation. *Im
leeren Zelt* appears to present a gloomy picture in the first paragraph : "...du bist im Gehen. Sicher gehst du nie," but the
narrator comes to face the fact that :

> "es reicht nicht aus, ich weiss es, dass ich gehe und die entlegenen
> Stellen aufsuche, wo ich hoffen möchte, dass dort nichts mehr
> sei und ich nichts zu tun brauche. Etwas tun muss ich, gleichviel,
> gut oder böse, aber tun auf Menschenweise. Fehlbar, werde ich

gehen müssen und vielleicht fehlen. Was kann es sein, was erwartet mich? Ich werde nicht warten dürfen. Ich gehe, bis an den Gaumen voll Furcht, und grüble. Ich muss etwas tun."[43]

The individual is standing at the crossroads with a decision to make : he must do something, whether good or bad, but as a man. This sums up the situation encountered in Gaiser's work overall with its implied plea for man to help man. Gaiser's choice of vocabulary with biblical elements, the choice of title for certain of his stories, even the odd touch of humour (which is never black humour), would confirm his own positive hopes in this direction. But in this age of flux it is as yet not an easy matter to choose instinctively and unhesitatingly the right path. The narrator of *Vergeblicher Gang* (also from *Gazelle, grün*) had difficulty in saying to himself parts of the Lord's Prayer : "Forgive us our Trespasses, as we forgive..." The words got stuck in his throat— again the German verb used is *"ersticken"*!—before he could successfully conclude : "But deliver us from Evil." The Lutheran Gaiser sees the problem of combating the present spiritual crisis as something personal and resting on the individual. And his approach to the problem is not so much cerebral and intellectual as emotional. He seeks from within the way to try to realize the sense of existence so hard to determine. As yet he is still "looking through a glass darkly". It was perhaps not without its point that Ness Kämmerer should hand to Oberstelehn a book (not surprisingly a favourite with Gaiser himself) entitled *El caballero de la Triste Figura.*

NOTES AND TRANSLATIONS

1. "I can't really picture the joys of being a writer at all. Writing is all-consuming. The desk is not my world." *Autobiographisches Nachwort* in *Revanche.*
2. "The Past he saw as bare and vain, the Present hostile and, like many of his kind, he viewed the Future as an empty word." (*Fehleisen.*)
3. "We went about and sought the beginning of life, rummaged after the remnants and were afraid." (*Von den Farben der vergangenen Tage.*)
4. "He viewed this world of upsurging materialism merely through a glass window. He had ceased to take part." (*Mittagsgesicht.*)
5. It seems that a second verse-collection entitled *Gesang von Osten* was prepared about 1943 but its existence is not known.
6. "of the shining shield, the golden spurs, hair flowing, hand holding the reins."
7. "Schwersenz fell silent. He was silent, first of all from surprise, then because he was perplexed and then finally through obstinacy."
8. "You can want a thing and fight for it, that's a splendid destiny.

You can want it and not fight for it, not worth mentioning. You can not want something and therefore refuse to fight for it, that can be very hard, but at least you retain your peace of mind. But not to want something, but still fight for it because of a certain set of circumstances, must mean you lose one way or another. There is no way out."

9. "Respectfully request. Will and yet not will."

10. "What is Peace? It is promotion-lists, thwarted ambitions, lies, shops, business by commission; doing your neighbour down so you can live better yourself. If that is impossible, buying him off—community spirit that's called. Everyday life, gasping with hate and irritation..."

11. "We have forgotten the meaning of order to such a degree, or destroyed it, that we now have to hold on to the little that still remains."

12. "Besides, history is a kind of swindle, particularly when we try to alter its course a bit. The temptation of man to openly show that he is greater than nature and is not prepared to put up with the situation."

13. "Grass and dust. Man is like grass, like the lowest form of life, a prey to chance, subject to cause and effect."

14. "Man must return to the earth again, even if he has been able to support himself in the air for a time. He can't remain up there." The same idea is contained in a sentence from *Gib acht in Domokosch*: "No man ever became master over this earth."

15. "He lay huddled, his legs tucked up under him, like a child in its mother's womb."

16. "The earth dreamed; God snatched man from the dream, selected him and let him loose. But he did not let signs be lacking."

17. "Take things as the dear God sends them, as raw material. It merely depends on what you make of it. He would seem to have had the intention of leaving you in life, and now you have to pass a test."

18. "It tormented them that they could not discover the meaning... there were days when God seemed dead or departed."

19. "There is always time to call out (for help)."

20. "Many of the troubles of that time stemmed perhaps from the fact that one no longer understood anything under the meaning of love."

21. "Death and the fulness of life come from one and the same darkness" (from *Der Hund von Scholm*).

22. "People were on the move, scared and lost, seeking each other with straining eyes and not finding each other."

23. "To view the world as being harmless is the worst possible deception."

24. *Allerleirauh, Viele schöne Kinderreime.* Suhrkamp, Frankfurt am Main, 1961.

25. "History as an ordered course? A so-called line of development or something of that kind? What a lot of nonsense! Everything is pure gamble and monstrosity."

26. "The history of this mountain consists of its springs, its summers, its autumns and its winters."

27. "It was always the same. The end recommenced to prepare the rise."

28. "In the state of consciousness everyone has a common world. In the state of sleep each person turns from that world into his own private one."

29. "What kind of an adventure have you let slip by you on that occasion, or what kind of one have you escaped from? Where in fact have you been? That sort of thing, though, we know but rarely."

30. "In a trance-like state everything is made clear for a time."

31. "It seemed to him that he already knew the land and had learned about it from maps. . . . Likewise in our dreams forests are illuminated, the paths to which are forgotten. They come before our gaze and although we know that we have never seen them, we know without a shadow of doubt: that is where we have come from."

32. "Too paralyzed twixt waking and sleep to know the time and to wait for something or other to happen."

33. "I fell asleep; how long, I don't know, until the awareness of a strange Presence slowly infiltrated my subconscious and finally woke me. I saw leaning against the wall Adjutant Hermes, *whom we had not been able to bury, because on a flight east to Turnu Magurele he had made a hole with his plane in the loamy earth that was deeper than a lift-shaft and the heat had burnt the shaft that it was like a red duct.* That immediately struck me when Hermes turned to me, but there was nothing special about him to notice; he was the same as always when he said, 'Get up when you have rested; we have time enough though. I'll accompany you'."

34. "Everywhere I looked, I saw this life stirring, straining, full of pain, and terminating."

35. *Concepts of Criticism.* Yale Press. 1963.

36. "One can create words in the air and a reality arises." Significantly, Gaiser continues: "in die Luft malen, das bleibt Chimäre." On the one hand it helps to illustrate Gaiser's need to turn to literature as against painting to provide the means of real expression for his experiences. On the other, it helps to shed light on the element of the nebulous in his work (e.g., the landscape of *Am Pass Nascondo*).

37. "Ball! what a lovely sound"
"Not for a forestful of monkeys"
"On the threshhold of death"
"We went in the warm shade, we went along under the hanging flowers across the farm towards the village, and then we went through the village along the middle-path."

38. "She was never overflowing with things, but then, she was never short of anything."
"Parched land, sad without a sign of tears, watering the dry earth and dispelling all gloom, quenching its thirst on the signs of grief."

39. "The noonday-goddess languidly raised a lid."

40. "Reality was the image, and the image reality. These moments did not recur, otherwise it would have been after death. It was no longer possible for us to live in a state of certainty, free of deceptions, something we had held out for."

41. "The image of the boat was inverted in the mirror, black and

sharply defined as if it were cut out; the inverted image much more real than the object itself; pure transposed realities "

42. "Never stagnation nor permanence" (from *Das Schiff im Berg*). This state of flux is ever present in Gaiser's works in his ample use of verbs expressing movement; his setting of scenes at railway-stations (as in *Die Sterbende Jagd, Schlussball, In fahrenden Zügen,* etc.); Gaiser's traveller-figure is rarely able to travel at leisure and as a sightseer, as the author himself points out in *Stunde hier, Stunde dort* in Akzente 1955/1.

43. "You are on the move . . . but never with any degree of surety." "It won't suffice, I know, to go and seek the distant places where I should hope nothing more exists and that I need do nothing. I must do something, good or bad, but do it as a human being. Fallible, I shall have to go and perhaps err. What can it be that is expected of me? I shall not be allowed to wait. I'll go, the roof of my mouth dry with fear, and meditate. I must do something."

SELECT BIBLIOGRAPHY

Published works

Reiter am Himmel. Gedichte Langen-Müller Vlg, München 1941.
Zwischenland. Erzählungen. Hanser Vlg, München 1949.
Eine Stimme hebt an. Roman. Hanser Vlg, München 1950.
Die Sterbende Jagd. Roman. Hanser Vlg, München 1953, Fischerbucherei 1957.
Das Schiff im Berg. Roman. Hanser Vlg, München 1955.
Revanche. Erzählungen und Autobiographisches Nachwort. Reclam Vlg, Stuttgart 1956.
Einmal und Oft. Erzählungen. Hanser Vlg, München 1956.
Revanche. Erzählungen und Autobiographisches Nachwort. Reclam Vlg, München 1957.
Aniela. Erzählung in *Einmal und Oft.* Hanser Vlg, München 1958.
Schlussball. Roman. Hanser Vlg, München 1958. Fischerbücherei 1961.
Sizilianische Notizen. Hanser Vlg, München 1959.
Gib acht in Domokosch. Erzählungen. Bücher der 19. 1959.
Am Pass Nascondo. Erzählungen. Hanser Vlg, München 1960. DTV paperback 1963.
Gazelle, grün. Erzählungen und Aufzeichnungen. Hanser Vlg, München 1965.

Secondary literature

H. Bienek. Interview mit Gaiser in *Werkstattgespräche mit Schriftstellern.* Hanser Vlg, München 1962.
G. Blöcker. Gerd Gaiser. Frankfurter Allgemeine Zeitung 13.9.1958.
C. Hohoff. Gerd Gaiser. *Werk und Gestalt.* Hanser Vlg, München 1962.
K. A. Horst. Sinn und Hintersinn bei Gerd Gaiser. Merkur 1956 (10).
W. Jens. Gegen die Uberschätzung Gerd Gaisers. Die Zeit 1960 (48).
H. Kreuzer. Auf Gaisers Wegen. Korrektur eines Bildes. Frankfurter Hefte 1960 (15).

K. Migner. Zwischen erlebtem Chaos und anerkannter Ordnung. Welt und Wort 1961 (16).

M. Reich-Ranicki. Der Fall Gerd Gaiser. In *Deutsche Literatur in West und Ost*. Piper Vlg, München 1963.

E. Stutz. Der Erzähler Gerd Gaiser. Arreli Sezione Germanica, Napoli 1960.

Heinrich Böll

Heinrich Böll

by W. E. YUILL
(Sheffield University)

Heinrich Böll was born in Cologne on December 21st, 1917, the eighth child of a cabinet-maker whose ancestors had come to Holland and the Rhineland from England to escape the persecution of Roman Catholics that followed the Reformation. After taking his Abitur Böll was apprenticed to the book trade and then studied German language and literature for a short time before his conscription into the Arbeitsdienst and the army. He served throughout the war, mainly on the Russian front, being wounded four times and never advancing beyond the modest rank of corporal. On his return from an American prisoner of war camp in 1945 he was employed by the statistical department of his native city, Cologne. At the same time he began to write, and his first short stories were published in 1946–47. These were followed by two war novels (*Der Zug war pünktlich* and *Wo warst du, Adam?*), but it was not until 1953 that Böll achieved large popular success with *Und sagte kein einziges Wort*. He was awarded the literary prize of Gruppe 47 in 1951. In 1955 Böll made his first visit to Ireland, a country which attracted him so strongly that in 1958 he purchased a small farm there. Apart from his novels and numerous short stories Böll is the author of many radio plays and of one stage play, *Ein Schluck Erde*. In 1942 he married Annemarie Cech, and he and his wife have published several translations from English and American authors, including *Playboy of the Western World*, Behan's *The Hostage* and *The Quare Fellow* and Salinger's *Catcher in the Rye* and *Franny and Zooey*.

HEINRICH BÖLL was born in the last year of the Kaiser's reign and the first of the Russian revolution. Almost all of his stories have the local and topical affinities that this suggests : they are mostly set in the city of his birth and deal with the tumultuous era of European history that coincides with his life. Like a character whom he describes in one of his short stories he is "as old as the hunger and the filth in Europe, and the war".

The local associations of Böll's work go beyond mere setting and local colour, for, as a writer, he displays many of the attributes of his fellow-citizens : traditional Catholic faith, unquestioned but not unquestioning, level-headedness and practicality, humour and a drastic wit. He has the disrespect for authority and the sound political sense that prompted the Cologne crowds to greet Hitler not with flowers but with flower-pots; he has, too, the introspective and faintly melancholy temperament that characterizes what he calls "the gin-drinker's Rhine"—the part of the river that extends from Bonn to the mists of the North Sea. For Böll, however, Cologne is not simply an urban landscape : the dimensions of space merge for him into that of time, for he is constantly aware of the past that literally and metaphorically lies buried beneath the present—not only the past of his own experience but the remote past of Roman settlers. The past is not thought of in terms of a "cultural heritage" but rather as a continuity of human experience linking the Roman colonist with the modern artisan or clerk. Certainly Böll's fascination by the past is not of the kind that one would expect to issue in the form of historical novels or stories that are quaintly local; it is an aspect rather of his imaginative insight into basic human situations—and perhaps also of his belief in the ultimate timelessness of human existence.

Böll has always been more than a local writer : he is concerned with the fate and experience of a whole generation of Germans and of the individual in the great materialistic urban societies of the modern world. It was as the spokesman of his own generation that Böll first came into prominence; he subsequently developed into a mentor and critic of all those who seemed to forget too easily the sufferings of that generation and the causes of that suffering. Like so many of his contemporaries Böll was a conscript. Even more disgusted than most by what he later called "the almost total senselessness of the military life" he found himself forced to defend a cause in which no German of his liberal and Christian principles could believe—to suffer "the frightful fate of being a soldier and having to wish that the war might be lost". The tone of Böll's early war stories is certainly not nostalgic or romantic, but neither is it as hysterical as that of Borchert's play *Draußen vor der Tür* : the writer's reaction is one of sober, sombre, seemingly dispassionate disgust. War is a total catastrophe, a blight, "a disease, like typhus". It is only in his latest work, *Entfernung von der Truppe*, that Böll, looking back over twenty years, can see his experience of war in a satirical and at time scurrilously comic light. In the early stories, when memories were still painfully fresh, there was no room for humour. In an age of conscription and mechanization war had lost whatever glamour it might formerly have had, and was unmitigated by heroism. There is certainly nothing romantic or heroic about the soldiers in *Der Zug war pünktlich* and *Wo warst du, Adam?* They are cannon-fodder. The railway station, which in Böll's stories so often epitomizes the impersonality, restlessness and rootlessness of modern life, becomes in war-time the ante-chamber of fate. Men are driven by "the grey authoritarian scourge" of loudspeakers into trains which, as symbols of destiny, carry them unresisting to a punctual death. Scarcely one figure in these early stories eludes death. Feinhals, in *Wo warst du, Adam?*, escapes until the last moment, only to be blown to pieces—by a random German shell—on the threshold of his own home. The stories are not designed, however, as hair-raising accounts of the horrors of battle, for the writer is concerned with deeper issues than physical ordeal and destruction. This is implied by the choice of title from Theodor Haecker's *Tag- und Nachtbücher*:

> Eine Weltkatastrophe kann zu manchem dienen. Auch dazu, ein Alibi zu finden vor Gott. Wo warst du, Adam? "Ich war im Weltkrieg."[1]

It is the demoralization and degradation, the spiritual maiming and blinding that are emphasized. The killing of men's bodies is not the worst; their souls are enthralled or crushed by mindless discipline. Böll dwells on the impact of the war on the individual in describing fear and nausea, the sensations of the wounded, the apathy of the exhausted, the nostalgia of bewildered youths in the vast squalid hinterlands of the front, the corruption and sultry atmosphere of impending violence in occupied lands. The vaunted discipline of armies is shown as the acme of inefficiency and futility: bridges are rebuilt only to be demolished again within minutes of completion; troops are rushed into action, incongruously, in brightly coloured furniture vans, as helplessly doomed as the Jews being similarly transported in the opposite direction; schoolrooms, hastily turned into operating theatres, receive back the maimed bodies of boys who sat there three months previously and mock them with patriotic emblems and slogans. War perverts institutions, shatters principles and wreaks havoc with the moral order far beyond the area of physical destruction. Families are torn apart, prostitution and adultery are fostered, and even where the marriage bond is preserved it is too often stripped of its sacramental character by makeshifts and sordid surroundings.

In the short story *Die Botschaft*, which describes a typical case of war-time adultery, the narrator concludes, "Da wußte ich, daß der Krieg niemals zu Ende sein würde, solange noch irgendwo eine Wunde blutete, die er geschlagen hatte".[2] Böll's stories are full of war-wounded and convalescents in the figurative sense, people for whom the war can never be "over"—not only the physically handicapped or the manifestly neurotic, but also those who are simply demoralized. The returning soldier and his attempts to adjust himself to life in post-war Germany naturally figure prominently in the stories. These "Heimkehrer" are not burdened like Beckmann, the hero of *Draußen vor der Tür*, with a sense of guilt, they do not succumb to hysterical despair. They suffer, rather, from an inarticulate malaise, a paralysis of will and feeling. The plight of such moral cripples is compared in a graphically banal metaphor with the effortless assimilation of the many :

Und als wir nach Hause kamen, sind sie aus dem Krieg ausgestiegen wie aus einer Straßenbahn, die gerade dort etwas langsamer fuhr, wo sie wohnten, sie sind abgesprungen, ohne den Fahrpreis zu bezahlen. Sie haben eine kleine Kurve genommen, und siehe da : das Vertiko stand noch ... man ließ sich ein bißchen entnazisieren—so wie man zum Friseur geht, um den lästigen Bart abnehmen zu lassen ... Wir aber fuhren weiter mit der Straßenbahn ... der Fahrpreis wurde immer teurer, das Tempo immer schneller, die Kontrolleure immer mißtrauischer, wir sind eine äußerst verdächtige Sippschaft.[3]

To this "dubious fraternity" belongs Fred Bogner, the hero (if one can use the term of a figure so unheroic) of Böll's first novel about post-war life. Bogner's experience as a telephonist during the war, undramatic and boring, has made him aware of the callousness of men. His response is an apathy rendering him incapable to cope with the squalor of civilian life. Only a frayed bond of religious faith holds him to his wife and family. It is not only the poor and the déclassés like Bogner who suffer from this lassitude. Albert and Nella in Böll's next novel, *Haus ohne Hüter*, although materially more secure, are equally apathetic and withdrawn. Not even the prospect of revenge for the death of her husband can stir Nella : brought face to face at last with the man responsible for it she can no longer summon up the hatred she has nursed for so many years : "She looked in vain for her hatred of Gäseler and sensed something quite different, something alien, cold and uncanny—boredom."

Bogner, Albert and Nella are typical central figures in these first novels of post-war life. They are moody and uncommunicative. It is symptomatic of their alienation that they prefer to speak on the telephone rather than face to face. They turn their backs on the reviving world around them and, young as they are, live in their memories. Reminiscence is the characteristic dimension of Böll's writing. He is fascinated by the counterpoint of time and place and by the changes worked through time and circumstance. This fascination is illustrated in a brief episode from the autobiographical sketch, *Stadt der alten Gesichter* :

"Zwei Bananen, bitte," sagte ich im Jahre 1929 zu einem fünfzehnjährigen Mädchen auf dem kleinen Platz vor St. Severin; die blühende Frische einer eben Schulentlassenen, die sorglos das Wechselgeld aus der grünen Stahlkassette nahm; dasselbe an derselben Stelle zur selben Person gesagt im Jahre 1959; erschreckend die rauhe, fast schon runzelige Hand der

Frau mittleren Alters, die bekümmert in die grüne Stahlkassette blickte. Nirgendwo deutlicher werde ich lesen, wie lange dreißig Jahre währen."

It is not unnatural that the drastic disruption of their lives by the war made the whole of Böll's generation obsessively conscious of a pattern of change and continuity. For characters like Albert and Nella in *Haus ohne Hüter* time is out of joint in a special sense. For them the past is the time before the war, the present is the time since, and between past and present lies a limbo, a gulf that has swallowed what might have been. Besides the actual past and present there is in their minds a potential time, "le temps perdu", "the third level", as Böll calls it. He is continually seeking metaphors to express all this : in *Haus ohne Hüter*, three "times" are visualized as discs superimposed upon one another and revolving eccentrically :

> Gegenwart und Vergangenheit schoben sich übereinander wie Scheiben, die den Punkt suchen, wo sie kongruent werden : die eine rotierte sauber und hatte den Drehpunkt in der Mitte, Vergangenheit, die er genau zu überblicken glaubte, die Gegenwart aber drehte sich heftiger als die Vergangenheit, eierte über diese hin, aus einem anderen Drehpunkt gesteuert ... und zwischen die eiernde Gegenwart und die scheinbar sauber rotierende Vergangenheit schob sich eine dritte, grellgelbe dahinsausende Scheibe : die Zeit, die nie gewesen, das Leben, das nie gelebt worden war ... wirres Geflimmer dreier Scheiben, die nie übereinander liegen würden, tödliche Inkongruenz, in der es keinen Ruhepunkt gab.[5]

Many of Böll's introspective characters, like the young widow Nella, cannot shake off the nostalgia for what might have been. They are haunted by the memory of a turning point in their lives. For these people time is essentially private and cannot be divorced from inner experience. The secretly rebellious traffic censor in the story *An der Brücke* rejects the notion of public time as a statistical factor : he scorns the "future perfect" of the planners and "embezzles" the minutes when the girl he secretly loves walks across the bridge—"these two minutes belong to me alone ..." The Man in the radio play *Klopfzeichen* remarks, "You can fall into time as you fall into a hole". Frau Fähmel in *Billard um halb zehn* has shrunk into a private world where all her experience is compressed into one day : "Today is Verdun, today Heinrich died, Otto was killed, today is the 31st May 1942." In his attempt to tell the story of his life Wilhelm Schmölder, the hero of *Entfernung von der Truppe* is repeatedly drawn back to the day when his mother died and when he first met his future

wife. In this story, impregnated as it is with irony, Böll himself
comments drily on his juggling with time structures :

Dieses Vor- und Zurückgreifen mag den Leser nicht nervös
machen. Spätestens im siebten Schuljahr weiß ja jedes Kind,
daß man das Wechsel der Erzählebene nennt.[6]

The notion of time as experience stored in the memory governs
the structure of *Billard um halb zehn*, the most ambitious and
perhaps most successful of Böll's novels. Here the author steps outside the bounds of a single generation and from the vantage point
of a single day constructs a story of multiple perspectives, scan-
ning the history of the Fähmel family over half a century as
recorded in the memories of the main characters. The pivotal
events are still those of the Nazi era and the Second World
War, the central figure Robert Fähmel a representative of Böll's
generation. As a structural designer deriving sombre satisfaction
from his war-time demolition tasks Robert displays a cold contempt
for the Nazis and their dubious political heirs in the booming post-
war society of Western Germany. At the same time he feels remorse
and guilt at his failure to protect the weak, the "lambs", from
oppression. The history of his family, and implicitly of the class
and faith they represent, is linked with the abbey of St. Anton—
built by Robert's father as the foundation of his prosperous
architect's practice, destroyed by Robert during the war as a protest against the toleration of the Nazis by the Church, re-built
with the help of Robert's son, who is dismayed to recognize in the
demolition diagrams on the ruins his father's hand.

In his disillusion and remorse Robert has withdrawn from
human contacts into the world of mathematical formulae. In his
daily "billiards at half past nine" he finds emotional and aesthetic
satisfaction—"music without melody, painting without pictures"—
and a quasi-religious absorption, "a kind of prayer-mill, a litany".
The game also serves as a kind of time-machine to carry him back
into the past to release a stream of memories addressed to his
confidant, Hugo, page-boy of the Prinz Heinrich hotel.

For many of Böll's characters besides Robert Fähmel habit is
an anodyne. Hypnotized by the notion of time, they often see in
habit a means of arresting its flow. In the sacramental form of
ritual, habit is a legitimate escape from time, an access to eternity,
the rituals of his Church playing a large part in Böll's stories. In a
secular context, however, habit can be a baleful force. The attempt
to resurrect the past by repetition may have harrowing effects :
Hans Schnier in *Ansichten eines Clowns* describes his abortive experiments in this respect and confesses that moments cannot be repeated. Habit can be an aid to survival, but it may also be an inert

weight that crushes individuality and impoverishes life. In the story entitled *Über die Brücke*, the narrator, passing years later over a railway bridge he regularly used to cross, observes with mingled relief and dismay that the windows of a house are being cleaned in exactly the same sequence as before the war : the daughter, having taken over from her mother, the hypnotic routine of the "Putzplan" is becoming the same kind of household drudge. It may be that Böll has here put his finger on a particular weakness of his nation—the fondness for ceremony and regulated routine. The satirical story *Nicht nur zur Weihnachtszeit* describes how a middle-class family's regard for the traditional Christmas gathering becomes a nightmare through the mania of an elderly aunt who insists on the celebration being repeated every night of the year. As the children wilt from repeated exposure to the rigours of a family Christmas and are replaced by tailor's dummies, the adults evolve a duty roster or are impersonated by hired actors. Some of the family are driven into monasteries, existentialist clubs or even emigration by a protracted diet of Christmas sweetmeats and perpetual singing of Christmas carols. The story, written in a parodied would-be "literary" style by one of them who is clearly in a state of repressed hysteria, is irresistibly comic. It is also an acute ironic comment on commercialization and the pathological desire of certain circles in Germany to ignore change and restore the empty forms of a sentimental, outmoded way of life.

The part played by time, memory and habit in Böll's works points to a concentration on emotion and inner sensation rather than on action. Only the satirical short stories tend to have definable plots : many others simply trace the changes of emotional climate in a character or the evolution of attitudes from a germ of experience. Even in the novels the external action—as distinct from reminiscence—rarely occupies more than a few hours. There is little of what one might call epic objectivity : frequently the author identifies himself with the protagonist, while the more complex works are built up from a series of private views.

The tone of the first person narrative so common in Böll is generally subdued, resigned, melancholy, often with a hint of the morbid; the apocalyptic intensity of *Steh auf, steh doch auf* is exceptional. As a true son of the "sombre and melancholy" lower Rhine described in *Undines gewaltiger Vater*, Böll shows a recurrent awareness of death as the one certainty in life. What Hans Schnier says in *Ansichten eines Clowns* would seem to apply to Böll himself : "The artist always has death by him as a good priest has his breviary." In many of his war stories Böll conducts his hero to the threshold of death—and sometimes, uncannily, beyond it. Fred Bogner is "always thinking of death" and, like the narrator in

Es wird etwas geschehen, haunts cemeteries and attaches himself to funeral processions. To the ideal of frantic activity for which his countrymen are renowned Böll opposes the ascetic motto of *memento mori.* Too few of his compatriots, he asserts, are capable of melancholy—the mark of humility and hence of true humanity. "Ein Mensch ohne Trauer," reflects one of the characters in *Billard um halb zehn,* "das ist doch kein Mensch mehr".[7]

Although often struck, this muted note is by no means the only one in the register of Böll's work. In many of his stories, particularly since about 1952 when symptoms of over-indulgence began to appear in German society, Böll looks round him with a critical eye, and the tone becomes ironical, sometimes hilariously satirical. *Dr Murkes gesammeltes Schweigen* tells the story of a fastidiously intellectual radio producer who is so surfeited by the endless stream of verbiage which he has to supervise that he collects the silences from recording tapes and "plays" them over to himself. During a re-recording session he torments with sadistic but entirely justified glee a time-serving popular philosopher who has the superb name of Bur-Malottke. The score or so of "God"-s which he has excised from the apostate philosopher's talk he adroitly inserts into a radio play—appropriating for himself the original "silences"—a fine example of Böll's skill in turning whimsy to satirical ends. A similar combination of fantasy and closely observed detail may be seen in stories like *Der Wegwerfer* and *Der Bahnhof von Zimpren.* The narrator in the former is employed by a company to destroy the masses of useless postal material that is a by-product of modern society. In the latter story the discovery of oil in a desolate rural district leads to the mushroom growth of a town complete with main-line railway station; the oil dries up, the station—decorated with a fresco by a distinguished modern artist—remains, sustained by the machinery of bureaucracy, staffed by redundant officials : a monument to reckless exploitation and the philosophy of "expansion" at all costs.

Böll's humour does not always have a satirical edge. In the earlier stories particularly it is sometimes gentler and not so pointedly topical. The hero of *Im Lande der Rujuks* devotes eighteen years of his life to learning the language of an obscure island race only to discover, when he goes to live among them, that they are mainly interested in whisky and Hollywood. Without more ado the scholar abandons his researches, returning to grow fruit on the Rhine and to exchange insulting postcards in Rujuk with his former professor. Böll later develops a more outspokenly critical attitude, the figures of the earliest novels and stories being too much concerned with their own traumatic experiences to pay much attention to the society around them, which in any case is disrupted by war and its immediate aftermath. As order and prosperity return, however, Böll's attacks on smugness and conformism become more severe. Although the passive and introspective characters in *Haus ohne Hüter* seldom voice a protest their bitter reflections convey the author's criticism of cultural pretensions, modish religion and the undying Philistinism of German middle-class life. Nella stigmatizes the unctuous manner of fashionable priests as "Seelenmassage", and speaks of the critics who batten on her dead husband's works as "cultural knackers". The heroes of Böll's latest works are no longer passive victims : if not actually rebels they are at least deliberate outsiders. Unlike Fred Bogner, Robert Fähmel in *Billard um halb zehn* has been capable of one act of protest, even though a covert act—the demolition of the abbey of St. Anton—and his withdrawal from society is disciplined and dignified, not a consequence of apathy and shiftlessness. Hans Schnier in *Ansichten eines Clowns* avails himself of the license traditionally granted to the comedian and is capable —at least over the telephone—of scathing attacks on smugness and hypocrisy. Most bitterly outspoken of all is Wilhelm Schmölder in *Entfernung von der Truppe* with his subversive appeal :

Es wird dringend zur Entfernung von der Truppe geraten. Zur Fahnenflucht wird eher zu- als von ihr abgeraten...[8]

In this context the "troops" are the forces of authority and conformism and all those who are dedicated to a ruthless ethic of success.

As we have seen, Böll tends to dwell in the minds of his characters, to convey his own view in their reflections and utterances. But it is not only their minds that he inhabits but their bodies as well. He sees with their eyes—it is perhaps significant that, when he describes the appearance of his protagonists, he often does so through the reflection in a mirror. Even more characteristically, he feels with them in the physical as well as the emotional sense : he feels the itch of stiff new uniforms, registers the peptic climate of his characters, is aware of their defective teeth. Above all, particularly in the later works, he seems to be sharply conscious of everyday smells : the sour reek of sweat and tobacco smoke in troop-trains, the pungent odour of boot-polish, the aroma of cooking, either stimulating or repulsive. Smell is even a feature of individual characterization, for a man may be identified by what Böll calls his "heraldic odour". Hans Schnier's sense of smell is so delicate that it responds to stimuli that are only imagined : "Ich kann durch das Telefon Gerüche wahrnehmen,"[9] he complains on one occasion.

Few German writers have evoked so effectively the familiar

texture and repetitive patterns of ordinary urban life. His meticu-
lous descriptions have a certain aura of professional craftsmanship
about them, and the writer's ancestry and upbringing may not be
without significance here. Among his models he names Charles
Dickens and Joseph Roth. His technique might in a specific sense
be called "realistic", but his realism is not simply objective, does
not consist only in accumulation of detail. It is largely subjective :
physical reality is nearly always apprehended through the senses
and minds of characters in the stories. Nearly always it is restricted
to features within the purview of one individual; we do not often
find extensive description of landscape, setting or background. The
author identifies himself with figures moving in urban surrounds
—often precisely named real localities—so familiar or so restricted
that the wider background is taken for granted. He operates, as it
were, with a very short focal length, sometimes creating an effect
that is almost obsessive or claustrophobic. One might perhaps
detect in Böll an absorption in familiar things and in particular a
leaning towards the drab and sordid that almost constitutes a kind
of inverted romanticism with which readers of Graham Greene will
be acquainted.

Böll's realism might be described as poetic as well as subjective.
A poetic quality is manifested on two levels. In the first place, Böll
imparts to the perceptions of the people in his stories the awareness
of an urban poet, a sense of the intrinsic strangeness of familiar
things. Secondly, as author, he invests objects with symbolic significance and employs them in thematic patterns. The sharp contours of everyday objects in the stories often give the impression
that these items of reality have been torn from their context by the
prehensile mind of the observer—it is not the natural coherence or
proportions of things in themselves that matters but their emotional
or emblematic associations. Familiar actions—the making of a
telephone call, for instance—may be seen in close-up or slow
motion, as it were, because the moment is fraught with emotional
significance. Trivial objects acquire meaning as the evidence of
fateful events : Bruno Schneider in *Die Postkarte* pores over the
scrap of paper that changed the course of his life—the registration
slip from his calling-up papers. Hans Schnier, remembering the
stained table napkin left by his sister when she went to her death,
realizes "wie furchtbar die Gegenstände sind, die einer zurückläßt,
wenn er weggeht oder stirbt".[10] The relationship, at once spiritual
and physical, between a man and a woman, between Schnier and
Marie Züpfner, is commemorated in a mosaic of trivial objects and
gestures. One of the charges that Schnier levels at Catholics is
precisely that they "have no sense of detail". It is in keeping with
Schnier's character that the obsession with what the song-writer

calls "these foolish things" descends into near-maudlin sentimentality; for Böll, as a writer a concern with the details of ordinary living is linked with his awareness that man is a psychosomatic entity, that the soul inhabits a body and must express itself in a world that is physically real. Mundane things and actions can readily acquire a sacramental significance : the sensuous pleasure of eating fresh bread so exactly described in *Das Brot der frühen Jahre* has sacramental implications.

The spell of inanimate objects and their associations is apparently so strong that they occupy the central place in some of Böll's stories—the bread-bag in *Abenteuer eines Brotbeutels*, for instance, becomes the passive hero of a satirical fable. In the whimsical tale *Schicksal einer henkellosen Tasse* the author identifies himself with the central object, just as he tends to identify himself with human characters in other stories. But even where significant objects do not occupy the central place they often recur as symbols in the narrative pattern. Symbols in Böll's stories are not always as explicit as the bread in *Das Brot der frühen Jahre* or the scales in *Die Waage der Baleks*. They may be more recondite, like the perfect circles described on the blackboard by the pupil in *Wir Besenbinder*, symbols of an intuitively comprehended cosmic harmony, or like the blood from the wild boar's carcass in *Billard um halb zehn* that drips on the pavement next to the printing works where "edifying things are being printed inexorably on white paper"—a darkly satirical juxtaposition of violence and conventional morality.

This kind of symbolism is one of the features that give Böll's stories depth and make them much more than evocations of mood and setting. Many are mounted on a framework of parable : singly and together marking out a moral universe which has the objective coherence that the physical world they describe seems to lack. Behind the topicality is a timeless reality. In the grouping of characters and in typical experiences they undergo one may detect a kind of theology : figures superficially somewhat diverse fall into opposing categories that have the unambiguity of those in a morality play. In *Billard um halb zehn* the characters are most distinctly grouped under the apocalyptic designations of "Büffel" and "Lämmer"—the beasts and lambs of God, apostles of violence and their innocent victims. In the short symbolic tale *Wir Besenbinder* a similar distinction is epitomized in the mathematics teacher and his meek, dreamy pupil, who suffers death and a kind of apotheosis on the Russian front. For all his mathematical skill and mephistophelian rationality the teacher has never mastered the art of drawing perfect circles free-hand, a feat which is effortlessly performed by the pupil whom he contemptuously describes as a "Besenbinder".

Those who have "partaken of the sacrament of the buffalo" are fettered to the physical world, are materialists, and are characterized by an overpowering physical presence. They have firmly marked features or impassive faces, with eyes cold or compelling; they are energetic, vital, self-confident. Their gospel is the traditional German ideal of hard work and ruthless efficiency, their overlord and archetype is Hindenburg. But physical presence and harsh authority is all that such characters possess—as Böll sees them they are literally soulless. Of Otto Fähmel, after his conversion to Nazism, it is said "only his shell remained". Into the minds of such characters (Werner Gäseler in *Haus ohne Hüter*, Frau Franke in *Und sagte kein einziges Wort*, the politician Nettlinger in *Billard um halb zehn*) Böll does not attempt to enter. Obersturmführer Filskeit, the sadistic concentration camp adjutant, is the only one of these evil characters to reveal a certain psychological complexity.

The "Lämmer", the meek in spirit, form the majority of characters in Böll's work and certainly absorb most of his attention. They are diverse in mental constitution, but the author enters into the minds of all of them. Their physical presence, on the other hand, is seldom described in detail—partly because the author identifies himself with them and has little occasion to describe it, but also because they tend to be by nature unimpressive and nondescript.

The division of characters into opposite moral types is not in itself an artistic weakness. However, the difference of approach to the two fundamental types, a consequence of Böll's theological view, might be considered an aesthetic drawback. It possibly deprives the stories of balance and involves a danger of oversimplification. The reluctance to fathom the "evil" character, or even to see him as problematic, and the habit of seeing him through the eyes of his anti-type suggest a certain limitation in the writer's imaginative range. The sympathetic characters, although superficially diverse, tend to share a resigned and inhibited temperament. Nevertheless, Böll's later works, particularly *Entfernung von der Truppe*, do suggest that he is acquiring more insight into bitterly rebellious or sardonic characters.

The "lambs" are hallowed by suffering and comforted by private religious experience : like Kathy Bogner in *Und sagte kein einziges Wort* they know "the infinite peace that radiates from the presence of God". In symbolic figures marked out as ministers or messengers of grace—"angels", Böll calls them—the long-suffering lambs also find consolation. These mysterious figures appear on the periphery of the stories, suggesting a metaphysical dimension. They appear in the earliest of the stories. Most often they are women—Ilona

HEINRICH BÖLL

153

in *Wo warst du, Adam?*, Henriette Schadel in *Haus ohne Hüter*, the waitress in the snack-bar in *Und sagte kein einziges Wort*, Henriette Schnier in *Ansichten eines Clowns* and many others. The smile that is the mark of angelic grace appears most frequently in youth—it is inherited, as it were, from Edith Fähmel by Hugo the page-boy. The messengers of grace may be anonymous, recognized by their bearing, and glimpsed so fleetingly that afterwards they seem mere phantoms. Sometimes the messenger looks ominous : Schrella in *Billard um halb zehn* seems to Robert's father "a dark angel . . . God's bailiff" come to set his seal upon Robert and claim him as a "shepherd" of the "lambs". It is perhaps significant for the development in Böll's attitude already mentioned that in *Entfernung von der Truppe*, he comments ironically on the angel figure : "Engel(bert) is not a symbol for an angel, although this is his name and he is described as looking like one."

Although the sacraments of his Church play an important part in Böll's stories, for him grace tends to flow through unofficial channels. The motto to *Ansichten eines Clowns* is a quotation from St. Paul's Epistle to the Romans : "Die werden es sehen, denen von ihm nichts verkündet ward, und die verstehen, die noch nichts vernommen haben" (Romans xv, 21) He champions the outsiders and criticises smugness and professionalism in the Church. He prefers what he calls "Instinktkatholiken" and elevates conscience above dogma. He attacks "the priests who live in large houses and have faces like advertisements for skin cream", the urbane practitioners like Schurbigel and Willibrord in *Haus ohne Hüter*, or Sommerwild in *Ansichten eines Clowns*. The religious procession in *Und sagte kein einziges Wort* is satirically paralleled by the contraceptive advertising of a congress of druggists. The specious modernity of Catholic "study groups" is exposed, the snobbish traffic in religious art is condemned.

Böll's criticism of the political aspect of Roman Catholicism may be less specific than the much-publicized attack launched by Hochhuth in *The Representative*; it is hardly less outspoken and all the more impressive in that it is based on the personal experience of a sincere and thoughtful Catholic. *Brief an einen jungen Katholiken* embodies the first direct attack on the political attitude of the Church. Böll notes that the Vatican was the first foreign state to seek an understanding with Hitler and recalls the religious instruction which he himself received as a conscript. This instruction was concerned almost solely with sexual morality never referring to the real moral dangers threatening young men pressed into the service of an evil totalitarian system; the concept of conscience hardly entered into it. In post-war Germany Böll sees the Church again in danger of becoming too closely identified with the Establishment, of ceasing to be a theological and moral power and becoming instead a political pressure group.

In the novels and stories true faith is seldom linked with efficiency, success and prosperity, and is not found in the loveless organizational religion of Frau Franke and her like. Faith is most authentic in failure, in squalid surroundings or where it verges on despair—a paradoxical truth familiar to readers of Graham Greene. It is perhaps the flourishing of faith in the midst of decay that attracts Böll in the slums of Dublin. In Ireland he finds a society which has not yet succumbed to the ethic of success and the tyranny of material values, and in which daily life is still informed by traditional faith. There is a danger that this kind of radical Catholicism may degenerate into obscurantism, but Böll would seem to be too intelligent and humane for this to be a real danger in his case.

It is in keeping with the theological implications of Böll's works that many of his central characters have a strong impression that their lives are pre-ordained, that they are in some cases subject to supernatural guidance. This sense of destiny reaches a climax in the "Grenzsituationen" of love and death :

> Den Liebenden und den Soldaten, den Todgeweihten und denen, die von der kosmischen Gewalt des Lebens erfüllt sind, wird manchmal unversehens diese Kraft gegeben, mit einer plötzlichen Erleuchtung werden sie beschenkt und belastet ... und das Wort sinkt in sie hinein.[11]

Andreas in Der Zug war pünktlich has a premonition of his death, a premonition that is punctually fulfilled, but in most of the stories it is love which strikes the hero with the force of revelation. Walter Fendrich's meeting with Hedwig Muller in Das Brot der frühen Jahre alters the course of his life in an instant. A sudden sense of communion that defies reason and convention compensates for years of physical and spiritual hunger. Wilhelm Schmölder in Entfernung von der Truppe is similarly led to his wife by a supernatural intelligence. The kind of love shown in these encounters is not narrow and selfish; it initiates a reconciliation with mankind at large. Love emancipates the individual from isolation and imagined self-sufficiency, breaks down a psychic blockage and, as Walter Fendrich indicates in a characteristically somatic metaphor, purges a man of hatred : "Haß, der längst aus mir herausgeflogen ist wie ein Rülpser, der hart im Magen gedrückt hat."[12] The experience is not necessarily as instantaneous as with Fendrich, and not necessarily erotic in complexion. Through a cumulative affection for Hugo, Robert Fähmel is drawn back into the com-

munity of his fellow-men. For Fred Bogner the revelation of love
is a moment of truth after years of familiarity. Undisturbed, he
sees his wife in the street and, suddenly and paradoxically, seeing
her as a stranger, he "knows" her. It is not simply that they have
shared a bed, that she has borne his children. There is a closer
bond : they have prayed together. This moment of truth leads
Bogner back to the family from which he has drifted in apathy,
guilt and disgust; it initiates, if not a conventional happy ending,
at least an uncertain glimmer of hope.

Love, in Böll's view, even in its basest manifestations is never
totally devoid of a sacramental element. Its true culmination, however, is in marriage and family life. Marriage is not simply a social
institution; it is a sacrament as distinct from a ceremony, a communion of souls ordained in heaven and independent of—even on
occasion in contravention of—social sanction. The harmony of
souls in marriage is a facet of the divine cosmic order. This is
delicately suggested in the little story *So ward Abend und Morgen*,
in which the young husband, in moments of repose when he lies
awake at night, senses the meaning of the Biblical Creation :

> Gott schuf die Erde und den Mond, ließ sie über den Tag und
> die Nacht walten, zwischen Licht und Finsternis scheiden, und
> Gott sah, daß es gut war. So ward Abend und Morgen. (cf.
> Genesis i, 14–19.)

This fabric of sympathy and intimacy is the true foundation of
family life, and the family is, in its turn, the repository of charity
and integrity. It was in fact, Böll tells us, the sound moral atmosphere of his own family which preserved him from the contagion
of Nazism.

Among the writers of post-war Germany Heinrich Böll has
earned a prominent place as a literary artist and moralist. His
works appeal not only as authentic renderings of atmosphere,
setting and mood, but also because they clearly embody emblematic
characters and situations demonstrating moral problems and truths.
They deal with ideas and experiences that are none the less profound because they can be understood by the great majority of
people. In this, as in more obvious senses, Böll is a democrat.
Unlike many German writers he is not hampered by philosophical
systems or fettered by a pretentious "literary" tradition. It is hardly
a compliment to a writer to say that his language is "simple", but
Böll's idiom is at any rate not obscure or difficult : "workmanlike"
might be the best word to describe it. Clear it certainly is and
always to the point. That he is capable, however, of considerable
sophistication is evident from the stories written in a parodistic

style and also from the complex structure of works like *Billard um halb zehn* and *Entfernung von der Truppe*. Although his themes and settings may not be very diverse, the range of Böll's technique is in fact much wider than it might appear at first sight. The form in which Böll is most obviously at home is the short story, and even the novels, with their brief span of "real" time and their episodic structure, have the economy of short stories. Nevertheless, within the novels and in individual short stories there is a considerable variety of idiom, ranging from laconic description of incident, through impressionistic evocation of atmosphere to the regular structure of *Novellen* like *Die Waage der Baleks* or *Wir Besenbinder*, forming altogether a body of work remarkable for humour and perceptiveness.

As a Christian moralist Böll tries to apply the values of a traditional faith to the problems of modern man, isolated as he often is in an over-populated environment where economic considerations are paramount. The moral issues of the urban lower and middle classes with which Böll principally deals are not sensational. Men are corrupted in a banal fashion, "as in second-rate films". The integrity of a young poet in the radio play *Zum Tee bei Dr. Borsig* is threatened by the rewards of commerce; the hero of *Kerzen für Maria* is infected by the world's slow stain :

> Ich war wie ein Kübel Wasser, der lange an der Luft gestanden hat : er sieht sauber aus, nichts entdeckt man in ihm, wenn man ihn flüchtig betrachtet... alles ist klar, ruhig, und doch, wenn man hineingreift in dieses Wasser, rinnt durch die Hand ein unfaßbar widerlicher feiner Schmutz, der keine Gestalt, keine Form, fast kein Ausmaß zu haben scheint... ein sattes, fast bleiernes Sediment aus diesen unsagbar feinen Schmutzkörnchen, die der Luft der Anständigkeit entnommen sind.[13]

This typical urban metaphor is echoed in *Dr. Borsig*. Böll wishes men to cleanse themselves of the grimy sediment that is deposited in an atmosphere of mere "respectability", he wishes to lead them back to a positive faith, to the humanistic nucleus of Christianity, to charity. Where he satirizes the social provisions of our industrial society it is because he fears their dehumanizing influence. Where he criticizes his Church it is because he fears that it is falling into dogmatism, working for sectional interests, becoming modish rather than modern. The motive behind much that Böll writes is compassion. In this compassion there is an element of sentimentality that has led one critic to speak of "allegorical confectionery", but nearly everywhere—and particularly in his latest works—the sweetness is neutralized by the acid of satire. It is the critical vein in Böll's writing as well as his technical skill that has kept him in the *avant-garde* of German writing and given him an appeal and authority far beyond the membership of his Church. He is a complex figure, both compassionate and critical, a writer of whom one might say in the words which he himself borrows from Hölderlin :

Fest bleibt das mitleidsvolle Herz.[14]

TRANSLATIONS

1. A world catastrophe may serve many ends. Amongst other things it may provide an alibi before the judgement of God. Where hast thou been, Adam? "I was in the war."

2. Then I knew that the war would never be over as long as somewhere there still bled a wound that it had inflicted.

3. And when we came home they got out of the war like out of a tram that had slowed down just where they lived, they jumped off without paying the fare. They veered off a few steps, and just look! the dresser is still there . . . they had themselves de-Nazified, as you go to the barber to have that tiresome beard removed . . . But we went on with the tram . . . and the fare got more and more expensive, the speed grew faster and faster, the inspectors more and more suspicious, we are a thoroughly dubious fraternity.

4. "Two bananas, please," I said in 1929 to a fifteen year old girl in the little square in front of St. Severin; the fresh bloom of a young girl just out of school who nonchalantly took my change from the green cash-box; the same thing said in the same place to the same person in 1959; alarming to see the rough, almost wrinkled hand of the middle-aged woman who peered anxiously into the green cash-box. Nowhere shall I read more clearly how long thirty years is.

5. Present and past were superimposed like discs seeking the point at which they would coincide : one rotating evenly with its pivot in the middle, the past, which he felt he could survey precisely, but the present was rotating more violently than the past, wobbling over it, mounted on a different pivot . . . and between the wobbling present and the apparently regular rotation of the past a third disc was interposed, a garish yellow disc that spun rapidly round : the time that had never been, the life that had never been lived . . . confused flicker of three discs which would never coincide, deadly inconsistency in which there was no point of repose.

6. This moving backwards and forwards in time should not upset the reader. In his seventh year at school at the latest every child knows as a matter of course that this is called variation of narrative level.

7. A man without melancholy is no longer a man.

8. Removal from the forces is urgently recommended. Desertion is to be encouraged rather than discouraged.

9. I can detect smells over the telephone.

10. How fearful are the objects left behind when someone goes away or dies.

11. To those in love and to soldiers, to the doomed and to those who are imbued with the cosmic power of life, this faculty is occasionally and unexpectedly granted, they are gifted and burdened with a sudden illumination . . . and the Word sinks deep into their beings.

12. Hatred which has long since fled from me like a belch that had pressed hard on the stomach.

13. I was like a tub of water that has stood for a long time in the open air: it looks clean, you can't see anything if you just glance at it . . . it's quite clear, still, and yet, if you put your hand into this water, a repulsive, intangible fine dirt runs through your fingers; it seems to have no shape or form, it hardly has dimensions . . . a thick almost leaden sediment composed of those inexpressibly fine grains of dirt that come from the atmosphere of respectability.

14. Firm remains the sympathetic heart.

SELECT BIBLIOGRAPHY

Published works

Below is a chronological list of Böll's novels and the main collections of short stories. Individual stories have been published in a variety of journals and editions and this list is not a certain guide to the exact dating of particular works. Böll's publisher until 1951 was Verlag Middelhauve; thereafter his works have been brought out by Kiepenheuer und Witsch.

1949. *Der Zug war pünktlich.*

1950. *Wanderer, kommst Du nach Spa* . . . (25 short stories).

1951. *Wo warst du, Adam?*

1953. *Und sagte kein einziges Wort.*

1954. *Haus ohne Hüter.*

1955. *Das Brot der frühen Jahre.*

1957. *Irisches Tagebuch.*

1958. *Dr. Murkes gesammeltes Schweigen und andere Satiren. Brief an einen jungen Katholiken.*

1959. *Billard um halb zehn.*

1961. *Erzählungen, Hörspiele, Aufsätze* (an anthology).

1962. *Ein Schluck Erde* (drama).

1963. *Ansichten eines Clowns. 1947 bis 1951* (short stories).

1964. *Entfernung von der Truppe.*

Secondary literature

Articles on individual works by Böll are too numerous to list here. The following more general publications are a good introduction to his work and personality.

Der Schriftsteller Heinrich Böll, ed. Ferdinand Melius, Kiepenheuer und Witsch, Cologne/Berlin, 1959, contains appreciations by various English and German critics as well as some autobiographical sketches.

Hermann Stresau, *Heinrich Böll,* Colloquium Verlag, Berlin, 1964.

Paul Celan

Paul Celan

by SIEGBERT PRAWER

(Westfield College, University of London)

"Paul Celan" is the pseudonym of Paul Antschel, born in Czernovitz (Roumania) in 1920. He finished his course at the local Staatsgymnasium in 1938, went to France to study medicine; but in the following year returned to Czernovitz and took up the study of Romance languages and literature. His native province became part of the Soviet Union in 1940 and was occupied by German and Roumanian troops in 1941. Celan found himself, because of his Jewish origins, confined to a ghetto, and had to see his parents sent (in 1942) to a concentration camp from which they never returned. He himself managed to escape and spent some time in a Roumanian work-camp before returning to Czernovitz and resuming his studies in 1944. In 1945 he left the Soviet Union and went to Bucharest, where he lived as translator and publisher's reader until his migration to Vienna in December 1947. In that year his first poems were published. Celan moved to Paris in 1948 and has stayed there ever since. He studied German literature and philology, obtained his Licence-ès-Lettres in 1950, and makes his living as author and translator. His wife, Gisèle Lestrange, is a graphic artist. Paul Celan has won two important literary prizes: The *Literaturpreis der Freien Hansestadt Bremen* in 1958, and the *Georg-Büchner-Preis* in 1960.

DIE Landschaft, aus der ich—auf Umwegen! aber gibt es das denn : Umwege?—die Landschaft, aus der ich zu Ihnen komme, dürfte den meisten von Ihnen unbekannt sein. Es ist die Landschaft, in der ein nicht unbeträchtlicher Teil jener chassidischen Geschichten zu Hause war, die Martin Buber uns allen auf deutsch wiedererzählt hat. Es war, wenn ich diese topographische Skizze noch um einiges ergänzen darf, das mir, von sehr weit her, jetzt vor Augen tritt,—es war eine Gegend, in der Menschen und Bücher lebten."[1] Thus Paul Celan describes his origins in the remote parts of the Austro-Hungarian Empire, in a Jewish community whose religious genius and intellectual power is now a matter only of historical recollection. His first language, and his first reading, was German—his dream, unrealizable after Hitler's annexation of Austria, was to reach what he considered the cultural capital of his Bukovinian enclave: Vienna. The harsh winds of our time blew him first into the orbit of France (during his year of medical studies at Tours, 1938–39); then that of Russia (his native Czernovitz became part of the Soviet Union in 1940);

and at last into the nightmare world of ghetto and camp which has provided some of the central images of his poetry. Unlike his parents, he escaped with his life, to settle in Paris with the one possession that had remained throughout :

> Erreichbar, nah und unverloren blieb inmitten der Verluste dies eine : die Sprache.
> Sie, die Sprache, blieb unverloren, ja, trotz allem. Aber sie mußte nun hindurchgehen durch ihre eigenen Antwortlosigkeiten, hindurchgehen durch furchtbares Verstummen, hindurchgehen durch die tausend Finsternisse todbringender Rede. Sie ging hindurch und gab keine Worte her für das, was geschah : aber sie ging durch dieses Geschehen. Ging hindurch und durfte wieder zutage treten, "angereichert" von all dem.
> In dieser Sprache habe ich nun, in jenen Jahren und in den Jahren nachher, Gedichte zu schreiben versucht : um zu sprechen, um mich zu orientieren, um zu erkunden, wo ich mich befand und wohin es mit mir wollte, um Wirklichkeit zu entwerfen.[2]

Out of his experience of exile and horror, out of his wanderings in German, Jewish, Slav and French cultural and ethnic regions, Paul Celan has managed to fashion a German poetry whose compelling force has been acknowledged even by those who are most disturbed by its occasional preciosity and its sometimes all-too-wilful obscurity.

If one opens *Mohn und Gedächtnis*, Celan's first important volume of poetry, one is caught up straight away, on the first page, into a grave, melodic dance.

> Ein Kranz ward gewunden aus schwärzlichen Laub in der
> Gegend von Akra :
> Dort riß ich den Rappen herum und stach nach dem Tod
> mit dem Degen.
> Auch trank ich aus hölzernen Schalen die Asche der
> Brunnen von Akra
> Und zog mit gefälltem Visier den Trümmern der Himmel
> entgegen.
> Denn tot sind die Engel und blind ward der Herr in der
> Gegend von Akra,
> Und keiner ist, der mir betreue im Schlaf die zur Ruhe
> hier gingen.
> Zuschanden gehaun ward der Mond, das Blümlein der
> Gegend von Akra :
> So blühn, die den Dornen es gleichtun, die Hände mit
> rostigen Ringen.[3]

The predominantly dactylic lines make the whole world dance
—but in a dance of death. However autonomous the poem may
seem, however removed from the *Erlebnislyrik* of earlier generations, however incomprehensible in detail (what are those "flowering hands with rusty rings that vie with thorns"?), its central
suggestions of disaster, defeat and foiled searching for metaphysical meaning are inescapable. With its images of blood, fire,
ruin, the drinking of ash, rust, destruction and darkness the poem
sets the mood of the whole collection.

The opening poem has one other characteristic that gives *Mohn
und Gedächtnis* its special note. Its technique is post-Symbolist,
near to French Surrealism, near, above all, to the manner of
Paul Eluard and Yvan Goll; but the images it uses, and its
language too, are remote, uncontemporary, Romantic. "Dort riß
ich den Rappen herum..." "Und zog mit gefälltem Visier..." "Es
sickert das Blut durch die Spangen..." "Noch fühl ich den Brand
auf den Wangen..."—do we not feel in this poem, as in so many
others, the effect of an early diet of Uhland as well as Stefan
George? It is the language of a disrupted tradition, of childhood
memories that merge with the modernism of another tradition, a
modernism that in this early volume becomes occasionally a matter
of verbal tricks. The surrealist genitive metaphor especially—the
union of the disparate through a simple genitive construction—is
overworked; a reader quickly tires of such locutions as "Haus des
Vergessens", "Wage des Leids", "Sonne des Tiefschlafs", "die
heiligen Schwüre des Sandes", "im Uhrwerk des Schwermut"...[4]
Celan himself seems to have realized this, for the genitive metaphor
has all but disappeared from his later work.

There are other ways too in which earlier traditions of German
poetry break into the complex, modern world of Celan's work. A
title may allude to such traditions: "Die feste Burg," for instance,
deliberately reminds us of Luther's hymn about the "mighty
fortress" God, recalls a belief, and a church poetry, that are to
be negated in the poem that follows. A familiar tune may be struck
up—that of Novalis's *"Wenn alle untreu werden"*, for instance, in
the strange poem:

So bist du denn geworden
wie ich dich nie gekannt:
dein Herz schlägt allerorten
in einem Brunnenland,

wo kein Mund trinkt und keine
Gestalt die Schatten säumt,
wo Wasser quillt zum Scheine
und Schein wie Wasser schäumt...[5]

At times we are even reminded of the all too plangent sweetness of poems like Hermann von Gilm's *Allerseelen*—the kind of poem that the young Richard Strauss liked to set to music. "Ich steh im Flor der abgeblühten Stunde..." "So schneeig weiß sind, Nacht-wind, deine Haare..."; can we not hear behind that the very tune of Gilm's *"Stell auf den Tisch die duftenden Reseden"*? It is diffi-cult to say how deliberate such echoes are; but they serve, in the end, to underline the distance that divides Celan's complex, mysterious poetry from the simple plangencies of a poet like Gilm.

In his notable analysis of the "depersonalization" of the lyric since the days of Mallarmé and Rimbaud, Hugo Friedrich (in *Die Struktur der Modernen Lyrik*, Rowohlt Vlg, Hamburg 1956, p. 116) tells us that modern poetry has "become a 'cool' affair". Nothing could be less true of the work of Paul Celan. Granted that the "I" of his lyrics is at a further remove from the poet's empirical "I" than that of, say Mörike;[7] granted that much of his work is verbal collage, or experiment in which the sound and shape of one word suggests the next—yet there is no mistaking the real involve-ment of the poet, not only in the act of making his poem (an island of meaning in a universe whose meaning is so difficult to fathom) but also in the world out of which the poem has grown.

> Wir höhlten die Hände zu schöpfen den sickernden
> Sturzbach :
> das Wasser der Stätte, wo's dunkelt und keinem gereicht
> wird der Dolch.
> Du sangst auch ein Lied, und wir flochten ein Gitter im
> Nebel :
> vielleicht, daß ein Henker noch kommt und uns wieder
> ein Herz schlägt;
> vielleicht, daß ein Turm sich noch wälzt über uns, und ein
> Galgen wird johlend errichtet;
> vielleicht, daß ein Bart uns entstellt und ihr Blondhaar
> sich rötet....[8]

There is nothing "cool" about the fears and terrors we can hear within and behind these lines, with their evocations of prisons and hangmen, gallows and blood, jeering crowds and disfiguring beards—images which we know all too well from newsreels, but which have here been experienced with greater immediacy and found their place in a poetry that may be recognized as the pro-duct at once of the weighing, ordering intellect and the feeling heart.

The title of this first collection, with its characteristic mingling of the concrete (*Mohn*) and abstract (*Gedächtnis*), of the hallucina-tory and forgotten with the known and remembered, is taken from

what is recognizably a love-poem : or one, at least, which *begins*
as a love-poem and then moves from the personal, circumscribed
and detailed to the general and abstract.

Mein Aug steigt hinab zum Geschlecht der Geliebten :
wir sehen uns an,
wir sagen uns Dunkles,
wir lieben einander wie Mohn und Gedächtnis,
wir schlafen wie Wein in den Muscheln,
wie das Meer im Blutstrahl des Mondes.

Wir stehen umschlungen im Fenster, sie sehen uns zu
                               von der Straße :
es ist Zeit, daß man weiß !
Es ist Zeit, daß der Stein sich zu blühen bequemt,
daß der Unrast ein Herz schlägt.
Es ist Zeit, daß es Zeit wird.

Es ist Zeit.[9]

"Wir sagen uns Dunkles..."—a key-line, clearly, not only for
this poem but for the whole of Celan's work. What is said is "dark"
not only in the sense that it is deep and obscure, but also in the
other sense that it is sinister, unthinkable, unspeakable. Love is
poppy and mandragora, bringing forgetfulness; but it also brings—
as Rilke knew!—memories of what is hidden, buried, of what one
tries to push down and forget. The conjuring final lines insist that
the repressed be brought into light, the hidden into knowledge :
"Es ist Zeit, daß man weiß ... Es ist Zeit..."; and they are followed, in *Mohn und Gedächtnis*, by that "fugue of death" which
is also, as its closing lines show, a fugue of frustrated love, and on
which the poet's reputation most securely and justly rests.

Todesfuge occupies among Celan's works the place that *Guernica*
has among Picasso's : a supreme technical achievement, a formal
masterpiece in a radically modern idiom, which deals overtly with
forces of society that have immediately affected the artist's personal life and have had repercussions, too, in the lives of his
potential readers. Like *Guernica*, *Todesfuge* confounds those who
would divorce modern art from experience, who refuse to recognize the presence, within such art, of personal, social and political
concomitants. Once again we are caught up in that dactylic
melody which now, more than ever, we feel to be a dance of
death : for the subject of the poem is the torture and death of those
concentration camp victims whose sufferings continue to haunt
even the most apparently abstract poems Celan has written. The
construction of the poem, as well as its melodiousness, justifies the

musical metaphor of its title : a number of motifs are suggested ("black milk of dawn", playing with snakes, ashen hair, blonde hair, and—most terrible and explicit of all—the digging of graves while musicians are forced to strike up a dance-tune) and these are then intertwined and played off against each other in ever new combinations and variations. Here the traditional motif of the dance of death has found its most powerful and unforgettable modern treatment :

> Er ruft spielt süßer den Tod der Tod ist ein Meister
> aus Deutschland
> er ruft streicht dunkler die Geigen dann steigt ihr als
> Rauch in die Luft
> dann habt ihr ein Grab in den Wolken da liegt man
> nicht eng[10]

The complete absence of punctuation marks only underlines Celan's control over his material (one notes such felicities as the sudden use of rhyme to suggest the climactic killing : "der Tod ist ein Meister aus Deutschland sein Auge ist blau/er trifft dich mit bleierner Kugel er trifft dich genau"[11]); but such control is used to heighten rather than diminish the emotional involvement which has been secured from the very opening lines.

> Schwarze Milch der Frühe wir trinken sie abends
> wir trinken sie mittags und morgens wir trinken sie nachts
> wir trinken und trinken
> wir schaufeln ein Grab in den Lüften da liegt man nicht
> eng[12]

The opening "wir" identifies poet and reader with the suffering Jews; and the famous surrealist metaphor of the first line is felt to suggest a perversion of the order of nature, to be sign and symbol of a paradoxical, a hideously distorted world. The final lines of the poem then juxtapose, in a last statement of two motifs that have been heard several times before, the image of two women, and at the same time the image of two peoples fatally involved with each other.

> dein goldenes Haar Margarete
> dein aschenes Haar Sulamith[13]

That final vision of ashen hair, of the irreparable wrong done to the Jewish people, colours the whole of Celan's poetry, from the early *In Ägypten* to the opening of his latest volume, *Die Niemandsrose* :

> Es war Erden in ihnen, und
> sie gruben.

> Sie gruben und gruben, so ging
> ihr Tag dahin, ihre Nacht. Und sie lobten nicht Gott,
> der, so hörten sie, alles dies wollte,
> der, so hörten sie, alles dies wußte.[14]

The persistent death-theme of Celan's work has its roots deep in his life and in the life of our times.

In his speech at Bremen in 1958 Paul Celan has himself denied the possibility of a "time-less" poem—but he has spoken, in the very same breath, of an urge to "thrust through time" which is a characteristic feature of his poetry.

> Das Gedicht ist nicht zeitlos. Gewiß, es erhebt einen Unendlich-keitsanspruch, es sucht, durch die Zeit hindurchzugreifen—durch sie hindurch, nicht über sie hinweg.
>
> Das Gedicht kann, da es ja eine Erscheinungsform der Sprache und damit seinem Wesen nach dialogisch ist, eine Flaschenpost sein, aufgegeben in dem—gewiß nicht immer hoffnungsstarken —Glauben, sie könnte irgendwo und irgendwann an Land gespült werden, an Herzland vielleicht. Gedichte sind auch in dieser Weise unterwegs : sie halten auf etwas zu.
>
> Worauf? Auf etwas Offenstehendes, Besetzbares, auf ein ansprechbares Du vielleicht, auf eine ansprechbare Wirklichkeit.[15]

That confronts us with two difficulties of communication which are closely related : the difficulty of finding a "Thou" to address (to whom is the poet speaking?), and that of finding a reality, an ultimate truth, to which poetry may bear witness. The image of the message in a bottle is a significant one in this context. The "I-Thou" relationship to which all Celan's formal experiments are directed is a relationship with a reader who has yet to be found, who has indeed, in a real sense, to be created; but it is also a thrust towards "something beyond", towards a principle that shapes and directs our life : and this too, in our post-Nietzschean age, has to be found again and to be created. In another address, at Darmstadt in 1960, he says :

> Ich denke, daß es von jeher zu den Hoffnungen des Gedichts gehört, gerade auf diese Weise auch in *fremder*—nein, dieses Wort kann ich jetzt nicht mehr gebrauchen—, gerade auf diese Weise auch *in eines Anderen Sache* zu sprechen—wer weiß, vielleicht in eines *ganz Anderen* Sache.[16]

The consequence of this thrust towards the "wholly other", towards a transcendence felt to be at once impossible and within reach, is a tendency to fall silent, to gesture mutely towards a beyond of which one cannot speak :

Das Gedicht zeigt, das ist unverkennbar, eine starke Neigung zum Verstummen. Es behauptet sich am Rande seiner selbst; es ruft und holt sich, um bestehen zu können, unausgesetzt aus seinem Schon-nicht-mehr in sein Immer-noch zurück.[17]

Invocations, araphora aposiopesis, the union of a deliberately "grey" language with musical spell-weaving—all these characteristic devices of Celan's poetry find their explanation here. He laments the silence that the "Thou", metaphysical or human, opposes to the "I"; and the consolations he suggests, in poems like "Aus Herzen und Hirnen" (*Mohn und Gedächtnis*, p. 68), are due to contact achieved against all odds.

That Celan's second collection of poems, *Von Schwelle zu Schwelle*, takes its name from a line in the first is an external mark of an internal continuity and coherence. The metaphysical thrust, the incantatory quality, the sense of terror and of loss, persist as before—so do the old symbols, stone and jug, hair and eye, poplar and slope. But the second collection has more self-reflecting, inturned poems, more poems about poetry, than the first:

> Dies ist ein Wort, das sich regt
> Firnen zulieb,
> ein Wort, das schneewärts geäugt,
> als ich, umsommert von Augen,
> der Braue vergaß, die du über mich spanntest,
> ein Wort, das mich mied,
> als die Lippe mir blutet' vor Sprache.
>
> Dies ist ein Wort, das neben den Worten einherging,
> ein Wort nach dem Bilde des Schweigens . . .[18];

and towards the end of the new volume Celan gives us what may be felt to be the most accurate and complete description of his own work that he ever attempted. In *Sprich auch du* we have the modern poet's sense of being a late-comer, the end of a development; we are made to feel that importance of facing the shadow-side of life, the negative as well as the positive aspects of experience; we hear once again the melody of death; we are given a strange sense of isolation, of losing the ground under our feet, while being impelled, at the same time, towards a beyond that seems—or does it?—to be putting out feelers to meet our groping.

> Blicke umher :
> sieh, wie's lebendig wird rings—
> Beim Tode ! Lebendig !
> Wahr spricht, wer Schatten spricht.

Nun aber schrumpft der Ort, wo du stehst :
Wohin jetzt, Schattenentblößter, wohin?
Steige. Taste empor.
Dünner, wirst du, unkenntlicher, feiner!
Feiner : ein Faden,
an dem er herabwill, der Stern :
um unten zu schwimmen, unten,
wo er sich schimmern sieht : in der Dünung
wandernder Worte.[19]

It is significant that the most memorable poem of *Von Schwelle zu Schwelle*, the much-anthologized *Assissi*, should conjure up the image, not only of a place, but of a saint on whose meaning for our time another German-Jewish poet, Yvan Goll, had also insisted. St. Francis, the man who serves the earth and yet looks beyond it, may be seen as a counter-image to the figure of Job which has haunted the poetry of Wolfskehl, Goll, Nelly Sachs and so many others, and whose hidden presence informs that of Paul Celan as well.

A poem like *Assissi* shows consolation to be not easily achieved, lets us hear the melody of death as insistently as ever. In this it is typical of the whole collection in which it appears, and whose tone and tenor may be exemplified by the poem *Abend der Worte*.

Abend der Worte—Rutengänger im Stillen!
Ein Schritt und noch einer,
ein dritter, des Spur
dein Schatten nicht tilgt :

die Narbe der Zeit
tut sich auf
und setzt das Land unter Blut—
Die Doggen der Wortnacht, die Doggen
schlagen nun an
mitten in dir :
sie feiern den wilderen Durst,
den wilderen Hunger . . .

Ein letzter Mond springt dir bei :
einen langen silbernen Knochen
—nackt wie der Weg, den du kamst—
wirft er unter die Meute,
doch rettets dich nicht :
der Strahl, den du wecktest,
schäumt näher heran,
und obenauf schwimmt eine Frucht,
in die du vor Jahren gebissen.[20]

The genitive metaphors are still with us, and the dactylic tune is there too, though more muted, perhaps, enshrined in less expansive lines. The romantic imagery has also persisted, notably in the "dowsers", wielders of the divining-rod, of the opening line. The central motifs too are by now familiar—we can guess at the origin of those images of blood that floods the land as the wounds of time are opened, and of those dog-images that faintly recall the "Rüden" of *Todesfuge* :

> er pfeift seine Rüden herbei
> er pfeift seine Juden hervor läßt schaufeln ein Grab in
> der Erde . . .[21]

But the dogs now bark within the mind and soul; they belong to that "night of words" which gives the whole poem its title, a "night" in many senses. "Abend der Worte," "Wortnacht"—the poetry of a late-comer in the "evening" of time; the poetry of one who lacks certainty, who gropes in the dark; a poetry in which sudden voices clamour, terrifyingly, in the gloom of the subconscious. Anyone who takes the trouble to examine the pattern of vowels and consonants, and the contraction and expansion of the lines, in ll. 8–12 can see for himself how skilfully, with what physical immediacy, Celan has managed to render this sudden clamour out of darkness. Typical of his poetry are the bare landscape ("Nackt wie der Weg, den du kamst . . ."); the Klopstockian comparatives ("den wilderen Durst,/den wilderen Hunger") which push the image away from the natural world from which it is taken towards the frontier of the inexpressible; the eating and drinking metaphors that Celan uses with something of the force with which these same images are used by Novalis; the sense of danger and frustrated hopes of rescue; and the presence, as in the final lines, of an ineluctable past. Such poems are indeed what the title of two others in this same collection proclaim : a "Schibboleth" (p. 55) and an "Argumentum e silentio" (p. 62).

Among the complex of images so far isolated in *Von Schwelle zu Schwelle* two important ones are missing : those of the net (e.g. "Aus dem Meer", p. 17) and of the cage (e.g. "Schibboleth", p. 55) which merge in the poem that ends the collection :

> so rudern die Fremden und Freien,
> die Meister vom Eis und vom Stein :
> umläutet von sinkenden Bojen,
> umbellt von der haiblauen See.
>
> Sie rudern, sie rudern, sie rudern :—
> Ihr Toten, ihr Schwimmer, voraus !
> *Umgittert auch dies von der Reuse!*
> Und morgen verdampft unser Meer![22]

This image of the cage, or trellis, or fence, we now find again, significantly, in the title of Celan's third collection of poems, *Sprachgitter*; a title which is also that of one of the poems in the collection, where it suggests a prison of the soul, with an eye peering through it in search of communion.

> Augenrund zwischen den Stäben.
> Flimmertier Lid
> rudert nach oben,
> gibt einen Blick frei.
> Iris, Schwimmerin, traumlos und trüb :
> der Himmel, herzgrau, muß nah sein....[23]

But the "fence" of language is more than something that confines and shuts out. It is also a pattern (traced by the very shape of the poem on the page) arranged about its interstices or pauses. The word *Sprachgitter* thus suggests the making of order and meaning —and the most moving experience this collection affords its readers is in fact that of feeling meaning break through apparent meaninglessness (a stone, or a puddle on the floor, suddenly speaks to the heart), of feeling communication achieved, against all odds, between an "I" and a "Thou" that have only just been strangers.

In one other sense the title *Sprachgitter* is significant. It suggests a landscape of language—a poetic world in which the material of experience has been wholly transmuted into a verbal construct, a fence transformed into a "language-fence". This transmutation is in fact achieved again and again in the poems that follow—notably in that subtlest and most intricate of all Celan's poems, *Engführung*, in which "hurricanes" turn into "flurries of particles" ("Orkane, von je,/Partikelgestöber") and "grass" is "written apart" ("Gras, auseinandergeschrieben"). This kind of transmutation is the ultimate development of Hölderlin's attempt, in poems like *Mein Eigentum*, to find in poetry itself the "home" that others possessed on the apparently more solid earth; the ultimate development, too, of Rilke's endeavours, in his later poetry, to "transmute" the world in order to make it "arise invisibly in us".

The verse of *Sprachgitter* is more spare than that of the earlier volumes—the rhythm wants to flow but is held back and checked, so that lines containing only one, or two, syllables are frequent. Yet through this contained, controlled verse there breaks, again and again, the old song of death.

> *Stimmen,* vor denen dein Herz
> ins Herz deiner Mutter zurückweicht.
> Stimmen vom Galgenbaum her,
> so Spätholz und Frühholz die Ringe
> tauschen und tauschen.[24]

These lines come from the opening poem, in which the voice of
Jacob, weeping for a brother who has become his enemy, and a
voice from within the Ark, weeping for a world that is perishing,
are joined by other, stranger voices. Through the rubble, through
the slime, something is trying to reach us, something eternal, something that speaks to the heart :

> *Stimmen*, kehlig, im Grus,
> darin auch Unendliches schaufelt,
> (herz-)
> schleimiges Rinnsal[25]

until, in the end, voices cease, and something else, a "late sound",
"strange to the hour", makes itself heard, uncanny yet full of
promise :

> *Keine*
> *Stimme*—ein
> Spätgeräusch, stundenfremd, deinen
> Gedanken geschenkt, hier, endlich
> herbeigewacht . . .[26]

Through the lamentations breaks, slowly but irresistibly, a song
of praise which sounds hesitantly in the final poem, the splendid
Engführung

> Chore, damals, die
> Psalmen. Ho, ho-
> sianna.
>
> Also
> stehen noch Tempel. Ein
> Stern
> Hat wohl noch Licht.
>
> Nichts,
> nichts ist verloren.
>
> Ho-
> sianna.[27]

The broken lines convey perfectly the resistance against which the
new song of praise has to assert itself—a resistance made explicit
in the terrible poem "Tenebrae". (The title of this poem alludes,
of course, to the Holy Week mass, the *officium tenebrarum*, with
its opening words "tenebrae factae sunt", while also suggesting the
darkness that hangs over Celan's poetry.)

Nah sind wir, Herr,
nahe und greifbar.

Gegriffen schon, Herr,
ineinander verkrallt, als wär
der Leib eines jeden von uns
dein Leib, Herr.

Bete, Herr,
bete zu uns,
wir sind nah.

Windschief gingen wir hin,
gingen wir hin, uns zu bücken
nach Mulde und Maar.

Zur Tränke gingen wir, Herr.

Es war Blut, es war,
was du vergossen, Herr.

Es glänzte.

Es warf uns dein Bild in die Augen, Herr.
Augen und Mund stehn so offen und leer, Herr.

Wir haben getrunken, Herr.
Das Blut und das Bild, das im Blut war, Herr.

Bete, Herr.
Wir sind nah.[28]

These are the shadows that hide the divine from us. The sufferings
of man (in ll. 3–6 we faintly perceive images of the clawing dead
in the gas-ovens of the death-camps) pervert the relationship between the human and the divine. Celan's opening lines in fact
invert and parody Hölderlin's famous lines, at the beginning of
Patmos, on the nearness of the divine and the difficulty of "seizing"
it :

> Nah ist
> Und schwer zu fassen der Gott.

There is a dreadful semantic ambiguity about ll. 14–15 : is it
God's own blood that has been shed (the blood of the Saviour,
drunk by the faithful) or it is man's blood, shed by a destructive

Lord who must now pray to man to redeem Him? No answer is possible—the re-iterated "Herr" inextricably merges submission, reproach and exhortation, while the very shape of the poem on the page shows how strongly it is built up around its pauses. In true *Sprachgitter* fashion, the lines are there to enshrine the essential mystery between them, to let us divine through them what can only be hinted at.

These lines from *Nacht* are a description at once of a landscape, of language. Through the heath of *Sommerbericht* runs an empty line ("Eine Leerzeile, quer/durch die Glockenheide gelegt"), the grass of *Engführung* is "written apart", in order to create a realm of poetry where, in Beda Allemann's formulation, "observed reality and linguistic description do not fall apart ... as object and subject".[29] It is also a landscape of the heart (the word "herzgrau", which occurs twice in the title-poem, is wholly characteristic), an inner landscape, a landscape that speaks of states of mind and spiritual realities.

> Kies und Geröll. Und ein Scherbenton, dünn,
> als Zuspruch der Stunde.[30]

These lines from *Nacht* are a description at once of a landscape, of a state of mind and of the tone and texture of Celan's poetry. A work like *Köln, Am Hof* announces its geographical setting and occasion in the title but transports its reader, with its very first word, out of clock-time into a "time of the heart" :

> Herzzeit, es stehn
> die Geträumten für
> die Mitternachtsziffer.
>
> Einiges sprach in die Stille, einiges schwieg,
> einiges ging seiner Wege.
> Verbannt und verloren
> waren daheim.
>
> Ihr Dome.
>
> Ihr Dome ungesehn,
> ihr Ströme unbelauscht,
> ihr Uhren tief in uns.[31]

This is an unmistakable Celan poem, with its awareness of exile and loss (Celan is fond of words beginning with the prefix "ver-", suggesting loss and misdirection), its descent into dream, its listening into the silence, its passage from grammatically ordered—if not immediately comprehensible—statement to anaphoristic, verb-

less conjuration, its spare, short lines into which the old dactylic
tune irrupts on occasions to be immediately checked again, its
power of converting abstract into concrete, its word-music and
rhythmic control, its power to create a realm of poetry in which
the uncommunicable is somehow communicated.

Das Unsägliche geht, leise gesagt, übers Land.[32]

That line from one of Ingeborg Bachmann's poems characterises
not only her own work, but also that of Paul Celan.

Celan's latest volume to date, *Die Niemandsrose* published in
1963, seems concerned, at times, to reverse the direction of *Sprachgitter* and reconquer the relative simplicity of pre-twentieth century
poetry. Rhyme, significantly, is more frequent in this than in
earlier collections; there are many reminiscences of children's
songs; and several poems—like the moving dialogue with Nelly
Sachs entitled *Zürich, Zum Storchen*—are wholly without obscurity. But to complement this, we are given poems that fall
silent, not just in the middle of a sentence, but in the middle of a
word ("Einem, der vor der Tür stand...", p. 41); poems which
combine conjugation, apostrophe and paradox in the manner of
Helmut Heissenbüttel:

> ich weiß,
> ich weiß und du weißt, wir wußten,
> wir wußten nicht, wir
> waren ja da und nicht dort,
> und zuweilen, wenn
> nur das Nichts zwischen uns stand, fanden
> wir ganz zueinander;[33]

poems which try to reach an ultimate meaning through deforma-
tions of speech, through letting language take over, meanings develop through the momentum of sound, and which are quite un-
translatable, e.g.:

> Wann,
> wann blühen, wann
> wann blühen die, hühendiblüh,
> huhediblu, ja sie, die September-
> rosen?
>
> Hüh—on tue ... Ja wann?
>
> Wann, wannwann,
> Wahnwann, ja Wahn ...

The realm of the sayable is not, after all, to be so easily conquered;

and a poem that quotes a famous line from one of those late odes
of Hölderlin's which seemed—until recently—to have reached the
very limits of language, ends on a note of defeat and resignation :

> Käme,
> Käme ein Mensch,
> Käme ein Mensch zur Welt, heute, mit
> dem Lichtbart der
> Patriarchen : er dürfte,
> spräch er von dieser
> Zeit, er
> dürfte
> nur lallen und lallen,
> immer-, immer-
> zuzu.

> ("Pallaksch. Pallaksch.")[34]

Utterance seems to have become more rather than less difficult—
the words take a run, stumble, start again, stumble and fumble
on, to end in stuttering repetition and meaningless onomatopoeia.

The title of this latest collection clearly recalls the epitaph Rilke
wrote for himself at the very end of his life :

> Rose, oh reiner Widerspruch, Lust,
> Niemandes Schlaf zu sein unter soviel
> Lidern.[35]

But "Niemand", "No-One", had played, in *Sprachgitter*, a part
very different from Rilke's "pure contradiction"—it had symbolized the emptiness between man and his gods, the goal of his ever-
thwarted but ever-renewed metaphysical aspirations. In *Ein Tag
und noch einer*, for instance :—

> ein Morgen
> sprang ins Gestern hinauf, wir holten,
> zerstoben, den Leuchter, ich stürzte
> alles in niemandes Hand;[36]

or in *Ein Auge, Offen* :

> Das nicht mehr zu Nennende, heiß,
> hörbar im Mund.

> Niemandes Stimme, wieder.[37]

Now, in a poem that epitomizes Celan's art as it is to-day, "No-
one" becomes, paradoxically, the recipient of a psalm of praise.

Psalm

Niemand knetet uns wieder aus Erde und Lehm,
Niemand bespricht unsern Staub.
Niemand.

Gelobt seist du, Niemand.
Dir zulieb wollen
wir blühn.
Dir
entgegen.

Ein Nichts
waren wir, sind wir, werden
wir bleiben, blühend :
Die Nichts-, die
Niemandsrose.

Mit
dem Griffel seelenhell,
dem Staubfaden himmelswüst,
der Krone rot
vom Purpurwort, das wir sangen
über, o über
dem Dorn.[38]

This is the language of a natural God-seeker who has failed to find
God, yet cannot leave off calling into nothingness and emptiness
in the hope of an answer; of a man who tries to find a home in
tradition, and therefore uses a vocabulary and imagery that are
almost ludicrously old-fashioned, and who yet finds that the traditional modes to which he resorts, from the Psalms to Rilke, are in-
adequate to his experience; of a man who desperately seeks communion with others (the persistent "Wir" persona, the second person plural that Celan uses so often from *Todesfuge* to *Psalm*, is one
indication of this search), but who finds himself forced again and
again to a mode of utterance that is private, all but incomprehensible; of a man who tries to speak soberly and directly, but finds
himself ever stumbling over his words, finds utterance receding (as
in the first section of the poem just quoted), and is driven to have
recourse (as in the final section) to devices of language that conjure rather than state.

A particularly striking feature of *Die Niemandsrose* is its conscious Jewishness. The volume is dedicated to the memory of
Ossip Mandelstamm, a Russian poet of Jewish origin who fell

victim to Stalin's purges in the 1930s—and the "lyric I" of the
final poem of Celan's volume speaks of bringing Slav as well as
Jewish elements into Western Europe.

Die Niemandsrose opens, as has already been seen, with a clear
reminiscence of *Todesfuge*; it has a poem dedicated to Nelly Sachs,
whose subject is the Jewish God; it has mottos from Heine and
Marina Zvetaieva that refer directly to the problems of Jews in
a Gentile world; it quotes a Jewish folk-song (in the original
Yiddish), mentions Jewish religious festivals, refers to the legends
around Rabbi Loew of Prague, and is full of Hebrew words like
Kaddish, Yiskor, Havdalah, Tekiah. It seems, in fact, as though
the fate of the Diasporean Jew has become, for Celan, the symbol
par excellence for the fate of man in our time—where *Todesfuge*
had contrasted the golden hair of the German Margarete with the
ashen hair of the murdered Jewish Sulamith, *Mandorla* equates
"the lock of the Jew" with "the lock of man". The author of
Todesfuge is not likely to forget the truth of what Leo Baeck, the
spiritual leader of German Jewry, wrote from his exile in New
York in December 1945 :

> Für uns Juden aus Deutschland ist eine Geschichtsepoche zu
> Ende gegangen. Eine solche geht zu Ende, wenn immer eine
> Hoffnung, ein Glaube, eine Zuversicht endgültig zu Grabe
> getragen werden muß. Unser Glaube war es, daß deutscher und
> jüdischer Geist auf deutschem Boden sich treffen und durch
> ihre Vermählung zum Segen werden könnten. Dies war eine
> Illusion—die Epoche der Juden in Deutschland ist ein für alle
> Mal vorbei.[39]

Yet as a poet conscious of his Jewish origins who writes in German
and for Germans—though not, significantly, on German soil—
Celan is preparing the ground, tentatively, for a new start. The
past, it is true, is not to be forgotten. The "twelve years" to which
the title of the poem on p. 18 refers are those of Hitler's rule over
Germany, and the image of the Nazi crematoria (merging, now,
with images of that Siberian exile in which Mandelstamm found
his end) persistently recurs; but Hölderlin's famous promise that
what has been parted will be reunited—"Alles Getrennte findet
sich wieder"—finds a significant variation in *La Contrescape* :

was abriß, wächst wieder zusammen[40]

Paul Celan has been trying, of late, to extend the reach of his
poetry—notably through forays into sinister nonsense like the somewhat embarrassing *Gauner- und Ganovenweise gesungen zu Paris
Emprès Pontoise von Paul Celan aus Czernowitz bei Sandagora*[41]
and contributions to G. B. Fuchs's anthology *Die Meisengeige*; but

the range of his themes as well as his vocabulary remains strictly limited. Nor do the elements of his work always coalesce satisfactorily: his old-fashioned, romantic imagery seems sentimental at times, seems to sort ill with the surrealist and post-symbolist manner he has taken over, and developed, from Yvan Goll, Paul Eluard and René Char. Some of the more expansive verse of his first two volumes, especially, has not worn too well; with its all-too-obtrusive genitive metaphors and other verbal tricks it lends itself easily to parody. But no poet of Celan's generation has more successfully transmuted the special horror and inhumanity of our age into verse which neither trivialises them nor renders them so starkly that aesthetic distance is totally annihilated; none has managed to fashion more fascinating verbal constructs, which seem self-contained and yet strike us as immediately relevant to our own lives, and relevant, also, to the life of their maker; none has conveyed more powerfully and directly the alienation of modern man and his need for communion, for contact with a human "Thou" and beyond that with an impossible—but oh so necessary! —transcendence. We cannot tell which of the poems of our time will live; but it is hard to think that posterity will altogether reject such poems as Celan's *Todesfuge, Tenebrae, Engführung, Zürich, zum Storchen* and *Psalm*.

TRANSLATIONS AND REFERENCES

1. *Ansprachen bei Verleihung des Bremer Literaturpreises an Paul Celan*, p. 10. "The landscape from which I come to you by round-about ways—but is there such a thing as a round-about way?—will probably be unfamiliar to most of you. It is the landscape in which a not inconsiderable part of those Chassidic stories was at home which Martin Buber has retold us in German. It was—if I may supplement this topographic sketch with something that comes to me now from very far away—a region in which men and books lived."

2. *Ibid.*, "In the midst of all losses one thing remained within reach and not lost: language./In spite of everything, language was not lost. But it had to pass through its own inability to answer, through a terrible falling silent, through the thousand and one darknesses of death-dealing speech. It passed through and yielded no words for what was happening; but it did pass through all that happened. Passed through and was allowed to reach daylight again, 'enriched' by it all./In this language I have tried, since those years and afterwards, to write poems: in order to speak, in order to orientate myself, in order to find out where I stood and where I was being led, in order to sketch reality."

3. "A wreath was wound out of blackish leaves in the region of Akra; there I turned my steed and stabbed at death with my sword. I drank, too, from wooden bowls the ash of the wells of Akra, and with closed

visor I drew towards the ruins of the heavens. For the angels are dead and the Lord went blind in the region of Akra, and there is no one to guard for me, in sleep, those who went to their rest here. The moon was hewn to pieces, and the little flower, in the region of Akra: thus flower those who rival the thorns, the hands with rusty rings." (The "Akra" of this poem is probably Harak on the Red Sea—in so far as any definite geographical region is envisaged at all in this landscape of death.)

4. "House of forgetting," "scales of sorrow," "sun of deep sleep," "the sacred oaths of the sand," "in the clockwork of melancholy."

5. "You have become, then, as I never knew you—everywhere your heart beats as in a land of wells, where no mouth drinks and no form borders the shades, where water gushes, seeming, and seeming foams like water . . ."

6. "I stand in the flowering of the faded hour," "Your hair, o night-wind, is so snowy-white." "Stand the sweet-smelling mignonettes on the table." Gilm's poem on All Soul's Day is conveniently reprinted in *Das Buch der Lieder und Arien*, ed. P. Douliez and H. Engelhard, Winkler (München), 1956.

7. An interesting comparison between Celan and Mörike is in Beda Allemann's essay *Gibt es abstrakte Dichtung?*, *Definitionen*, ed. Frisé, pp. 157–184.

8. "We hollowed our hands to draw from the oozing torrent: the water of the place where it grows dark and where the dagger is reached to no one. You sang a song, too, and in the mists we braided a fence: perhaps a hangman will come and a heart will beat for us again; perhaps a tower will yet roll over us and gallows will be raised amidst bawling; perhaps a beard will disfigure us and her fair hair turn red . . ."

9. "My eye descends to the sex of the beloved: we regard each other, we say dark things to each other, we love one another like poppy and memory, we sleep like wine in the shells, like the sea in the moon's blood-ray./We stand in the window, embracing, they watch us from the street: it is time men knew! It is time for the stone to condescend to flower, for unrest to acquire a heart-beat. It is time it should be time./It is time."

10. "He calls out play sweeter death's music death is a master from Germany he calls out stroke darker the strings and you shall rise as smoke into the air then you will have a grave in the clouds where there is room enough to lie"

11. "Death is a master from Germany his eyes are blue his leaden bullet will strike you reaching its mark"

12. "Black milk of dawn we drink it at nightfall we drink it noon and morning we drink it at night we drink and drink we are digging a grave in the air where there is room enough to lie"

13. "Your golden hair Margarete your ashen hair Shulamith"

14. "There was earth in them and they dug. They dug and dug, and so their day passed, and their night. And they did not praise God who—so they heard—wished all this, who—so they heard—knew all this."

15. *Ansprachen . . .*, p. 11. "A poem is not timeless. True, it claims infinity, it seeks to reach through time—through time, not over and above

it./Since poetry is a form of language and since, therefore, it is essentially
a dialogue, it can serve as a message in a bottle, cast on the waters in the
belief (not always very hopeful) that it might somewhere, at some time,
be washed on land, on a land of the heart perhaps. Thus poems are on
the way—they move towards something./Towards what? Towards something that stands open, something that may be occupied, perhaps a
'Thou', or a reality, that may be addressed."

16. *Der Meridian*, p. 16. "From time immemorial it has, I think, been
one of the hopes of poetry that it might speak on behalf of something
strange—no, this is not a word I can use any more now—on behalf of
something Other; perhaps, who knows, on behalf of something Wholly
other . . ."

17. "Poetry is showing an unmistakable tendency to fall silent. It
balances on the very edge of itself; it calls out and in order to maintain
itself at all it has constantly to bring itself back from 'Not any More' to
'Still' or 'Yet'."

18. "This is a word that moves for the sake of snowy peaks, a word
that eyed towards the snow when I, with the summer of eyes all about
me, forgot the brow that you stretched over me, a word that avoided me
when my lip bled with speech./This is a word that went by the words'
side, a word in the image of silence."

19. "Look about you—see, how all around things are springing to life—
to life, by Death! Who speaks shadows, speaks true. But now the place
on which you stand contracts: whither, shadowless one, whither? Rise.
Grope your way upwards. You are becoming more slender, less recognizable, finer. Finer—a thread by which a star wants to climb down in
order to swim below, below where he sees himself shimmering, in the
ground-swell of wandering words."

20. "Eventide of words—dowsers in the silence! A step, another, yet a
third, whose trace your shadow does not obliterate:/the scar of time is
opened and floods the land with blood—the mastiffs of the night of
words, the mastiffs now give tongue in the very midst of yourself: they
celebrate the wilder thirst, the wilder hunger . . . /A last moon springs to
your aid: a long silver bone—bare as the way you came—he throws into
the pack, but this cannot save you: the jet you awakened foams nearer,
and on top of it swims a fruit into which you bit years ago."

21. "He whistles his dogs to his side, he whistles his Jews out has them
dig a grave in the earth . . ."

22. "Thus row the strange and the free, masters of ice and of stone:
with sinking buoys clanging about them, with the shark-blue sea barking
about them./They row and row and row—precede them, you dead ones,
you swimmers! This also fenced in by the bow-net! And tomorrow our
sea will evaporate."

23. "The circle of an eye between the bars./The lid, shimmering
beast, rows upwards, opens a prospect./Iris, swimmer, dreamless and
clouded: the sky, heart-grey, must be near . . ." A good analysis of this
poem will be found in R. N. Maier's *Das moderne Gedicht*, pp. 144–8.

24. "Voices before which your heart recedes into that of your mother.

Voices from the gallows-tree, where late-wood and early-wood change and re-exchange rings."

25. "Throaty voices in the rubble in which something infinite is burrowing. (Heart-) slimy streamlet."

26. "No voice—a late sound, strange to the hour, given to your thoughts, here, at last brought hither by watching."

27. "Choirs, in those days, the Psalms. Ho, Hosanna./Temples, then, are still standing. A star, I suppose, still has light. Nothing, nothing is lost./Hosanna."

28. "We are near, Lord, near and within grasp./Grasped, Lord, already, clawed into each other, as though the body of each of us, Lord, were Thy body./Pray, Lord, to us, we are near./Crooked we went before the wind to bend down to crater and trough./We went to the watering place./It was blood, it was, Lord, what Thou hadst shed./It shone./It cast your image into our eyes, Lord. Eyes and mouth, Lord, stand so open and so empty./We have drunk, Lord./The blood and the image that was in the blood, Lord./Pray, Lord. We are near."

29. Beda Allemann, "Non-representational German Poetry", in: Reality and Creative Vision in German Lyrical Poetry, ed. A. Closs, Butterworths, London, 1963, p. 79.

30. "Gravel and rubble. And a sound of shards, thin, as the hour's word of comfort."

31. "Heart-time, the dreamt stand for the midnight numeral./Something spoke into the quietness, something kept silent, something went on its way. Exiled and Lost were at home./O you cathedrals—you unseen cathedrals, unheard streams, clocks deep within us."

32. Ingeborg Bachmann, Die gestundete Zeit, Piper, München, 1957, p. 26. "The Un-sayable, quietly said, walks the land."

33. "I know, I know and you know, we knew, we did not know, we, after all, were in one place and not in another, and at times, when only Nothingness stood between us, we found our way wholly to each other."

34. "If there came, if there came a man, if a man came into the world, to-day, with the light-beard of the patriarchs: he could, if he spoke of this time, he could only stammer and stammer, ever, ever again-gain./('Pallaksh. Pallaksh.')."

35. R. M. Rilke, Sämtliche Werke, Vol. II, Insel, Wiesbaden, 1956, p. 185. "Rose, O pure contradiction, delight to be no one's sleep under so many lids."

36. "A morrow leapt up into yesterday; scattered we fetched the lamp, I cast everything into No one's hand."

37. "That which can no longer be named, hot, audible in the mouth./No one's voice, once again."

38. "No one kneads us again out of earth and clay. No one conjures our dust. No one./Blessed art Thou, No one. For Thy sake we will blossom. Towards Thee./Nothing we were, are, shall remain, blossoming: the Nothing-rose, the No one-rose./With soul-bright pistil, heaven-wasted stamen, the crown of our corolla red from the scarlet word we sang over, over the thorn."

39. Selbstzeugnisse des deutschen Judentums, 1870–1945, ed. A. v.

Borries, Fischer Bücherei 1962, p. 45. "For us Jews from Germany an epoch has come to an end. One may speak of the end of an epoch whenever a hope, a belief, a confident trust must finally be carried to its grave. It was our belief that the German and the Jewish spirit could meet on German soil, and that their marriage would be a blessing. This was an illusion—the epoch of the Jews in Germany is over, over once and for all."

40. What tore apart, grows together again. *Die Niemandsrose.*

41. *A robber and rascal song, sung in Paris, Emprès Pontoise, by Paul Celan from Czernowitz near Sadagora.*

BIBLIOGRAPHY

The Works of Paul Celan

Der Sand aus den Urnen. Gedichte. Wien: A. Sexl, 1948.

Mohn und Gedächtnis. Gedichte. Stuttgart: Deutsche Verlags-Anstalt, 1952.

Von Schwelle zu Schwelle. Gedichte. Stuttgart: Deutsche Verlags-Anstalt, 1955.

Arthur Rimbaud: Das trunkene Schiff. Ubertragung aus dem Französischen. Wiesbaden: Insel, 1958.

Alexander Block: Die Zwölf. Ubertragung aus dem Russischen. Frankfurt: Fischer, 1958.

Ansprachen bei Verleihung des Bremer Literaturpreises an Paul Celan. Stuttgart: Deutsche Verlags-Anstalt, n.d.

Sprachgitter. Gedichte. Frankfurt: Fischer, 1959.

Ossip Mandelstamm: Gedichte. Ubertragung aus dem Russischen. Frankfurt: Fischer, 1959.

Paul Valéry: Die junge Parze. Ubertragung aus dem Französischen. Frankfurt: Insel, 1960.

"Gespräch im Gebirg", in: *Die Neue Rundschau*, 1960, pp. 199–202.

Der Meridian. Rede anläßlich der Verleihung des Georg-Büchner-Preises. Frankfurt: Fischer, 1961.

Sergej Jessenin: Gedichte. Ubertragung aus dem Russischen. Frankfurt: Fischer, 1961.

Gedichte. Eine Auswahl, ed. K. Wagenbach. Frankfurt: S. Fischer Schulausgaben, 1962.

Drei russische Dichter. Block—Mandelstamm—Jessenin. Frankfurt: Fischer Bücherei, 1963.

Die Niemandsrose. Gedichte. Frankfurt: Fischer, 1963.

"Abzählreime" and "Großes Geburtstagsblaublau mit Reimzeug und Assonanz" in:

Die Meisengeige. Zeitgenössische Nonsensverse, ed. G. B. Fuchs. München: Hanser, 1964.

Some Comments on his Work

Allemann, Beda: "Paul Celan", in: *Schriftsteller der Gegenwart. Deutsche Literatur*, 53 Porträts, ed. K. Nonnenmann, Olten & Freiburg: Walter, 1963.

Allemann, Beda: "Gibt es abstrakte Dichtung?", in: *Definitionen. Essays zur Literatur*, ed. A. Frisé, Frankfurt: Klostermann, 1963.

Anderle, Martin: Strukturlinien in der Lyrik Paul Celans. *Wort in der Zeit 1960* (6) December.

Anderle, Martin: Das gefährdete Idyll. *German Quarterly 1962* (35).

Grimm, Reinhold: "Montierte Lyrik", *Germanisch-Romanische Monatsschrift*, N.F., VIII, 1958.

Heselhaus, Clemens: "Paul Celans Sprachgitter", in: *Deutsche Lyrik der Moderne*, Düsseldorf: Bagel, 1961.

Hohoff, Curt: "Steine sollen blühen", *Kölnische Rundschau* 4.7.1964.

Holthusen, Hans E.: "Fünf junge Lyriker", in: *Ja und Nein. Neue kritische Versuche*, München: Piper, 1954.

Holthusen, Hans E.: "Das verzweifelte Gedicht", *Frankfurter Allg. Zeitung* (Literaturblatt), 2.5.1964.

Jens, Walter: Zu einem Gedicht Paul Celans. *Merkur 1961 (15)*.

Jokostra, Peter: Zeit und Urzeit in der Dichtung Paul Celans. *Eckart 1960 (29)*.

Kalow, Gert: "Das ganze Leben". Interpretation eines Gedichtes von Paul Celan, *Frankfurter Allg. Zeitung*, 9.1.1964.

Klessmann, Eckart: "Paul Celan: Die Niemandsrose", *Neue Deutsche Hefte*, XCVIII, 1964.

Krolow, Karl: "Landschaften des Gedichts", *Hannoversche Allg. Zeitung*, 8/9.2.1964.

Lohner, Edgar: "Dem Verderben abgewonnen". Paul Celans lyrische Kunst. *Die Zeit*, 26.2.1965.

Maier, Rudolf N.: "Paul Celan: Sprachgitter", in: *Das moderne Gedicht*, Düsseldorf: Schwann, 1959.

Prawer, Siegbert: "Reflections on Recent German Poetry", *German Life and Letters*, N.S., XIII, 1959.

Seidensticker, P. and Butzlaff, W.: Zwei Bemühungen um ein Gedicht. (—Paul Celans *Todesfuge*), *Der Deutschunterricht*, Stuttgart 1960 (12).

Weinrich, Harald: "Semantik der kühnen Metapher", *Deutsche Vierteljahrsschrift für Literaturwissenschaft und Geistesgeschichte*, XXXVII, 1963.

Ingeborg Bachmann

Ingeborg Bachmann

by GEORGE C. SCHOOLFIELD

(University of Pennsylvania)

Ingeborg Bachmann was born at Klagenfurt, Austria in 1926. After studies in Innsbruck, Graz and Vienna, she received the doctorate in 1950 with a dissertation on the critical reception of Heidegger's existential philosophy. From 1951 until 1953 she was employed by Radio Rot-Weiss-Rot in Vienna. Her libretto for Hans Werner Henze's ballet, *Der Idiot*, was published (with the piano score) in 1952, the year in which she held her first reading before the Gruppe 47. Her position in contemporary letters was won by her two books of lyrics, *Die gestundete Zeit* (1953) and *Anrufung des Grossen Bären* (1956). From 1953–57 she resided in Italy, which provided the scene for her first radio-play, *Die Zikaden* (1954); her second work in this genre, *Der gute Gott von Manhattan* (1958) has an American setting—she had visited the United States in 1955, at the invitation of Harvard University. As guest-lecturer in poetics at the University of Frankfurt (1959–60), she lectured on *Literature as Utopia*; another work in collaboration with Henze, the opera *Der Prinz von Homburg*, after Kleist, had its debut at the Hamburg State Opera in 1960. A collection of stories, *Das dreissigste Jahr*, appeared in 1961; a selection from her poetry, drama, narratives, and essays was issued by the Piper-Verlag, Munich, in 1963.

THE title of Ingeborg Bachmann's first collection of verse *Die gestundete Zeit* was bound to attract the reader who, having barely escaped the Third Reich's grandeurs and miseries, found himself confronted directly by the Cold War. The official-sounding past participle of the title had an air of *Payment Deferred*, and, to the imaginative ear, of time broken down into its hourly segments, a kind of living from hand to mouth. The title was ominous, it made the reader nervous; but it had its consolations, too—reminding him that he did not have to pay up, as yet, it made the nuclear demon seem somehow less horrible, since it put the jinn in the fragile but amusing manacles of business jargon. A wry verbal joke, cast at history, it seemed to be planning an enormous and final prank against humanity. Lured inside the book, the reader found a language which presented, for the most part, no greater initial difficulties than the metaphors with which Rilke had trained his followers to cope in such late poems as *Ausgesetzt auf den Bergen des Herzens*. Bachmann also used the heart metaphorically, warning her audience that it should not become too attached to the time allowed it, or the time to which it had been sentenced :

> Fall ab, Herz, vom Baum der Zeit,
> fallt, ihr Blätter, aus den erkalteten Ästen,
> die einst die Sonne umarmt',
> fallt, wie Tränen fallen aus dem geweiteten Aug ![1]

And whoever had been trained in poems about *Abschied* (parting, departure) by Rilke's numerous variations on this favourite theme of German verse, had no difficulty in following what Bachmann had to say on the subject. Rilke gave rather personal advice that *possessionless love* is the best kind, since partings render all possession void. Bachmann's manual of farewells is not intended for the happy few who would be wise lovers; she tells us that we shall all have to leave this dying summertime of ours. "Die grosse Fracht des Sommers ist verladen" and :

> Das Sonnenschiff im Hafen liegt bereit,
> und auf die Lippen der Galionsfiguren
> tritt unverhüllt das Lächeln der Lemuren.[2]

It is made quite clear; the world, albeit about to become the lemurs' prey, has been and is a fair place. Bachmann early learned an important lesson : departure from an earthly semi-paradise is much more poignant than from an earthly hell. The world as beheld by many contemporary poets deserves to be exploded, the sooner the better. But we are genuinely saddened to leave Bachmann's pleasant land.

A peculiarity in the emotional make-up of Old Austria was the inclination to make the inevitable seem less so, or to beautify the hideous extreme, e.g. the apocryphal communiqué of the Imperial and Royal Army : "The situation is hopeless but not desperate." Bachmann has a difficult task as she searches for ways to make the thought of an approaching Armageddon bearable. We may, she suggests, feel responsibility only toward ourselves, seeking personal pleasures; but we shall regret it :

> Lasst uns eine Reise tun ! Lasst uns unter Zypressen
> oder auch unter Palmen oder in den Orangenhainen
> zu verbilligten Preisen Sonnenuntergänge sehen,
> die nicht ihresgleichen haben ! Lasst uns die
> unbeantworteten Briefe an das Gestern vergessen !
> Die Zeit tut Wunder. Kommt sie uns aber unrecht,
> mit dem Pochen der Schuld : wir sind nicht zu Hause.
> Im Keller des Herzens, schlaflos, find ich mich wieder
> auf der Spreu des Hohns, im Herbstmanöver der Zeit.[3]

The poem whose last strophe has just been quoted, *Herbstmanöver*,
is an example of Bachmann's ability to make a lyric look two ways
at once—again an explanation of her popularity, for some members of her audience will decipher its message about the past,
others its message about the present. *Herbstmanöver* has some
tactful reminders to her German readers about the unpleasant
matters during Hitler's reign (written at a time when collective
guilt was discussed more keenly than it is today); but it also has
an admonition that all of us—not just Germans—must obey the
categorical imperative of our humanity. We may *not* forget what
we read in the newspapers :

> In den Zeitungen lese ich viel von der Kälte
> und ihren Folgen, von Törichten und Toten,
> von Vertriebenen, Mördern und Myriaden
> von Eisschollen, aber wenig, was mir behagt,
> Warum auch? Vor dem Bettler, der mittags kommt,
> schlag ich die Tür zu, denn es ist Frieden ...[4]

And if we do travel through the lands of uneasy peace, looking for
distraction, then we find that the beggar (not to be understood only
as a symbol of social misery) pursues us. In Paris, with our arms
"voll Blumen,/Mimosen aus vielen Jahren"[5] (the dreams long
cherished about the City of Light), we discover that the light is
cold, and that subways run beneath the ground :

> Aufs Rad der Nacht geflochten,
> schlafen die Verlorenen
> in den donnernden Gängen unten ...[6]

Or we may visit England, and, since we do not wish to be seen, we
leave it without having known it; if we are Germans (of 1953), we
are afflicted both by twinges of guilt from the past, and anxiety
for the future, in which not only England but the whole world of
the lyricist's dreams will be devoured.

Not so long ago, in Bachmann's youth, Saint-Exupéry wrote
about the romance of flight, considering it a means to expand the
human spirit, not a means to go swiftly from one place to another. But flight changed, and the fliers, cooped into pressurized
cabins, no longer heeded the Frenchman's words. The title of
Saint-Exupéry's best-known book *Vol de Nuit*, Bachmann—with
her customary skill at cool linguistic irony—used for her poem
Nachtflug. We are carried along over places we shall never know,
and over persons, significantly enough, whose degree of "guilt" can
never be determined—"guilt" is a condition to membership in the
human club. We care nothing about the ghosts below, because
we are unable to care, trapped in our swift isolation; and they

care as little about the ghosts above. We have left a harbour where return counts for nothing (a nostalgia for the more circumstantial, the more "human" departure of the passenger liner may be detected here) :

> Wir sind aufgestiegen, und die Klöster sind leer,
> seit wir dulden, ein Orden, der nicht heilt und nicht lehrt.[7]

Bachmann's verb, "dulden", is difficult to translate into English; "suffer" implies that something is befalling us, "endure" that we shall survive. The lukewarm "put up with [it]" is probably the most accurate if technically least practicable rendering. We are disengaged, members of an order that neither heals nor teaches, and our pilots are no better than we are :

> Zu handeln ist nicht Sache der Piloten. Sie haben
> Stützpunkte im Aug und auf den Knien ausgebreitet
> die Landkarte einer Welt, der nichts hinzuzufügen ist.[8]

The reader is expected to imagine the last step for himself. There is nothing to add to this smooth, uneventful, and impersonal flight save a crash at its end.

The gesture of escape in Bachmann's poetry is brought up short, its tether consisting of a moral imperative. No matter what our gain in comfort or pleasure might be, we should not take the night flight; we must not allow ourselves to be degraded into indifference, however absurd our concern with others seems in a world preparing itself for a supreme gesture of indifference. We must not accept the patience which is thrust upon us by our comfortably hopeless situation. The programme poem of *Die gestundete Zeit*, *Alle Tage*, opens with a description of war as it has been since the 1930s :

> Der Krieg wird nicht mehr erklärt,
> sondern fortgesetzt. Das Unerhörte
> ist alltäglich geworden. Der Held
> bleibt den Kämpfen fern. Der Schwache
> ist in die Feuerzonen gerückt.
> Die Uniform des Tages ist die Geduld,
> die Auszeichnung der armselige Stern
> der Hoffnung über dem Herzen.[9]

It should be noted that there is a profound caesura between lines fixe and six, in the passage which follows upon the description of the "new" war, the hero's "new" role, and the "new" role of the weak. The uniform of the war must be kept quite distinct from the decorations pinned onto it. A uniform is something that draftboards, or governments, force us to wear, making us all alike. In it, we are expected to show endless patience, while waiting for the end. As for the decoration : have the authorities (or heroes) given it as a sign of shame? The star sewn onto a garment—again we recall how much Bachmann is a product of her time and place—reminds us inevitably of the Star of David which the Third Reich bestowed upon its Jewish citizens. It has become, almost magically, a pathetic star of hope, to which we must hold if we do not wish to be reduced to uniformed sheep. To win it, we must not allow ourselves to be herded to the slaughter. (Another double time-perspective : we think of our own lot, and of those ghastly but timely arguments as to why the Jews of Central Europe allowed themselves to be butchered.) In its true meaning, the badge is given on the following grounds :

> ... für die Flucht von den Fahnen,
> für die Tapferkeit vor dem Freund,
> für den Verrat unwürdiger Geheimnisse
> und die Nichtachtung
> jeglichen Befehls.[10]

It is a different kind of escape altogether : not to the lands of vulgar sunsets but from the lands of thoughtless power. Very little imagination is required to understand the speed with which the poem *Herbstmanöver*—and much else that can be read in and between the lines of Bachman's first book—appealed to the young men who wrote *ohne mich* on German walls. Likewise, very little imagination is required to see how the escape of the moral man in *Herbstmanöver* could be perverted into an escape from moral commitment, something which Bachmann condemns. More maliciously than the case would warrant, Marcel Reich-Ranicki has observed that Bachmann's metaphorical formulations of historical, social, and moral events are "vague and thus extensive enough to justify each and every interpretation". Poets are forever being confused with philosophers or political scientists; they do not construct airtight systems, they reflect their times and react to them.

Reich-Ranicki is also piqued at Bachmann because she presents a kind of poetic discussion "which, despite all appearances, treats the German reader of the 1950s considerately and in fact kindly goes halfway to meet him". Certainly, this is true in one respect, if not quite in the way the critic meant it; Bachmann presents her opinions and observations in language of unusual beauty, unusual, at any rate, in an age which no longer expects the lyric to provide the well-turned formulation or a depiction of beautiful things. Indeed, Bachmann distrusts this urge to beauty within herself. In *Herbstmanöver*, sparing herself no more than others, she says :

... und manchmal
trifft mich ein Splitter traumsatten Marmors,
wo ich verwundbar bin, durch Schönheit, im Aug.[11]

An eye struck by beauty may lose its moral sharpness.

Awareness of a fault makes it more easily controlled; it may even be used to advantage. In two major poems of *Die gestundete Zeit*, Bachmann has combined her awareness of her weakness for beauty with her distrust of beauty for beauty's sake, producing works in which beauty is used against itself. One is about Germany, the other about Austria. Both can be understood only with the aid of some knowledge of the cultural traditions involved; both are products of their time, yet neither will be ephemeral on that account. The first, *Früher Mittag*, has to do with German guilt, German recovery, and German efforts to make the past forgotten, by Germans and by others.

Having been offered a platter with the German heart, the lyric traveller opens it, looks inside, and comments on what he finds: Germany's past misuse of idealism, and its present effort to disguise the past with the simple heartiness of the beer-garden. It is the kind of cruel and perceptive attack on German failings at which the Austrians have long excelled—think of Nestroy's parodies on Hebbel and Wagner—save that here the target is not artistic pomposity but something far worse:

Sieben Jahre später
fällt es dir wieder ein,
am Brunnen vor dem Tore,
blick nicht zu tief hinein,
die Augen gehen dir über.

Sieben Jahre später,
in einem Totenhaus,
trinken die Henker von gestern
die goldenen Becher aus.
Die Augen täten dir sinken.[12]

Nugget after nugget from the treasury of German musical and literary culture is made to pass through our minds; Schubert, Goethe, and the atmosphere of the *Volkslied* are conjured up: "am Brunnen vor dem Tore," "die Augen gehen dir über," "trinken ... die goldenen Becher aus," "Die Augen täten dir sinken." But is the parody spoken with hatred or contempt? Germany is a beheaded angel who, all unashamed, gives us its heart to eat; but it *is* an angel just the same. It is also another winged being, the bird of the fairy-tale, rising again in the midst of a ruined ideal landscape:

Schon ist Mittag,
schon regt sich im Brunnen der Strahl
schon hebt sich unter den Scherben
des Märchenvogels geschundener Flügel,
und die vom Steinwurf entstellte Hand
sinkt ins erwachende Korn.[13]

Bachmann says what many of us have thought about Germany : it
it, or was, a place where sublimity readily grows base. It is, or
was, a land where hangmen drink from the golden goblet of
Goethe's "*Es war ein König in Thule*", a king who, it will be remembered, was "faithful unto the grave". How many Germans
defended their actions with a reference to their oath of loyalty to
a monstrous régime? It was a land where a Hitler delighted in
Wagner and Bruckner, where a Hess spouted Goethe and Schiller.
But the hand that lifts a stone against the one Germany—and who
may cast the first stone?—will strike and kill its twin as well. The
poem ends :

Das Unsägliche geht, leise gesagt, übers Land :
schon ist Mittag.[14]

"Das Unsägliche" is an abstract noun with two quite disparate
implications; unspeakable crimes and unutterable beauty come
into our mind, and beyond these two connotations lies a hint : that
there are problems whose complexity defies expression.

One of the great film successes of the post-war years was Carol
Reed's *The Third Man*, where, against a background of zither
music and a shattered Vienna, a question of some import was
argued : whether the achievement and preservation of beauty is
worth the sacrifice of human life. No one who has seen the film
will have forgotten Harry Lime's words about Switzerland and
the cuckoo-clock, spoken after Lime has been carried through the
air on the Prater's *Riesenrad*. Bachmann's *Grosse Landschaft bei
Wien* has the scenery of *The Third Man*, the giant ferris wheel
and the baroque ruins. Any doubts as to what rôle the film played
in the poem's creation are removed by the poem's penultimate
strophe, which makes a direct reference to a church, partially destroyed in the war and used as the background for a chase-episode
in *The Third Man*, within Vienna's inner city :

Maria am Gestade—
das Schiff ist leer, der Stein ist blind,
gerettet ist keiner, getroffen sind viele,
das Öl will nicht brennen, wir haben
alle davon getrunken—wo bleibt
dein ewiges Licht?[15]

The Gothic church has been ravaged, the oil used in the altar's lamp and in the sacraments of baptism, confirmation, and extreme unction has been consumed—by the communicants of the church, who drank freely of it and yet found it was of no value in the last days of a civilization's destruction. The church has withdrawn from the earth, a victim of history, even as the spirit of Austrian (or European) culture has gone away. Certainly, the external signs of that culture are fast disappearing. Earlier in the poem, a detail from Viennese life during the first years of the four-power occupation is adduced, when Vienna was a happy-hunting-ground for antique dealers from one side of the Iron Curtain, and for collectors of reparations from the other :

> Alles Leben ist abgewandert in Baukästen,
> neue Not mildert man sanitär, in den Alleen
> blüht die Kastanie duftlos, Kerzenrauch
> kostet die Luft nicht mehr . . .[16]

The city is dead, as its inhabitants are, although the military authorities have taken medical and nutritional steps to make survival possible.

The poem is an elegy, a late realization, quasi after the fall, of the fears which beset Ferdinand von Saar in his *Wiener Elegien* (1893). Yet what distinguishes the poem from the customary lament at Austria's destruction (poems, *Novellen*, dramas, and novels on this theme comprise a good part of Austrian literature) is an odic element particularly apparent at the poem's start and finish. In fact, the elegy is enclosed within a tragic ode :

> Geister der Ebene, Geister des wachsenden Stroms,
> zu unsrem Ende gerufen, haltet nicht vor der Stadt ![17]

("Ende" has a triple meaning : a "region" of the world, a land's end projecting into the sea beyond, and the end of civilization.) A characteristic of the German ode-tradition, from Celtis and Mellissus Schede to Hölderlin, has been to use the great stream to illustrate both geographical vastness and cultural change : the poet can follow the movement of cultures along its course. For the odists just mentioned, the river, Rhine or Danube, was both a guardian of the old and a bringer of the new; for Bachmann, the odist of a later time, the Danube carries the nation's life away. Before we come to Vienna, we have been shown the barren landscape of the Marchfeld and the drilling towers of the Zistersdorf oil fields. The shining but undrinkable water reminds us that the land's old spirit has been lost in industrial improvements; once we have finished reading the poem, we also see how a "profane" oil has replaced the oil of faith. The poetic course of the Danube is not the same as its real one; we pass the Prater, where the ferris wheel stands and where "we play the dances no more", suddenly to find ourselves by the Neusiedlersee, which lies far to the south of the Danube's course. Geographical accuracy does not count; what does matter is the set of references, all of which seem "eastern" and threatening to the Viennese eye and ear : the steppe, the oil fields (whose existence played a major role in Russian hesitance to sign an Austrian peace treaty), the Prater, which lay in the Russian-occupied wards of the capital, the big and shallow lake on the Austrian-Hungarian border. The poem's first section is concluded by a single line, standing alone :

Asiens Atem ist jenseits.[18]

The best, it seems, that can be made of the situation is abandonment to a "trunkenes Limesgefühl," "a drunken feeling of the *limes**," a resignation to the enjoyment of beauty—while it lasts. Bachmann is careful to make us think of ancient Rome; like an archaeologist digging at Carnuntum (the Roman border town east of Vienna), she will accept the end. Uncommitted, she will abandon herself to the aesthetics of decline and fall.

But does Bachmann—in this respect, too, a keen student of Rilke—intend a pun with her *Limesgefühl*, of which she experiences such an intoxicating attack? Are we to think of Harry Lime as well, who abandoned his moral self in order to enjoy the profits and pleasures to be had from Vienna's beautiful corpse? The ode, of course, is used not only for the depiction of vast cultural developments; Horace and Hölderlin make it an instrument of scolding and of accusation. The *limes-feeling* is subjected to bitter criticism. In the poem's centre there is a catalogue of the "miracles of disbelief". A series of mocking imperatives are listed; by obeying them, one can persuade oneself that one has come to terms with the situation. Nor does Bachmann exempt herself from chastisement. Feeling the hurricane approach from the east, she loses herself once again in the *limes-feeling*.

Possessed by beauty and driven by a superb formal sense, she lets the Danube flow on toward the black seas (another solemn pun), bearing faith with it :

So sind auch die Fische tot und treiben
den schwarzen Meeren zu, die uns erwarten.[19]

Yet, she adds, we reached the river's mouth long ago, carried along by other streams; we were not finished by the loss of a formal faith, but by the "Sog" ("suction") of history's course. The poem

* A fortified frontier, for example, the *Limes Germanicus*.

might have ended here; it does not. The last lines of the elegy-ode must be read with irony :

> Die Türme der Ebene rühmen uns nach
> dass wir willenlos kamen und auf den Stufen
> der Schwermut fielen und tiefer fielen,
> mit dem scharfen Gehör für den Fall.[20]

Even though we knew we were at the world's end : we should not have accepted it patiently, enjoying, with our keen hearing, the nearness of destruction. The poem is not meant for Austrians alone.

The times have been kind to *Die gestundete Zeit*; if little Austria has seen a mild improvement of her situation since the book appeared, the rest of the world has not; Bachmann's words about our predicament are not of mere historical interest. The collection published four years later, *Anrufung des Grossen Bären*, seemed, after first examination, to have struck out on new paths. The patent or lightly disguised temporal references, which made *Die gestundete Zeit* into a vade-mecum of instructions for dealing with a brief phase of European history, are missing. Like the majority of her contemporaries, the poetess has moved away from her direct concern with the events of the Nazi and occupation periods. She seems even to have forgotten her affection for humanity. The new collection has poems at central points which indicate an intensified concern with the poetic art as such, and an effort to enrich that art by the dropping of shafts into forgotten layers of myth below, or outside the limits of history. The first section of the *Anrufung des Grossen Bären* ends with the poem, *Mein Vogel*, which both Professor Rasch and, more pointedly, Professor Schlotthaus have interpreted as a poem with an old-fashioned sort of theme—a summoning of the muse. Poets used to make the gesture without any embarrassment whatsoever; but during the last hundred years, the muse has been called down only partially (as in Rilke's *Der Dichter*, where we catch sight of her wings alone) or in deep disguise. However, in our century, natural history is still an acceptable field for image-ransacking; Bachmann's muse is a bird. As a matter of fact, we are told what sort of bird it is, an owl. We should probably have recognized it even if Rasch and Schlotthaus had not aided us, for the eyes of the owl are mentioned in the poem's first strophe; a bird of prey, it perches on the speaker's shoulder, is "ice-grey", its eyes can pierce the dark, and are surrounded by the characteristic circle of plumage, the *Schleier* or veil. The owl is Athene's wise old bird, and we cannot help imagining the poetess, likewise wise-eyed and demurely dressed, a helmet atop her head, dealing out aid to a triumphant young Athens. But the world in which Athene stands is a wild one, not primeval (before Athens was founded) but after the final catastrophe, after Athens' last successor has been bombed out of existence. The war is over, the boundaries—armed boundaries, of course, like that between East and West—are no longer maintained, because there is no one to mount guard along them, and no one to attempt to cross them. The poem starts with this view of the aftermath :

> Was auch geschieht : die verheerte Welt
> sinkt in die Dämmrung zurück,
> einem Schlaftrunk halten ihr die Wälder bereit,
> und vom Turm, den der Wächter verliess,
> blicken ruhig und stet die Augen der Eule herab.[21]

And our Athene (who has survived the catastrophe by some miracle) behaves in a by no means Athene-like way; naked, she is engaged in a savage dance :

> Wenn auch im Nadeltanz unterm Baum
> die Haut mir brennt
> und der hüfthohe Strauch
> mich mit würzigen Blättern versucht,
> wenn meine Locke züngelt,
> sich wiegt und nach Feuchte verzehrt,
> stürzt mir der Sterne Schutt
> doch genau auf das Haar.[22]

The tones of erotic frenzy in these lines cannot be overlooked; likewise, the results of the excitement are described in considerable detail :

> Wenn ich befeuert bleib wie ich bin
> und vom Feuer geliebt,
> bis das Harz aus den Stämmen tritt . . .[23]

Yet the sensational dance, quite without seven veils, should not cause us to forget what actually occurs during the spell of ecstasy : *Schutt*, refuse, but refuse from the stars, falls directly on to the dancer's head. The resin that the heat of the dance's fire produced will wrap the earth in a warm cocoon; the watch-tower is replaced by a nobler if less specific height. Whatever may happen, the poet will know the ecstasy of creation, and out of this ecstasy some good will come to the ruined world. The flight of the muse-bird, calmed by creation, toward some splendid and dimly seen goal is as old as the poetic hills. The new elements in the poem are (1) that the events take place after an imaginary destruction of the world and, at the same time, in preparation for that destruction; (2) that the wisdom the bird confers is of a very "deep" or "mythic" kind—no classical Greek sun shines on this northern forest landscape; (3) that the poetic frenzy is described in erotic terms. In *Anrufung des Grossen Bären*, taken as a whole, the predicament of man in the middle of the twentieth century is not ignored, but the consolation provided is now of a nature which, in a way, only poets can appreciate : the song, by some wonder, will survive. And the singer, also surviving, may be able to return to the sources of mankind's wisdom, out of which (we guess) a fresh and better start can be made. Finally, in his search for inspiration, the singer discovers what we are often told is the last refuge of free expression for a mankind trapped in its own technology : the act of love. *Mein Vogel* states, then, themes which, albeit variously transformed, are the principal ones of the new collection.

The first century of Norse settlement on Iceland was called the *landnámstid*; Bachmann describes her march into the interior of her new-found land in the poem *Landnahme*. It is a lonely place, almost worse than that deserted forest in which the muse-bird visited her, but it has a major gift to offer :

> Ein Horn stak im Land,
> Vom Leittier verrannt,
> ins Dunkel gerammt.[24]

The pioneer withdraws the horn from the earth, and, made powerful by it (for it is like the horn of the 92nd Psalm,* both a symbol of strength and a musical instrument), she sounds it :

> Um dieses Land mit Klängen
> ganz zu erfüllen,
> stiess ich ins Horn,
> willens im kommenden Wind
> und unter den wehenden Halmen
> jeder Herkunft zu leben.[25]

The poem has a title which calls up memories of a glorious episode in Germanic tradition, and a climax which uses a passage from the Old Testament in its imagery. The immediate historical past, of Germany at any rate, will be put aside now, or regarded simply as a part of the "origin" in the poem's last line. Instead, poetic use of a deeper and more distant past will enable us to make our way into the unknown island of poetry.

The land, despite the horn blast which has echoed through it, is scarcely all filled with hope; memories of the recent past, whose

* "But my horn hast thou exalted like the horn of the wild-ox."

ghost was apparently just laid, crop up again and again, although
it is worth noting that they have more to do with individual experience, less with questions of general guilt. The autobiographical
poem, *Curriculum vitae*, carries the subject through the violent
dreams of childhood and the confusions of youth, only to reach
those events which marked every European, and many Americans,
of Bachmann's time :

> Verloren in den Feuerfontänen,
> in einer Nacht neben einem Geschütz,
> das nicht feuert, verdammt lang
> ist die Nacht, unter dem Auswurf
> des gelbsüchtigen Monds, seinem galligen
> Licht, fegt in der Machttraumspur
> über mich (das halt ich nicht ab)
> der Schlitten mit der verbrämten
> Geschichte hinweg.[26]

Thinly disguised as another conqueror, retreating from Moscow,
Adolf Hitler and his "Ende mit Schrecken" are easily discernible.
Then, leaving one kind of winter for another, an elegy, *Nebelland*,
laments the transformation of the world into a realm of cold fog,
where the "beloved", who persistently puts off her lover, hides
among the animals of the wood, the trees of the forest, the fish of
the waters; her heart is of mist, and she changes form without
regret. We roam the "mist-land", seeking a target for our affection, but the answer is mockery; our beloved is a witch, like Baba
Yaga in Mussorgsky's *Pictures at an Exhibition*, and ceases pluck-
ing her chickens only to throw us a white collar bone. We may try
magic ourselves, becoming heroes or heroines, but our heroic deeds
are transformed into empty rhetoric or circus tricks :

> Vom hohen Trapez im Zirkuszelt
> spring ich durch den Feuerreifen der Welt . . .[27]

A couplet from the poem, *Die blaue Stunde*, which begins like
Nebelland, discussing love and love's problems. Before the girl
embarks upon her career of would-be heroism, she has had dis-
appointing experiences, both of too little possession and too much,
with an old and a young man. Yet it would not be completely
correct to call *Nebelland* or *Die blaue Stunde* love poems; although couched in terms of romantic love, they put a larger question into the mouth of the pioneer in *Landnahme* : for whom do I
blow my horn? Is there anyone in the world to hear it? *Erklär
mir, Liebe*, however, is a love poem out and out : must I live without love during the world's last days?

> Erklär mir, Liebe, was ich nicht erklären kann :
> sollt ich die kurze schauerliche Zeit
> nur mit Gedanken Umgang haben und allein
> nichts Liebes kennen und nichts Liebes tun?
> Muss einer denken? Wird er nicht vermisst?[28]

Still, *eros* has not replaced Bachmann's familiar *caritas* altogether. We must not spend our lives concentrated within ourselves, and love, of the erotic kind, may be the wedge which opens the way to charity. At the end, the questioner tells love he need not reply; she already knows the answer. The questioner has beheld a beast which knows no pain :

> Erklär mir nichts. Ich seh den Salamander
> durch jedes Feuer gehen.
> Kein Schauer jagt ihn, und es schmerzt ihn nichts.[29]

But who would wear the salamander's skin? Putting it on, in order to insulate ourselves against suffering, we are human beings no longer. Instead, we have joined folklore's menagerie.

The journey through the new-found land continues; the land is changed from a place half myth and half Northern Europe to the Mediterranean South. The North, we suspect, has become too "civilized", too little like the forest of *Mein Vogel* and the grazing lands of *Landnahme*; it has grown up-to-date, filled with neon signs that flash the salamander's message :

> Wohin aber gehen wir
> *ohne sorge sei ohne sorge*
> wenn es dunkel wird und wenn es kalt wird
> *sei ohne sorge* . . .[30]

In the collection's third section, the traveller tries to begin again, confronted with the starkness of the real primitivity of the South (as compared to a Northern primitivity that exists only in the imagination) :

> Und als ich mich selber trank
> und mein erstgeborenes Land
> die Erdbeben wiegten,
> war ich zum Schauen erwacht.[31]

We are in that first-born land, from which our civilization came and where the poet learns to see cruelty and beauty in a clear light, naively, no longer with the aid of musical and literary memories, as once he did in Germany. Indeed, the poem which closes the third section of *Anrufung des Grossen Bären* is an ode to the sun, the most precious of whose qualities is that it allows sight :

Drum werde ich nicht wegen dem Mond und den Sternen und
   nicht,
Weil die Nacht mit Kometen prahlt und in mir einen Narren
   sucht,
Sondern deinetwegen und bald endlos und wie um nichts sonst
Klage führen über den unabwendbaren Verlust meiner Augen.[32]

The sun beholds the misery of the *mezzogiorno* (*In Apulien*), it
teaches us to perceive decayed splendour even at night (*Brief in
zwei Fassungen* and *Römisches Nachtbild* are examples of
"realistic" southern poetry, seen by a kind of dark light). But,
above all else, the sun makes us seize the burning moment of love
before death's darkness descends. The happiest of the erotic poems
in the third or Italian section of *Anrufung des Grossen Bären*
deals with the swift coming of love, death close behind. The poem
is, incidentally, one of Bachmann's first unqualified successes in the
short lyric form; hitherto, her talent has shown itself to most
advantage in the longer genres, where her great skill at the creation
of dignified lines (and at allusion and irony) have full play;
here, however, she triumphs by sheer intensity and concentration :

> Leicht ruht der Pfeil der Zeit im Sonnenbogen.
> Wenn die Agave aus dem Felsen tritt,
> wird über ihr dein Herz im Wind gewogen
> und hält mit jedem Ziel der Stunde Schritt.
>
> Schon überfliegt ein Schatten die Azoren
> und deine Brust der zitternde Granat.
> Ist auch der Tod dem Augenblick verschworen,
> bist du die Scheibe, die ihm blendend naht.
>
> Ist auch das Meer verwöhnt und glanzerfahren,
> erhöht's den Spiegel für die Handvoll Blut,
> und die Agave blüht nach vielen Jahren
> im Schutz der Felsen vor der trunknen Flut.[33]

Love has long been prepared for (the agave is also called the
century plant), just as death has (the pomegranate is one of
antiquity's symbols of mortality); but the supreme moment of the
one will occur before the other's coming—a moment mirrored in
the sea, which, although accustomed to many splendours, will be
intoxicated by the agave's brief return to life. There is a touching
braggadocio in these lines.

   Love ends, however, and death does not always follow its ending; the cycle of fifteen poems, *Lieder auf der Flucht*, which con-

cludes Bachmann's second book of poetry, has a wintry Naples as
its scene, and love, no longer requited, as its theme. Ice coats the
city of passion :

> Ich aber liege allein
> im Eisverhau voller Wunden.
> Niemand liebt mich und hat
> für mich eine Lampe geschwungen![34]

Hans Egon Holthusen has noted an echo of a poem by Sappho
in the first line, while even eyes poorly trained in the classics will
spy the reference to the story of Hero and Leander. Sappho and
the lovers of the Hellespont have led the poet to another new land,
revealed to us in the poems (about love's past delights) which form
the centre of the cycle :

> Innen sind deine Augen Fenster
> auf ein Land, in dem ich in Klarheit stehe,
> Innen ist deine Brust ein Meer,
> das mich auf den Grund zieht.
> Innen ist deine Hüfte ein Landungssteg
> für meine Schiffe, die heimkommen
> von zu grossen Fahrten.[35]

The passion can take verbal forms which are almost distasteful,
but then, lovers caught unawares may look grotesque :

> Innen ist dein Mund ein flaumiges Nest
> für meine flügge werdende Zunge.[36]

There is an openness of expression in the cycle, beginning with
the phrase, *"Niemand liebt mich"* (which has overtones not only
of Sappho, but of the bad popular song), which will move the
reader to a superior smile, unless he takes the trouble to remember
that Ingeborg Bachmann has decided to take an enormous chance :
to put reserve aside, to depend entirely upon intensity of expression.
The moral engagement which informs the best poetry of *Die
gestundete Zeit* has become emotional engagement of the most
intimate nature; the results can be ludicrous failure or stunning
success.

However, has moral engagement vanished for good? The cycle's
last poem recapitulates the lesson of *Nach vielen Jahren* about
love's brief triumph and death's longer one, and then reminds us
that we, we humans, have no lasting victory :

> Die Liebe hat einen Triumph und der Tod hat einen,
> die Zeit und die Zeit danach.
> Wir haben keinen.[37]

We possess only the splendour of the decline, and the song which will survive our mortality :

> Nur Sinken um uns von Gestirnen. Abglanz und
> Schweigen.
> Doch das Lied überm Staub danach
> wird uns übersteigen.[38]

The resemblance to the climax of Rilke's *Sonnets to Orpheus* has been noted by both Professor Prawer and Professor Holthusen : "Einzig das Lied überm Land/heiligt und feiert."[39] Holthusen has spoken, in this connection, of a "flight into aestheticism". Or, to put it another way, Bachmann has succumbed to the *"Limes-gefühl"*. But are we completely safe in assuming that the flight has taken place? Is not the song an expression of humanity's irrepressible desire *to be human*? It should not be forgotten that Rilke's lines have a tiny poem of Jens Peter Jacobsen as their parent, just as they are the parent of Bachmann's words :

> Lys over Landet—
> Det er det, vi vil.[40]

Men must keep their humanity, their light ; they must keep the song which is humanity's truest expression.

Those who believe that Bachmann has fled into aestheticism could support their arguments with the title poem of *Anrufung des Grossen Bären*, where—it seems plain—Bachmann has decided that nothing can be done to save the world, hurtling toward a final judgement which man has brought down upon his own head. The poem has been subjected to excellent, accurate, and altogether terrifying interpretations by Professors Jens, Schadewaldt, Heselhaus, and Rasch. It is agreed that the great bear who is invoked :

> Grosser Bär, komm herab, zottige Nacht,
> Wolkenpelztier mit den alten Augen,
> Sternenaugen . . .[41]

will bring about the end of the world. The shaggy beast that a blind man shows at carnivals and the *Ursa major* of the stars are combined into a single force, which may very well break loose, destroying us all, pushing the fir-cone of our world over the brink, and as a matter of fact, all the other worlds with it. Thinking that the bear was solidly chained, we summoned it for our amusement at the poem's start, knowing all the while that, if it were free, it would kill our herds and ourselves. We have got ourselves into the predicament ; the parallels with contemporary history do not need to be pointed out, and the commentators have provided us with a wealth of theological parallels as well, Professor Rasch remarking that the story of the last judgement, the fall of man, and the fall of angels are present, somewhat helter-skelter, in the poem's conclusion. He would make us think, then, that from the Christian point of view, things are going along as they should : our destruction is founded not only on the *contretemps* in which history and technology find themselves, but on religious tradition. Yet, without the Great Bear, man could not have navigated the seas, for it points to the polestar. If man had remained quietly in paradise, if he had not been brave, foolhardy, or curious enough to summon the bear, he would not be in his present predicament, and he would not be man at all. Is *Anrufung des Grossen Bären* as accusatory toward human kind as it at first may seem? Or is Bachmann still a "patriot of humanity", as Erika Mann called her father? Or, if Reich-Ranicki's condescending words are preferred, is she "a Cassandra with a soft heart"?

The substantial additions made to Bachmann's *oeuvre* during the last decade have been in the radio-play and the prose narrative. Her first radio play, *Die Zikaden*, was written while she was still at work on *Anrufung des Grossen Bären* (where the poem, *Lieder von einer Insel*, touches on the play's theme) and broadcast for the first time in 1954; it was followed, four years later, by *Der gute Gott von Manhattan*. Both plays have certain characteristics in common. They take place outside the German language realm, one on a resort-island in the Mediterranean (with a second island, a penal colony, in the vicinity), the other in the borough of Manhattan. Both have a chorus, rendered by technical means (the tape recorder) : the droning and wordless song of the cicadas in the former, the high-pitched chatter of the sinister squirrels, Billy and Frankie, in the latter. And both plays deal, in essence, with a theme central to Bachmann's work : the responsibility of one human being for another.

The sunny island of *Die Zikaden* is inhabited by the sort of people literature has taught us to expect to meet in such vacation spots : those who desire to capture (or re-capture) affection or youth or money or adventure or even self-respect, while not, however, giving wholly of themselves. There are the American tourists the Browns, the handsome Antonio, the ageing beauty Jeanette, the runaway boy Stefano, the painter Salvatore, a left-over prince Ali, and the newspaper editor Benedikt who, coming to the island as a political refugee, has remained to lead a senseless existence. Benedikt resembles two other persons on the island, Robinson and "the prisoner". Robinson, "the castaway", claims that he has "no history, no guilt, and no misfortune". He is "indifferent", his heart has turned to mist. However, he is made to regain his humanity by "the prisoner", a man who has escaped from the penal colony, and to whom Robinson, after initial hesitations (are not his emotions dead?), offers his suit and his passport. The prisoner is recaptured, but he has done something with his life that Benedikt, the successful escapee (and, in fact, the island's prisoner), has not. For Robinson, with the prisoner's aid, has freed himself by his willingness to help.

Die Zikaden is closed by a narrator who explains the action to us, in case we have not understood it. "Die Insel und die Personen, von denen ich erzählte, gibt es nicht. Aber es gibt andere Inseln und viele Menschen, die versuchen, auf Inseln zu leben. Ich selbst war einer von ihnen, und ich erinnere mich, dass mir eines Tages, als ich zum Strand hinunterging, einer entgegenkam und wegsah. Ich verstand sogleich, weil ich selbst nicht gesehen werden wollte."[42] But the sudden chorus of the cicadas breaks loose, and the two strollers look at one another. "Denn die Zikaden waren einmal Menschen. Sie hörten auf zu essen, zu trinken und zu lieben, um immerfort singen zu können ... verzaubert, aber auch verdammt, weil ihre Stimmen unmenschlich geworden sind."[43] Without human involvement, the song becomes something monstrous. The play is a pendant and recapitulation of the central plea of *Die gestundete Zeit*; it has a connection, chronological and thematic, with Bachmann's second verse collection as well.

The second radio-play, *Der gute Gott von Manhattan*, recounts a simple fable. One steamy summer evening in New York, a young woman meets a young man in Grand Central Station. They have a tedious adventure together, complicated by the young woman's tendency to make extremely "poetic" remarks and the young man's inclination in the opposite direction. At length, the young woman is blown to pieces by a bomb which "the good god of Manhattan" has sent her. The god's trial comprises both the frame and certain interior episodes of the play; the squirrels, mentioned above, have been the god's accomplices and spies. The young man meanwhile, having escaped the bomb and romance, returns to his old life and to Europe, from whence he came. (It is a refreshing feature of Bachmann's *Märchenspiel*—for it is a fairy tale play, like those of Andersen and Raimund, with its mixture of magic and satire, childishness and sublimity—that the young woman, capable of sustained emotional flights, is an American, the somewhat dull young man a European.) What does the play mean, apart from its retelling of the sort of love-story one finds in women's magazines? The point lies in magic : the transformation of a commonplace story, step by step, into the tale of the education with sublime love as its goal—the love of which Jennifer, the girl, is capable almost from the start, and of which Jan, the boy, led onward and upward like a Dante or a Faust, becomes capable for a little time.

That the play ends with an explosion (it is never decided whether the good god has committed a crime or not) should not surprise us, any more than the return to earth of the hero does. The echoes of Faustian language in the close of the tale of Jan are audible enough : "Er war gerettet. Die Erde hatte ihn wieder. Jetzt wird er längst zurück sein und bei schlechter Laune und mit mässigen Ansichten lange leben."[44] These words are spoken by the good god, and end much less grandly than they have begun. But the Judge adds : "Und vielleicht nie vergessen. Ja."[45] The adventure, which carried Jennifer, accompanied by a nervous Jan, through the stages of hell and purgatory to paradise, has left Jan somewhat better than he was before. The play can be taken as a commentary —or, if not that, then a parallel reading—to *Anrufung des Grossen Bären*, and to its title poem.

That, however, is a weakness of Bachmann's plays : we read them as ancillary material to her lyrics, because we sense that in her poetry she is a far surer artist than in the radio-play. And cannot a similar criticism be made of Bachmann's narratives in *Das dreissigste Jahr* (1961)? Are they not in fact prose-poems, depending a little too much on the mood they weave? *Jugend in einer österreichischen Stadt* is a suite of reminiscences from the author's life in Klagenfurt, from childhood to the air raids of the war; *Das dreissigste Jahr* is a portrait of a young man—an Anatol of the occupation years?—who cannot quite settle down until life and life's milestones take him in hand. *Alles* is about a not particularly happy couple whose only child, nicknamed Fipps, has been the apple of his father's eye—an apple which, as the child grows more independent and less innocent, has been allowed to fall out of the father's life; then the child falls in reality—he is killed in a climbing accident during a school outing. *Unter Irren und Mördern* is a portrait-gallery, old friends who meet and talk in post-war Vienna about their experiences in the *Wehrmacht* or in exile abroad; *Ein Schritt nach Gomorrha* is a picture of two women, the older of them ready to submit to the seductive arts of the younger. *Ein Wildermuth* returns to the single subject, a jurist who thinks he is in love with Truth, but who experiences more and more trouble in deciding whether "Truth is here to be used or not". Finally, *Undine geht* is a feigned monologue of the water-fairy (i.e., the sensitive woman, another version of Jennifer and of the hesitant Charlotte in *Ein Schritt nach Gomorrha*), whose experiences in the world of men have taught her how hard it is for the inhabitants of the two spheres to understand one another.

But is it fair to dismiss these prose works as reminiscences or portraits? Do they not present facets of a single "plot" or theme : the "plot" by which human beings become more and more aware of their isolation—from their pasts and their presents, their ideals and their hopes? And the "plot" is expanded by the attempts which men make to break their isolation. The attempts may lie in the simple act of remembering, as in the Klagenfurt sketch. They may be artificial, as in the reunion of old Viennese friends, in truth no friends at all, or self-deceiving, like Wildermuth's search for truth in an extra-marital affair, and like Charlotte's temptation. They may be pathetic, like the father's notion that Fipps asked for his parents as he lay dying; or comical, like the thirty-year-old's decision to continue his life, despite the discovery of a white hair. Or they may take the form of an almost hopeless and yet bold statement, Undine's penultimate words: "Beinahe ver-stummt,/beinahe noch/ den Ruf/ hörend."[46] The attempts to break the ring of isolation are made, for all their absurdity.

The tale of Undine ends in poetry, not prose; Bachmann's stories slide readily into the form of expression where she (like Undine returning to the depths) is most at home. But she will never become a hermit in the cool water-world, living there only for herself. The poems of Bachmann are her most valid work, not only because she offers in them an example of contemporary lyric language at its finest, at once arresting and lucid, but because the lyric is the instrument by which she best expresses her concern for humanity. And does her Undine sink beneath the waves for good? The last words of the water fairy are :

> Komm. Nur einmal.
> Komm.[47]

TRANSLATIONS

1. Fall off, heart, from the tree of time,
   fall, you leaves, from the chilled branches,
   which once the sun embraced,
   fall, as tears fall from the widened eye.

2. The great freight of the summer has been loaded
   The sun-ship lies all loaded in the harbour,
   and on the prow's carved figures, unconcealed,
   the smiling of the lemurs is revealed.

3. Let's take a trip! Let's go see sunsets
   which have no equal, see them under cypresses
   or under palm trees too, or in the orange-groves,
   see them at reduced rates! Let's forget
   the letters to yesterday we've left unanswered!
   Time works wonders. And if it comes inopportunely,
   giving guilt's knock at the door, we're not at home.
   In the heart's cellar, sleepless, I'll find myself again
   on the chaff of scorn, in the autumn manoeuvre of time.

4. In the papers I read a great deal about the cold
   and its results, about foolish people and dead ones,
   about refugees, murderers, and myriads
   of ice floes, but I read little that suits me.
   Why should I? I'll slam the door in the beggar's face
   who comes at noon, for it is peacetime...

5. ... full of flowers, mimosas from many years...

6. Tied on to the wheel of night,
   The lost are sleeping
   in the thundering passages below...

7. We have ascended, and the cloisters are empty,
   since we endure—an order, which does not heal nor teach.

8. Action is not the pilots' business. They keep
   their eyes on bases, and spread out on their knees
   the map of a world to which there's nothing to add.

9. War is not declared any more,
   it's continued instead. The unheard-of
   has become commonplace. The hero
   stays away from the battles. The weak
   have moved into the line of fire.
   The uniform of the day is patience,
   the decoration the pathetic star
   of hope above the heart.

10. ... for desertion from the colours,
    for valour in the presence of the friend,
    for the betrayal of shameful secrets
    and the refusal to obey
    every command.

11.   ... and sometimes
    a splinter of dream-sated marble strikes me
    where I am vulnerable, through beauty, in the eye.

12. Seven years afterwards
    it occurs to you again,
    at the spring before the gate,
    don't look to deeply within,
    your eyes overflow.

    Seven years afterwards,
    in a house of the dead,
    yesterday's hangmen are drinking
    the golden cup to the end.
    Your eyes did downward sink.

13.   ... It is already noon,
    the jet already stirs within the spring,
    already the fairy-tale bird's flayed wing
    is lifted beneath the débris,
    and the hand, distorted by casting of stones,
    sinks into the wakening grain.

14. The unutterable, gently uttered, goes over the land:
    it is already noon.

15. Maria am Gestade—
     the nave is empty, the stone is blind,
     no one is saved, and struck are many,
     the oil will not burn, we have all
     drunk of it—where is
     your eternal light?
16. All the life has migrated in construction cases,
     New despair is ameliorated sanitarily, in the avenues
     the chestnut blossoms without its smell, the air
     tastes candle smoke no more . . .
17. Spirits of the plain, spirits of the swelling stream,
     Called to our end, do not halt before the city!
18. Asia's breath lies yonder.
19. Thus the fish are dead, too, and are borne
     toward the black seas which wait for us.
20. The towers of the plain send our praise after us:
     that we came without wills and fell on the steps
     of melancholy and fell deeper still,
     with a keen ear for the fall.
21. Whatever happens: the world laid waste
     sinks back into the twilight,
     the woods have a sleeping draught ready for it,
     and from the tower which the sentry deserted
     the eyes of the owl look down, steady and calm.
22. Even though my skin burns in the needle-dance
     beneath the tree
     and the hip-high bush
     tempts me with spicy leaves,
     when my locks turn into tongues
     and sway and are consumed by a thirst for dampness,
     the stars' refuse plunges nonetheless
     straight down on to my hair.
23. When I stay enflamed as I am
     and loved by the fire,
     until the resin emerges from the trunks . . .
24. A horn stuck in the land,
     left there by the herd's leader,
     rammed into the dark.
25. In order to fill this land
     wholly with sounds,
     I blew into the horn,
     willing to live in the coming wind
     and under the billowing stalks
     of every origin.
26. Lost in the fountains of fire,
     in a night beside an artillery piece,
     which doesn't shoot, the night
     is damned long, beneath the discharge
     of the jaundiced moon, its bilious

light, there sweeps over me in the track
of a dream of power (I can't hold it off)
the sleigh with braid-hung
history.

27. From the lofty trapeze in the circus hurled,
I leap through the fiery hoop of the world.

28. Explain to me, love, what I cannot explain:
Ought I to spend this brief and awful time
only in company of thoughts, and, alone,
know naught of love and do no deed of love?
And must one think? Will he not be missed?

29. Explain naught to me. I see the salamander
pass through every fire.
No fear pursues him, and he knows no pain.

30. However, whither shall we go
without care be without care
when it grows dark and when it grows cold
be without care

31. And when I drank myself
and the earthquakes cradled
my first-born land,
I was awakened to sight.

32. Therefore, not for the moon's sake nor the stars' and not
because the night boasts with its comets and seeks a fool in me,
but for your sake and soon without end and as for naught else,
shall I lament the inevitable loss of my eyes.

33. Time's arrow lies but light upon the sun-bow.
When the agave from its rock descends,
Above it, in the wind, your heart is cradled
and keeps pace with the hour's several ends.

A shadow flies across the Azores; trembling,
the pomegranate across your breast appears.
Though death has sworn allegiance to the moment,
you are the mark which blinds him as he nears.

And though the sea's grown spoiled and wise on splendours,
it lifts its surface for the hand of blood,
and the agave, after long years' passage,
rock-sheltered blooms against the drunken flood.

34. But I lie alone
in the icy entanglement full of wounds.
No one loves me and has
swung a lamp for me!

35. Within, your eyes are windows
on to a land where I stand in clarity,
Within, your breast is a sea
which draws me down to its depths,

Within, your hip is a jetty
for my ships, which come home
from too long journeys.
36. Within, your mouth is a downy nest
for my fledgling tongue.
37. Death has a triumph and love has one,
time and the time afterwards.
We have none.
38. Only the sinking of constellations about us. Splendour reflected
and silence.
Yet the song above the dust afterwards
will rise above us.
39. Only the song over the land
hallows and praises. (*Sonnets to Orpheus*, I, 19.)
40. Light over the land—
that is what we want.
41. Great bear, come down, shaggy night,
Furry beast of clouds with ancient eyes,
eyes of stars . . .
42. "The island and the persons about whom I have told my story do
not exist. But there are other islands and many people who try to live on
islands. I myself was one of them, and I recall that when I went down to
the beach one day, someone came toward me and looked away. I understood immediately, because I did not want to be seen either."
43. "For the cicadas were people, once upon a time. They stopped
eating, drinking, and loving, in order to be able to sing on and on . . .
enchanted, but also damned, since their voices have become inhuman."
44. "He was saved. The earth possessed him again. He's long since
home by now, and will live for a long time in a bad temper and with
moderate opinions."
45. "And perhaps will never forget. Yes."
46. "Almost gone mute,/almost still/hearing/the call."
47. Come. Only once.
Come.

SELECT BIBLIOGRAPHY

Published works

Die gestundete Zeit. Gedichte. Frankfurt 1953. Now in Piper Vlg,
München.
Die Zikaden. Hörspiel. Frankfurt 1955. Now in Fischerbücherei Band
378.
Anrufung des Großen Bären. Gedichte. Piper Vlg, München 1956.
Der gute Gott von Manhattan. Hörspiel. Piper Vlg, München 1958.
Das dreißigste Jahr. Erzählungen. Piper Vlg, München 1961.
Gedichte, Erzählungen, Hörspiel, Essays. Bücher der 19. Piper Vlg,
München 1964.

Libretti for Hans Werner Henze

Der Idiot. Ballet-Pantomime nach F. M. Dostojewski von Tatjana Gsovsky. Mainz 1952. Also in *Die gestundete Zeit*.

Nachtstücke und Arien für Sopran und Orchester nach Gedichten von Ingeborg Bachmann. Mainz 1957.

Prinz von Homburg. Oper in drei Akten nach dem Schauspiel von Henrich von Kleist. Mainz 1960.

Der junge Lord. Oper. Mainz 1965.

Secondary literature

Ingeborg Bachmann—eine Einführung contains essays by J. Kaiser, G. Blöcker, S. Unseld, W. Rasch, W. Weber and H. Beckmann, also a Biographisch—bibliographischer Abriß. Piper Vlg, München 1963.

Other later articles include:

A. Doppler. Die Sprachauffassung Ingeborg Bachmanns. Neophilologus 1963 (10).

J. K. Lyon. The Poetry of Ingeborg Bachmann: A Primeval Impulse in the Modern Wasteland. German Life and Letters 1964 (4).

R. N. Maier. Zersetzte Weltsubstanz: Ingeborg Bachmann *Nebelland*, In *Das Moderne Gedicht*. Düsseldorf 1959.

W. L. Schlotthaus. Ingeborg Bachmann's Poem *Mein Vogel*: An Analysis of Poetic Metaphor. Modern Language Quarterly 1961 (3).

Günter Grass

Günter Grass

by ARRIGO SUBIOTTO
(University of Aberdeen)

Günter Grass was born of Polish-German parents on October 16th, 1927 in Danzig, a city that still spurs his imagination. He saw active service in 1944, was wounded and ended in American captivity. After 1946 his various jobs included monumental masonry in Düsseldorf where he began serious art studies, completing them in 1953 under Hartung and Schrieber in Berlin. Grass's breakthrough came when he won a radio poetry prize in 1955, and he then published regularly in *Akzente*, also making a name as sculptor, illustrator and playwright. He moved to Paris with his family in 1956 and there wrote *Die Blechtrommel* in straitened circumstances. The influential *Gruppe 47* awarded Grass a prize on the strength of the as yet unpublished novel and he has since been a force in the group. The first novel caused an immediate furore with critics and public and its success was confirmed by *Katz und Maus* and *Hundejahre*. In 1960 Grass settled in West Berlin, where his latest play, *Die Plebejer proben den Aufstand*, was staged in the winter of 1965–66; he is frequently a focus of literary and political controversy, and this play certainly makes him *persona non grata* in East Berlin.

A BARE seven years ago Günter Grass burst like an act of God upon the unsuspecting German critics and reading public; the thunder was caused by his novel *Die Blechtrommel*, excerpts of which had earlier caused prophetic rumblings and won a prize at a meeting of the literary coterie Gruppe 47. Walter Höllerer, editor of the periodical *Akzente*, had been publishing poetry and short plays by Grass for several years before 1959, when *Die Blechtrommel*, despite its length, leapt to the top of the best-seller lists. Detractors called the book pornographic, caused the award to Grass of the 1960 literary prize of the city of Bremen to be withdrawn, and by this familiar process of prudery doubtless multiplied the author's royalties. In 1963 Grass delivered another body-blow to the German consciousness with *Hundejahre* which covers much the same ground as *Die Blechtrommel*. An interlude was provided by *Katz und Maus*, a finely restrained *Novelle* which bears comparison with the best in that genre, written when Grass reached a point of stasis during the gestation of *Hundejahre*.

Grass belongs to that generation of Europeans, born in the late 1920s, that was caught up at the tail-end of the Second World

War, too young to have control and responsibility, too old not to know what it was all about. For these people, who had not experienced a formed pre-war world, the war is still traumatic, especially for a handful of German writers (Grass, Enzensberger, Walser, Siegfried Lenz, Rühmkorf, Heckmann were all born in the lustrum 1925–30) who went through evacuation, war adolescence, *Volkssturm*, mass flight from the East, post-war chaos and economic-miracle manhood. These are the angry young men of German literature who insist more than their elders (and to their discomfort) on raking over the happenings of the past forty years so as to analyse, ascertain, understand, accuse and warn. Some of these writers prefer verse for their invective; Grass seems to have found his touch in prose narrative allowing him to indulge a passion for evocative description and combine this with the correlative of actual historical documentation. The shape and style of Grass's novels is so characterized by this duality of feeling and fact that an ironical attitude to the novel form itself is generated. Thomas Mann's ghost looms large; a parody of parodies raises its complex head. One fascinating aspect of these novels is their form, another the authenticity of mood and social background created as if by chance and subordinate to the actions of the protagonists, just as earlier in Döblin's *Berlin Alexanderplatz* and Fallada's *Kleiner Mann—was nun?*

In *Die Blechtrommel* Oskar Matzerath, a thirty-year-old dwarf born in Danzig, narrates his life up to the point where he is lying in bed in a mental home to which he has been committed after having been found guilty of murdering a nurse. Oskar has evidence that would exculpate him but does not want the trial re-opened, he is cosy and protected from the molestations of the outside world and can contentedly (and literally) drum up his reminiscences to fill an inexhaustible supply of paper. He had arranged to become a dwarf physically by tumbling down some cellar steps and injuring himself at the age of three, and had a passion for playing tin drums with which the various guardians of his youth had to keep him supplied, for if these were not forthcoming he would emit glass-shattering cries. Though many elements in this book (the drum, the voice and other prodigious feats) are products of fantasy, the dates are precise, 1925–55, and the factual chronology in its surreptitious way ampler than that of many history books. Major and minor aspects of social and political events accompany and determine Oskar's life : Nazi rallies, anti-Semitism, the rise and recruitment of S.A. troops, the German campaign of propaganda then aggression against Danzig, the war, the Atlantic wall, elimination of the abnormal (attempts to put Oskar into an institution), air-raids, Russian troops, concentration camp survivors, the return of veterans, the black market, refugees, currency reform and the ensuing economic stabilization and recovery, guilt (satirically depicted in the Zwiebel Keller night-club where those who can afford the prices are able to weep copious, cathartic, onion-generated tears), the revisiting of theatres of war, and a final intolerably vacuous affluent society. Breadth of canvas in a nineteenth century, Tolstoy-like or Dickensian fashion is achieved by a welter of characters, Oskar's relatives and ancestors, acquaintances and neighbours, jostling in profusion, commandeering chapters, episodes and attention, all of them highly individualized.

Katz und Maus, a chip hewn from the block of *Hundejahre*, is a striking contrast, Grass here disciplining his ebullient inventiveness to delimit one personage, Joachim Mahlke, the schoolboy with an over-prominent Adam's apple and other outsize physical attributes who wins the Iron Cross when he joins up. Mahlke is consciously made to fill the book with his stature, as in a traditional *Novelle*, and even the narrator, one of Mahlke's group of schoolfellows, explicit jerks himself back from the temptations of digression to tell only of the hero, whom he often apostrophizes.

After the neat sinewy lines of *Katz und Maus* Grass returned beyond even the bloated fullness of *Die Blechtrommel* : *Hundejahre* begins further back than Oskar's life, in 1917, and thus implicitly catches in its net the Versailles treaty, the inflation, and other factors effectively paving the way for Hitler. Again the external events are not described independently but become emotional concomitants of the characters' lives, sometimes revealed with brutal directness, sometimes veiled in a pretence of allegory or fantasy. Instead of one narrator there are now three, taking consecutive turns at recounting the lives of Eduard Amsel and Walter Matern, the half-Jew and the Aryan, who, after various metamorphoses, survive into the present and are in fact the narrators. Around these two revolve a host of other personages, among them the third narrator, Harry Liebenau, who in his section uses the epistolary form. Of equal importance (and evidence of the interweaving satire in the book spun out of baroque-like "conceits") are : the dynasty of pedigree dogs culminating in Prinz, magnanimously accepted as a gift by Hitler; the manufacture of scarecrows by Amsel and later by Brauxel; the ability of Matern's miller father to predict the economic and political future by listening to mealworm augurs in a sack of flour. Again the story unfolds in Danzig, Grass's native city and favourite setting, and rides the flow of events like the sweep of the Vistula. The historical bearings of *Hundejahre* are marked out more copiously : there are the military careers of the fathers in the First World War; *Schlagball* (rounders) as a truly Germanic game; the gift of Prinz to the

Führer (an allusion to the Alsatian appearing with Hitler on so many photographs); a Zeppelin in the sky; left-wing pamphlets; the beating-up of Amsel and the belabouring of Jenny (who is of gipsy birth); the teacher who reveres Eichendorff and disappears in a concentration camp; schoolboys as *Luftwaffenhelfer*; the pernicious effect of Heidegger's philosophy ("we wanted to march East with Heidegger and Hölderlin in our knapsacks"); Stauffenberg's attempt on Hitler's life; the latter's birthday in 1945 and the ensuing twilight of the gods; Matern's plausible self-justification in the POW camp; the addresses of scattered acquaintances scratched on the urinal wall in Cologne Central Station; Matern like an avenging angel roaming through the land spreading syphilis in the families of those eager to forget the past; economic revival guided by the predictions of the meal-worms; the macabre Leichenhalle restaurant; the Cologne urinal "newly enamelled", inducing Matern to a vituperative attack on the white-washing of the past; a visit to East Germany that is found as corroded as the West; Matern's final descent into Brauxel's huge underground factory for producing scarecrows ("the Germans are the best models")—a Faustian, Inferno-like scene reminiscent also of the "magic theatre" of the human subconscious in Herman Hesse's *Steppenwolf*.

The historical framework in which the personal lives are embedded is conveyed in these novels by the technique of the "aside" inserted in the apparently fictional narrative, and is already very evident in *Die Blechtrommel* :

> "Ende Juli des Jahres nullnull—man entschloß sich gerade, das kaiserliche Schlachtflottenbauprogramm zu verdoppeln—erblickte Mama im Sternzeichen Löwe das Licht der Welt."[1]

and later :

> "Dienstag und Freitag Teppichklopfen, aber das knallte nur noch spärlich und fast verlegen an den zwei Wochentagen : seit Hitlers Machtübernahme gab es mehr und mehr Staubsauger in den Haushaltungen."[2]

The sentences are frequently long-winded and allusive, their oblique approach allowing the hard facts and real events to be smuggled into the narrative under cover of a humorous irony. Or a sharp irony results from a harsh juxtaposition, as when the S.A. decide to expel the musician Meyn for cruelty to his cats and on the same page set in motion the violent pogrom of the *Kristallnacht*, driving the toy-seller Markus to suicide, while Oskar's father, closing his shop and taking a stroll to see what's afoot, warms his fingers at the blaze :

"Der Berg (of synagogue furnishings) wurde in Brand gesteckt, und der Kolonialwarenhändler benutzte die Gelegenheit und wärmte seine Finger und seine Gefühle über dem öffentlichen Feuer."[3]

In such descriptions invention tips over into fact, and the historical nuances (here the culpable inaction of the ordinary citizen) are continually being woven in, not as an objectively static backcloth but as a vital constituent of the ferment in the author himself. Grass is not afraid to handle what Enzensberger calls "heisse Gegenstände" nor does he fight shy of indicting the grocer for "warming his feelings". A random example of the author's engagement, indicating that he takes up a critical position, is the compressed and virulent description of the soiled uniforms Amsel is given to clothe his scarecrows after the Nazi rally free-for-all :

"Diesmal waren es nicht nur SA-Uniformen. Auch das Zeug einiger simpler Parteigenossen fand sich darunter. Aber alles war braun : nicht das Braun sommerlicher Halbschuhe; kein Nüsschenbraun Hexenbraun; kein braunes Afrika; keine geriebene Borke, Möbel nicht, altersbraun; kein mittelbraun sandbraun; weder junge Braunkohle noch alter Torf, mit Torfspaten gestochen; keine Frühstücksschokolade, kein Morgenkaffee, den Sahne erhöht; Tabak, so viel Sorten, doch keine so bräunlich wie; weder das augentrügerische Rehbraun noch das Niveabraun zweier Wochen Urlaub; kein Herbst spuckte auf die Palette, als dieses Braun : Kackbraun, allenfalls Lehmbraund, aufgeweicht, kleistrig, als das Parteibraun, SA-Braun, Braun aller Braunbüsher, Braunen Häuser, Braunauer Braun, Evabraun, als dieses Uniformbraun, weit entfernt vom Khakibraun, Braun aus tausend pickligen Ärschen auf weisse Teller geschissen, Braun aus Erbsen und Brühwurst gewonnen; nein nein, ihr sanften Brunetten, hexenbraun nüssschenbraun, standen nicht Pate, als dieses Braun gekocht, geboren und eingefärbt, als dieses Dunghaufenbraun—ich schmeichle noch immer—vor Eddi Amsel lag."[4]

Apart from being highly emotive the above passage is also carefully calculated; these two aspects can be sensed throughout Grass's writing, determining his essential style and justifying the label of "mannerist" applied to him. In his book *Manierismus in der Literatur* G. R. Hocke lists some of the formal characteristics of the mannerist style at its peak in Europe from 1520–1620 :

"Manieristische Literatur bekundet folgende Grundtendenzen : affektvolle Übersteigerung oder kälteste Reduzierung des Ausdrucks, Verbergung und Überdeutlichkeit, Verrätselung und Evokation, Chiffrierung und ärgerniserregende 'Offenbarung'."[5]

At the heart of such writing there is always a dualism unable to come to terms with itself, its very essence and expression being a constant violent oscillation from extreme to extreme, a tension and vibration that emerges in a restless, unchecked form. The literary line that leads to Grass springs from Fischart and seventeenth century writers like Harsdörffer and Gryphius, and includes Laurence Sterne and Jean Paul Richter (whose *Vorschule der Ästhetik* is in many ways as applicable to the novels of Grass as to his own). The tendency to shapelessness and dissolution, the mingling of disparates, the grotesque and erotic, the "conceit", the labyrinthine, the riddle and cipher, shock and irritation, repetition that is both meaningful and tedious—these all stamp Grass's prose, which is worth looking at in some detail to see how the author has created a style that cries out from every page as unmistakably his.

If we place our faith in Thomas Mann's definition of the novelist and his art (*Die Kunst des Romans*, 1939) then Grass appears to be a narrative writer par excellence: "der Erzähler, dieser raunende Beschwörer des Imperfekts."[6] According to Mann the epic work is a vast undertaking "mit seinem gigantischen Miniaturismus, der auf das Einzelne versessen zu sein scheint, als sei es ihm alles, und dabei das Ganze unerschütterlich im Auge behält";[7] and, in famous words, the epic imagination

> "ist ein gewaltiger und majestätischer Geist, expansiv, lebensreich, weit wie das Meer in seiner rollenden Monotonie, zugleich grossartig und genau, gesanghaft und klug-besonnen; er will nicht den Ausschnitt, die Episode, er will das Ganze, die Welt mit unzähligen Episoden und Einzelheiten, bei denen er selbstvergessen verweilt, als käme es ihm auf jede von ihnen besonders an. Denn er hat keine Eile, er hat unendliche Zeit, er ist der Geist der Geduld, der Treue, des Ausharrens, der Langsamkeit, die durch Liebe genussreich wird, der Geist der verzaubernden Langeweile. Anzufangen weiss er kaum anders als mit dem Urbeginn aller Dinge, und enden mag er überhaupt nicht . . ."[8]

Though Mann and Grass may be poles apart in their aesthetics and philosophy, their actual working methods function in much the same way. At the beginning of *Die Blechtrommel* Grass ironizes sleights of hand aimed at revitalizing the novel form—then springs one of his own in the shape of Oskar drumming up his past:

> "Man kann eine Geschichte in der Mitte beginnen und vorwärts wie rückwärts kühn ausschreitend Verwirrung anstiften.

Man kann sich modern geben, alle Zeiten, Entfernungen weg-
streichen und hinterher verkünden oder verkünden lassen, man
habe endlich und in letzter Stunde das Raum-Zeit-Problem
gelöst."[9]

Oskar then reaches as far back as he can for the sources of his
story and cuts it short after his thirtieth birthday in 1955, an un-
avoidable *terminus ad quem* since Grass was actually *writing* the
novel then.

Epic breadth cannot be disputed to Grass's narration. An essential component of breadth is detail, which Grass supplies at every
opportunity; lyrical descriptions of geological specimens, old
clothes, the rules of rounders, sorts and qualities of corn, the
technicalities of monumental masonry, popular names for syphilis,
Amsel's experiments at constructing scarecrows and a pseudonym
—these are not capricious, but sparked off by a sensuous feeling for
words (as sound, evocation, representation) and convey the compact reality of things. In his minute and ironical particularizing
Grass operates in much the way that Jean Paul prescribes for the
humorous writer : "so heftet uns der Komiker gerade eng an das
sinnlich Bestimmte"[10] and "der metamorphotische sinnliche Stil des
Humors . . . individualisiert bis ins Kleinste".[11] This detailing of the
slight or unimportant often appears identical to the techniques of
le chosisme of the French *nouveaux romanciers* (Robbe-Grillet,
Butor, Sarraute), as when Oskar contemplates nurse Dorothea's
comb :

"Ich hielt ihn gegen die ungeschützte Glühbirne, liess ihn durchsichtig sein, folgte den beiden verschieden starken Sprossen-
gruppen, stellte das Fehlen zweier Sprossen in der schmäch-
tigeren Gruppe fest, liess es mir nicht nehmen, den Fingernagel
des linken Zeigefingers entlang den Kuppen der gröberen
Sprossen schnurren zu lassen, und erfreute Oskar während der
ganzen verspielten Zeit mit dem Aufleuchten einiger weniger
Haare, die ich abzustreifen mit Absicht, um keinen Verdacht zu
erregen, versäumt hatte."[12]

The similarity is deceptive, for the express intention of the
French writers is to release objects from their emotional depen-
dence on human circumstance; the effect being to isolate the individual in an alienating, static world of objects arbitrarily presented in terms of their pure existence (e.g., the rubber erasers in
Les Gommes). The result of Grass's detailed analysis is to create
an emotive effect (and emotions require sentient beings, they are
frivolous whimsy if referred only to things) : Oskar is in love with
this nurse, whom he has never seen, and in her absence needs to
investigate her room and belongings in utmost detail.

Another prominent feature of Grass's narrative style is its labyrinthine quality : this consists of circumlocutory detours as a means of approaching the centre; there is a retreat in order to advance, an arresting then a fresh flow of action; the reader is in the clenching-releasing grip of the author. On consecutive pages Oskar tells us about Meyn like successive waves of an advancing tide; in the way he does so our attention is fixed on "das Unglück" and the dubious virtue of the "sobriety" it induces :

"Es war einmal ein Musiker, der hiess Meyn und konnte ganz wunderschön Trompete blasen. In der vierten Etage unter dem Dach eines Mietshauses wohnte er, hielt sich vier Katzen, deren eine Bismarck hiess, und trank von früh bis spät aus einer Machandelflasche. Das tat er solange, bis das Unglück ihn nüchtern werden liess . . .
Es war einmal ein Musiker, der hiess Meyn und konnte ganz wunderschön Trompete blasen. In der vierten Etage unter dem Dach unseres Mietshauses wohnte er, hielt sich vier Katzen, deren eine Bismarck hiess, und trank von früh bis spät aus einer Machandelflasche, bis er, ich glaube, Ende sechsunddreissig oder Anfang siebenunddreissig in die Reiter-SA eintrat, dort als Trompeter im Musikerkorps zwar viel fehlerloser, aber nicht mehr wunderschön Trompete blies, weil er, in die geleederten Reiterhosen schlüpfend, die Machandelflasche aufgegeben hatte und nur noch nüchtern und laut in sein Blech stiess."[13]

This can of course be called a "conceit", though it is not carried through with the consistent and irresistible verve of Sterne. It also defines the narrator's tentative gropings to fix memories accurately (while retaining doubts as to the possibility of doing so) by making several approaches, as Oskar also does in his periodic and cumulative drumming through the events of his life, always in slightly different words. This is after all the subjective structure of memory :

"und ich begann zu trommeln, der Reihe nach, am Anfang war der Anfang : der Falter trommelte zwischen Glühbirnen meine Geburtsstunde ein; die Kellertreppe mit ihren neunzehn Stufen trommelte ich und meinen Sturz von der Treppe, als man meinen dritten sagenhaften Geburtstag feierte; den Stundenplan der Pestalozzi-Schule trommelte ich rauf und runter . . ."[14]

"Der grundsätzliche Zweifel" is paramount in Grass, according to Klaus Wagenbach, and this doubt is nowhere stronger than when he is trying to combat the lability of memory, to establish a past and a meaning. Lingering on detail, re-working and worrying it is thus for Grass not just a formal idiosyncrasy but a fundamental emotional necessity and an attempt to overcome the gap between mind and existence, akin to the inimitable virtues that Jean Paul saw in *Tristram Shandy* ("die uberfliessende Darstellung soll mit der Sinnlichkeit die Seele füllen".[15]) It is not enough for Grass to state that a pair of ballet shoes was not washed down a street drain, he needs to evoke Homerically the breadth of the city of Danzig through its network of sewers. Again irony (if not satire) lies just under the surface when we face the Biblical stamina with which the dynasty of dogs is enumerated whenever one of the lineage does something. Despite its bulk Grass's prose is precise and anchored to objects, even when it is most metaphorical. The joy in manipulating conceits pervades the smallest cell of these epic honeycombs; figurative phrases shun abstraction, rely entirely on evocation through the senses : for example, to indicate two snoring men :

> "Sie merkte nicht, dass Matzerath und ihr Jan hinter vorgehaltenen Händen verschieden starke Bäume ansägten . . ."[16]

or the effect on candles of the blast of an explosion :

> "Jan jedoch kam wieder die Angst an, als es die Tür unserer Briefkammer rüttelte und die Flämmchen der Talgkerzen nicht wussten, wie ihnen geschah und in welche Richtung sie sich legen sollten."[17]

or the lance-corporal offering his tram-seat to Tulla :

> "Der Gefreite machte aus seinen runden Sitzknien sofort faltenwerfende Stehknie."[18]

Such metaphors awaken preponderantly the visual, tactile and kinaesthetic senses, and not by chance : Grass studied drawing and sculpture professionally, illustrates his own volumes, designs their dust-jackets and creates a visual identity for his personages in innumerable sketches before committing them to words. The line drawings to the collections of verse *Die Vorzüge der Windhühner* and *Gleisdreieck* unmistakably reveal the sculptor who, of all artists, must primarily see objects in total physical isolation. Thus a fly, a locust, a hand, a spider, a hen or the dismembered parts of a doll stand on their own, filling the page. Grass turns this gaze on things in his writing too, and focuses his attention with equal magnification on each detail in turn to the momentary exclusion of others. Precise, single-minded observation is facilitated by the introduction of unusual perspectives, the dwarf's-eye or the dog's-eye view, for nothing alienates the familiar so easily as seeing it in a different perspective. As a result Grass achieves a certain type of objectivity : on the one hand he manages to exclude the human by ascribing human attributes to things, on the other he reduces the human to the status of objects, as, for instance, when Oskar squats under the table where three men are playing skat :

"Sechs Hosenbeine bespannten, verschiedene Fischgräten-
muster zeigend, sechs nackte, oder Unterhosen bevorzugende,
mehr oder weniger behaarte Männerbeine ... die oben, zu Rüm-
pfen, Köpfen, Armen vereinfacht und erweitert, sich eines Spieles
befleissigten ..." [19]

Many readers feel that these mannerisms are in the long run
affected and repetitive, yet beneath the apparently only artificial
decoration one can sense an irrepressible delight in the there-ness
of things, movement, life, time; an exuberant appetite of the
senses for everything that offers itself to them; a hunger for physical experience without which men can undertake nothing. Hence
the prominence in these novels of olfactory sensations, movements,
atmospheric conditions, feelings of cold and warmth, and above
all objects, that can be seen, held, caressed, weighed, kept. The
experiences of Grass's characters are defined in these terms, and
sensory precipitates are the reservoirs on which they draw to re-
enact experience through memory. Oskar (adopting a procedure
of Proust's) evokes his women by means of the smells associated
with them : vanilla, moss and mushrooms for Maria, the "säuer-
licher Geruch" of Lina Greff, Roswitha's Mediterranean odour of
"cinnamon and crushed cloves". Other powerful smells that form
part of his experience are the carpets in Zeidler's flat and the
corpse-like, cigarette-smoking, sweet-sucking, garlic-exuding Klepp.
In *Hundejahre* Brunies is first and foremost the smell of sweets on
his breath, and Tulla the aura of carpenter's glue that she has
absorbed at home. But it is essentially objects that carry the sensuous fullness of reality, which are presented in such a way as to
perform a dual function. In the first place they appear in their
own right with an existence of their own, detached from people,
unpossessed; in this way things acquire the independence of characters, move, change, lie still, arouse feelings, hurt, are acted upon
and fill with memories just like people. Such objects in *Die Blechtrommel* are Oskar's drum, the empty cartridge-case, his grandmother's skirts, the skat cards, Schugger Leo's fluttering white
gloves, the scars on Herbert's back, Oskar's penis and drum-sticks,
the Nazi Party badge, Korneff's boils, the Jew Fajngold's sterilizing
liquid, the ring-finger dug up by the dog, stiff white nurses' uniforms, the bag of sherbet powder. *Hundejahre* bursts with the
same plethora of things though now some of the more evident
and independent objects, such as the scarecrows, the miracle spec-
tacles and the meal-worms, take on allegorical value and invite
interpretation. However, in *Katz und Maus* objects most unequivocally appear as central, described as independent, irreducible
elements that simultaneously carry the action and absorb the per-

sonality of the hero. The story of Mahlke, who achieves his ambition of gaining the Iron Cross, is evoked retrospectively by his schoolfellow Pilenz, to whom the hero appears predominantly in terms of the objects he wears round his neck (leitmotifs counterpointed by another appendage of heroic size). The taciturn Mahlke's physical characteristic is his prominent Adam's apple (the "mouse" of the title) and this is adorned successively by a screw-driver on a shoe-lace, a chain and medal of the Virgin Mary, a tin-opener, tassels, a cravat, luminous badges and buttons, culminating in the Iron Cross (first a stolen one, then his own). The focal importance of these objects is seen in the way description is channelled through them : for example, it is the medal and chain that indicate the violent movements of Mahlke's gymnastic exercises :

> "wenn Mahlke also seine siebenunddreissig Kniewellen würgte, zog es ihm den Anhänger aus dem Turnhemd und das Silberding wurde siebenundreissigmal, immer seinen mittelbraunen Haaren voraus, um die knirschende Reckstange geschleudert, ohne vom Hals loskommen und Freiheit gewinnen zu können, denn Mahlke hatte ausser der bremsenden Gurgel jenen ausladenden Hinterkopf, der mit Haaransatz und deutlichem Knick dem rutschenden, durch Kniewellen entfesselten Kettchen Halt bot." [20]

The austere conciseness of the story is achieved by the economical introduction of such correlatives and another counterpart group : the wreck of the mine-sweeper with its encrustation of gull-droppings, the hole hacked in the ice, and the effects that Mahlke laboriously ferries out to the underwater radio room of the ship.

Since 1950 the theatre in particular (under the influence of Samuel Beckett) has stripped the philosophising overlay from Sartre's literary existentialism, which proclaimed an atheist belief in the essential meaninglessness and therefore absurdity of human life, and has tried to present existence in the naked implicitness of objects and situations. The term "absurd" applied to this type of play describes only the relationship of audience to it, not the play itself. It is not surprising that Grass has written several "absurd" plays, for his cult of things tends ineluctably in this direction. That his expeditions into the theatre have so far been unsuccessful is perhaps due to an inability to impose organization and directional force on his material; or, on the evidence of his novels, Grass's talent may be more immediately and aggressively satirical than is suited to the oblique criticism of contemporary society postulated in the very phenomenon of the "absurd" theatre. Grass is closer to Swift than to Ionesco and Pinter. He has recently completed a play, *Die Plebejer proben den Aufstand*, which he adds to the tradition of Coriolanus themes from Plutarch through to Brecht's adaptation of Shakespeare. The kernel is Brecht's refusal to side openly and unequivocally with the rioting East Berlin workers on June 17th, 1953, and in the nature of the subject-matter the treatment must almost inevitably be ironical and the effect satirical.

The link between Grass and the absurd, between Swift and Pinter, is the grotesque—a favourite word to describe Grass's work. Most of the elements of the grotesque, formulated clearly by Wolfgang Kayser in *Das Groteske in Malerei und Dichtung,* can certainly be found as structural principles in Grass's novels. The distortion of perspective shows things in Lilliputian isolation, angled and magnified from the floor, from under tables and platforms, through keyholes, from inside wardrobes with doors ajar. The reverse perspective of Brobdingnag appears in *Hundejahre* in the "puppet-master" Brauxel's makeshift desk model:

> "Der hier die Feder führt . . . hat sich mit dreiundsiebzig Zigarettenstummeln, mit der errauchten Ausbeute der letzten zwei Tage, den Lauf der Weichsel . . . auf geräumter Schreibtischplatte zurechtgelegt : Tabakkrümel und mehlige Asche bedeuten den Fluss und seine drei Mündungen; abgebrannte Streichhölzer sind Deiche und dämmen ihn ein." [21]

A second powerful and recurrent mark of the grotesque is the mingling of incommensurate spheres, of the animate and inanimate and especially of human and animal, a motif that Grass revels in rather than shuns. Memorable instances in *Die Blechtrommel* are the impaling of Herbert in the museum when attempting to violate the wooden female figure-head, or Oskar, wrapped in coconut matting, making love to nurse Dorothea. The grotesqueness generated in this fashion is intensified in *Hundejahre,* where the scarecrows are caricatured imitations of the animate and the lineage of dogs is handled with all the solemnity accorded by biographers to kings. The grand style of Harras' visit to the police kennels to beget pedigree scions, the details of his coition, the birth of Prinz and his inaccessibility after his elevation, the switching of the last defences of Berlin to search for him—these episodes contain elements of the animal fable, but the responsibility for the grotesque discrepancies is fixed firmly on human beings—we do not laugh at the dogs.

Exception is often taken to the scabrous and disgusting in Grass. He certainly does not spare the details of sexual, anal, coprological, furuncular and sacrilegious aspects of life, but to accuse the author of meretricious pornography for this reason is to misunderstand the part played by these episodes and possibly to condemn oneself. Grass does not introduce these incidents for lascivious or aesthetic effect, nor is he wilfully trying to *épater le bourgeois*. If he breaks through taboos with insouciance this is because the taboos themselves, if we are to give credence to Freud, are logical only to those who believe in them. The motivation for taboos probably lies in the conflict between the unconscious desire to break them and the fear of doing so; it could be this ambivalent attitude, haunting the world outside and our fantasies, that Grass lays bare. The shock occurs when he actually describes the nooks and crannies of the iceberg beneath the surface. At bottom, Grass is claiming no more than his artistic right in "dragging sacred values in the gutter", and fits into a long heritage of amoral, robust literature, where what is seemly, proper, becoming, decent and respectable, with all the firm values taken for granted in these words, has no relevance. Existence is not measurable by morals. The obscene in Grass, as in Chaucer, Boccaccio, Rabelais and his German adaptor Fischart, is an expression of vitality, an enjoyment of experience, a closeness to the movement of life, the hurt of growth and the squalor of decay, ultimately a sensual contact with existence expressing itself structurally in a welter of words and descriptions. It is not entirely by chance that these writers created their vernacular works at important formative points in their respective languages; their relish for life is reflected in their appetite for words. In Germany writers like Grimmelshausen and Harsdörffer in the seventeenth century display the same dual effusion and Grass, too, gives free rein to his fantasy and vitality. He is never satisfied that he has done with his personages, so they spill over from one book to the next. His linguistic effervescence is greater than that of any other contemporary German author (Gerd Gaiser and Martin Walser approach him in some respects) in the variety of idiom, slang, dialect, colloquial and official language, jargon and parodistic literary allusion that continually alters the tone and intent of his narration. In the total structure of a Grass work the obscene, parallel with other appetites from cooking to card-playing, fits into the overall dialectic of national events and individual lives, social and political criticism and personal amorality, and in this sense it has a patterning function. Altogether, Grass's narratives are concatenations of extravagant, out-of-the-way ideas and fantastical inventions just held in check by a real historical content—the basic formula for satire.

Inherent in the congested, exaggerated, effusive, essentially mannerist style (as a complementary pole to the strict severity aimed at by the "classical" writer) is the danger of formlessness. This is not simply a matter of length, for by this yard-stick Thomas Mann could be accused of greater mannerism and tedium than Grass. It is more a question of the author's position and intent, and a congruent structure to express these. Mann's "Langeweile" is aesthetically redeemed and made meaningful by levels of irony and connotation whereas Grass relies on addition rather than interaction. His aim is direct social depiction, there is one target for his arrow—ultimately satire, not irony. *Doktor Faustus* and *Die Blechtrommel* can legitimately be compared as both deal with the rise of the Nazis. In the former there is a fixed point of view : Mann, inventing for himself the intermediary of the narrator Zeitblom, analyses the "cases" of Leverkühn and Nazi Germany, creates ironic inter-relationships, but never shifts from his own absolute standpoint; his subject-matter is judged ontologically on the basis of "essential values" which are, inevitably, posited for the reader as well. This is the classical way of looking at things and is subject to the rigidity of self-imposed limitations in not entertaining even the possibility that its values may not be absolute. Grass displays no such total certainty; his doubt goes right to the core of his own position (or Oskar's) and can only be given shape in the shifting aspects of the novel. Time, or even identity, is not safely mastered by the narrator; there is no easy, reassuring, chronological progression; the present—interspersed with reflection—continually intrudes into the past or vice-versa with the frightening existential peremptoriness of memory. Grass cannot be complacently satisfied with a flailing of the Nazis, his contrapuntal censure of post-war society dialectically throws doubt upon the absolutes unhesitatingly invoked in condemning Nazi Germany. Doubt prompts questions, and if unimpeachable answers cannot be found the questions may be repeated. Mann stated his own rhetorical question in *Doktor Faustus* and the answer was self-evident to him. Grass, not armed with conviction, makes two major formulations of doubt : *Hundejahre* repeats *Die Blechtrommel,* only more insistently; that there is no answer, or that Grass expects none, does not invalidate the question.

It might be argued that Oskar is as if in the unassailable narrator's cockpit of Zeitblom in *Doktor Faustus,* describing and judging a period, yet immune to it. But Oskar's situation is inherently ambiguous : on the one hand he is a formal invention by the author, a framework to impose a shape on the exploding centrifugal material of thirty amorphous years; on the other he tells his own story and is too engaged in the telling to make judgements. In *Hundejahre* judgement is impeded even more firmly by a trinity of narrators with dissimilar viewpoints, each allotted a separate chronological section; yet, as nothing in the present can be evaluated without harking back to the past, and the past changes in the light of the present, the three strands are inextricable and the effect kaleidoscopic. A thick, tortuous, complex history is implied, not easily elucidated from any one point of view. The narrators form an "Autorenkollektiv", all three begotten in the author's mind yet adding up to something less than him. The ambiguity of the narrators' attitudes to events is emphasized by their use of the third person when speaking of themselves. In the opening paragraph the "Autorenkollektiv" argues about who is to start :

> "Erzähl Du. Nein, erzählen Sie! Oder Du erzählst. Soll etwa der Schauspieler anfangen? Sollen die Scheuchen, alle durcheinander? . . . Bitte, fangen Sie an! Schliesslich hat Ihr Hund damals. Doch bevor mein Hund, hat schon Ihr Hund, und der Hund vom Hund. Einer muss anfangen . . ." [22]

This presupposes an eager audience waiting to hear a tale that can be told indiscriminately by any one of the participants. As it is, the implied shared perspective is split into divergent paths, revealing the instability of the past revived in memory. Neither narrator nor reader is allowed to feel that the events happened only like this and in this order, and as such they can be mastered. Irony is constantly aroused by the uncertainty attending the relationship of narrator to story. Demarcation lines are agreed for the separate narrators and traditional phrases are introduced, inducing a false feeling of safe chronology : "Der junge Amsel, von dem hier fortan, wenn auch mit Pausen, die Rede sein wird . . ." or "der hier die Feder führt . . ." [23] Frequent is the interruption that "analyses" the act of narrating : in *Katz und Maus* Pilenz admits that the hard core of fact cannot be whittled away, however the narrator might wish otherwise; he implies something really happened, creates the effect of an authentic document and pretends to deny a place to fantasy and invention, though the facts actually issue as a *Novelle*. This leaves a final state of uncertainty whichever way the narrator is looked at. The function of the narrators themselves is thus ironized, unlike Mann's procedure of extracting irony from the contrast between the narrator and the material he handles. With Grass he is part of the material.

Documentary authenticity and ambiguity seem to be contradictories, yet Grass manages to hold them in equilibrium by suggesting ambivalences for apparently clear-cut facts. *Die Blechtrommel* (and *Hundejahre* less obviously) are to all appearances autobiographies (that Oskar oscillates between the appellations "ich" and "Oskar" is irrelevant—in *Dichtung und Wahrheit* Goethe referred to himself as "der Knabe"), yet consideration for that all-important structural factor, memory, is minimal. The time element is totally static and non-naturalistic, because Oskar has a mature adult mind from start to finish of his experiences, not only as the narrator but also as the putative growing hero; that his physical growth ceases at the age of three only accentuates the absence of a time perspective. There is a single fixed focus throughout and the traditional viewpoint of the autobiography, conditioned by the lability of memory and the flow of time, is cancelled : the reader experiences no sensation of memory tapering away into a past nor of a gradually expanding selection of facts nor of a blurring of sharpness with the passage of time. Each event in turn is jerked spatially and temporally into the range of the fixed-focus lens of Oskar's eye and each is equally clear-cut. Oskar depicts his grandmother (long before his own birth) in voluminous detail, remembers the Herz-Jesu-Kirche "from his christening ceremony" and where he sat ("zweiter Rang Seite, erste Reihe") on a childhood theatre visit. Whether minor details or whole chapters, such narration is a deliberate snub to an accepted form, a cheeky guying of representational obedience to time sequence that fits into a contrived structure in much the same way as do the "Life and Opinions" of *Tristram Shandy* where we get nearly half-way through the book before the hero's birth is achieved.

If these novels invite comparison with autobiography (Grass has said that he cannot write about what he has not experienced) they do so even more strongly with the autobiographical novel and *Bildungsroman*. One must look back through the nineteenth century to *Wilhelm Meister*, blend this earnest literary form with the picaresque novel of action or German *Schelmenroman* like *Simplicissimus*, temper the result with irony to produce parody as in Mann, to find some marked characteristics of Grass's prose works. They are utterly serious and at the same time tongue-in-cheek, recognitions of a literary tradition and a mockery of it. If in *Felix Krull* Mann was achieving a travesty of the *Bildungsroman* by parodistic inversion, in *Die Blechtrommel* Grass appears to be aping the parody of Krull. The similarities between the two heroes are so striking as to be suspect : both have a serious, dedicated outlook and a concern for the full development of their potential; Oskar is writing after his trial and in his "Pflege- und Heilanstalt", Felix from prison; both are beautiful boys, and while Oskar has hypnotic power over people with his voice, drum and hump, Felix exploits his seductive beauty and timbre of voice and a persuasive turn of phrase. Each has various names and personae, a chameleonic adaptability to new rôles. Both are convinced of their extraordinariness and are protected by Mercury, the patron of thieves and orators. *Die Blechtrommel* may not consciously imitate Mann's novel but it emerges as its parody since the "development" of the hero is now not even the central concern : he is relegated to being an accompaniment to a historical epoch.

Literary parody is to the fore not only in the overall shape of these novels; at any point Grass's language may break into imitations of Goethe or Kafka, Mann or Benn, modern philosophers or the Expressionists, Hitler or colloquial speech, the pomposity of a headmaster's mouthings or an ordinary person's attempt at lyrical description. This is not gratuitous derision, it serves as a springboard from which to criticize an ethos upheld by the writer and may be felt by Grass to be detrimentally influential. In *Hundejahre* Heidegger is consistently and viciously attacked through the pseudo-philosophical language typically indulged in by the Freiburg academic; as Störtebeker slaughters rats in the drains at army camp he muses thus :

"Die Ratte entzieht sich, indem sie sich in das Rattige entbirgt. So beirrt die Ratte, es lichtend, das Rattige mit der Irre. Denn das Rattige ist in die Irre ereignet, in der es die Ratte umirrt und so den Irrtum stiftet. Er ist der Wesensraum aller Geschichte." [24]

In Heidegger Grass saw a most destructive influence on his generation and seeks retaliation in this ridicule. The revenge has to be content with linguistic caricature as Matern fails to contact "Zipfelmütze" (Heidegger's notorious headgear in his post-war Black Forest retreat) despite an intensive search.

Mention has been made of Grass's dramatic attempts, chiefly with shorter pieces in the wake of playwrights of the "absurd"; as yet, however, he has not found his touch in this form, the structuring of sometimes unusual ideas lacks the unity of the novels, and tedium results from brevity. Nevertheless, these plays and the verse collections throw up images, ideas and fancies that constantly occupy the author's mind and feed his imagination : birds, seagulls, hens, cocks, nuns, dolls, cupboards and their contents, objects of all sorts thematically establish a subterranean unity in the whole of Grass's output and are nodal points for growth. The ramifications extend beyond the written word, when we remember that he is an active figurative artist and illustrates his own work. Perhaps more than any other writer in Germany today Grass expresses the nervous, sceptical, syncopated feeling of post-1945 Europe. This accounts for the restlessness and tension in his work, the groundswell that upsets received values, the undertow eroding the notion of absolutes and establishing the claims of the absurd and the grotesque. Hocke makes a distinction between two fundamental modes of apprehending and reacting to reality : "Der Klassiker stellt Gott in seiner Essenz, der Manierist Gott in seiner Existenz dar. Die Gefahr der Klassik ist die Erstarrung, diejenige des Manierismus die Auflösung." [25] Grass, baroque and mannerist, is frequently brought to the brink of disintegration through the congested tortuosity of his prose works; but this very form is a valid literary equivalent to an inherent formlessness in existence itself, and one factor that integrally affects the structure is Grass's lively vigilance responding to existence in a here and now. He denies that there are "timeless" works of art : literature has always been "in ihrer Zeit geschrieben, mit dem Blick aus dem Fenster, mit dem Ohr zur Strasse gewendet." [26] The description applies to the author himself, artist and writer, electing to live in the tense, dialectical ambiguity of Berlin (the only stimulating ambience he can find in Germany), non-engaged doctrinally but committed to life.

TRANSLATIONS

1. At the end of July in the year '00—it was just being decided to double the imperial warship building programme—mama saw the light of day under the sign of Leo.

2. ... Tuesdays and Fridays were carpet-beating days, but by now this banging was rare and almost self-conscious on the two weekdays: since Hitler had come to power more and more households had vacuum cleaners.

3. The pile (of furnishings) was set alight and the grocer took the opportunity of warming his fingers and feelings at the public blaze.

4. This time there were not just S.A. uniforms. There was stuff worn by rank and file Party members in the pile too. But everything was brown: not the brown of flat summer shoes; not a nut brown, witch brown; not the brown of Africa; not rubbed bark, not furniture, brown with age; not mid-brown sand-brown; neither new brown coal nor old peat, cut with peat spades; not breakfast chocolate, not morning coffee enhanced by cream; tobacco, so many brands, yet none so brownish; neither camouflaging fawn brown nor the Nivea tan of a fortnight's holiday; no autumn spat on the palette when this brown: shit brown, at all events clay brown, softened, sticky, when the Party brown, S.A. brown, the brown of all Brown Books, Brownshirt houses, Braunau brown, Evabraun, when this brown of uniforms, nothing in the least like khaki brown, brown from a thousand pimply arses shitted on to white bowls, brown acquired from peas and hot sausage; no, no, you gentle brunettes, witch-brown, nut-brown, were not the godmothers when this brown, cooked, born and dyed, when this dungheap brown—and I am still being flattering—lay before Eddi Amsel.

5. Mannerist writing displays the following basic tendencies: the emotional exaggeration or the dispassionate reduction of expression, obliqueness and over-explicitness, mystification and evocation, encoding and "revelations" of an offensive nature.

6. ... the story-teller, that murmuring invoker of the past tense.

7. ... with its description of minutiae on a grand scale, apparently obsessed by the individual detail as if nothing else were important, and yet keeping the whole firmly in view.

8. ... is a powerful and majestic spirit, expansive, packed with life, vast as the sea in its rolling monotony, grand in gesture but at the same time exact, full of swing yet carefully controlled, it is not after the part, the episode, it goes for the whole, the world with its countless episodes and details, on which it lingers dreamily, as if each were of prime importance. For it is in no hurry, it has unlimited time, it is the spirit of patience, fidelity, perseverance and a deliberateness that becomes a source of pleasure through the love with which it is handled; it is the spirit of bewitching boredom. It scarcely knows where to begin unless at the very source of all things, and it would like to go on for ever.

9. One can start a story in the middle and create confusion by striking out boldly backwards and forwards. One can pretend to be modern, cut out all epochs and distances and afterwards proclaim, or have someone proclaim, that one has finally and at the very last moment solved the space-time problem.

10. ... thus the humorous writer confines us rigidly to the sensuously precise.

11. ... the metamorphotic sensuous style of humorous writing... individualizes down to the tiniest detail.

12. I held it up to the bare light bulb, making it transparent, cast my eye along the two rows of teeth of different thicknesses and noted that two teeth were missing from the finer ones; I did not resist the temptation to run the nail of my left index finger along the tips of the thicker teeth, and, during the whole of the time spent playing in this way, delighted Oskar with the glint of a few hairs that I had deliberately omitted to remove so as not to arouse suspicion.

13. Once upon a time there was a musician called Meyn who played the trumpet marvellously. He lived in an attic on the fourth floor of a tenement, kept four cats (one of them was called Bismarck) and tippled from a gin-bottle from morning to night. This he did until the disaster sobered him up.... Once upon a time there was a musician called Meyn who played the trumpet marvellously. He lived in an attic on the fourth floor of our tenement, kept four cats (one of them was called Bismarck) and tippled from a gin-bottle from morning to night. This he did until, I think at the end of '36 or the beginning of '37, he joined the Mounted S.A., where, as a trumpeter in the band, he played far more accurately but no longer marvellously, because, when he slipped into the riding-breeches with the leather seat, he had given up the gin-bottle and now only blew soberly and loudly into his trumpet.

14. ... and I began to drum, everything in the right order, in the beginning was the beginning: the moth between the light bulbs drummed in the hour of my birth; I drummed up the cellar stairs with their nineteen steps and my fall from those stairs when my memorable third birthday was being celebrated; I drummed up and down the time-table of the Pestalozzi school...

15. ... the function of the overflowing description is to fill the soul with sensuousness.

16. She did not notice that Matzerath and her Jan, with their hands over their mouths, were sawing away at trees of different thicknesses.

17. Jan, however, got scared again when the door of the mail-room we were in rattled and the flames of the candles didn't know what was happening to them and in which direction to lie down.

18. The lance-corporal immediately turned his round sitting knees into sharp-creased standing knees.

19. Six trouser-legs of different herring-bone patterns were stretched over six more or less hairy male legs, some bare, some favouring long underpants; ... up above, extended and reduced to trunks, heads and arms, they were engrossed in a game ...

20. ... so when Mahlke struggled to complete his thirty-seven revolutions round the horizontal bar the medal came out of his gym vest and the silver thing was hurled thirty-seven times round the creaking bar, always just ahead of his light brown hair, without managing to break free from his neck and gain its freedom; for, apart from his throat acting as a brake, Mahlke had a projecting back to his head with a marked angle where his hair ended, holding in check the chain flung round by the revolutions.

21. The writer of these pages ... has laid out on the cleared desk-top the course of the Vistula with seventy-three cigarette stubs, the yield of two days' smoking: scraps of tobacco and powdery ash represent the river and its three mouths; used matches stand for the dykes and embankments.

22. You tell the story. No, you! Or let *him*. Should perhaps the actor begin? Or the scarecrows, all at once? ... Please, you start! After all, it was your dog that. But before my dog, yours did, and the dog of the dog. Someone must begin ...

23. Young Amsel, whose story we shall be telling from now on, though with interruptions ...
... the writer of these pages ...

24. The rat withdraws by concealing itself in the rodential. In so doing the rat misleads the rodential with confusion, while reducing its numbers. For the rodential has eventuated into confusion, in which it circles round the rat and thus gives rise to error. The latter is the sphere of being of all history.

25. The classical writer presents God in his essence, the mannerist in his existence. The danger in the classical is rigidity, that in mannerism disintegration.

26. ... written in its time, with the author looking out of the window listening to what goes on in the street.

SELECT BIBLIOGRAPHY

Verse and Prose

(Published mainly by Luchterhand Verlag, Neuwied):

Lilien aus Schlaf, 1954. Verse.
Die Vorzüge der Windhühner, 1956. Verse and Prose.
Die Blechtrommel, 1959. Novel.
Gleisdreieck, 1960. Verse.

Katz und Maus, 1961. Novelle.
Hundejahre, 1963. Novel.
Since 1955 frequent contributions to *Akzente,* including the dramatic pieces *Beritten hin und zurück* and *Noch zehn Minuten bis Buffalo,* 1958.

Plays
(The published text is often a revision of an earlier version):
Die bösen Köche (1956) in *Modernes deutsches Theater I,* Luchterhand, 1961.
Hochwasser (1956), Suhrkamp, 1963.
Onkel, Onkel (1958), Klaus Wagenbach Verlag, Berlin, 1965.
Die Plebejer proben den Aufstand was performed in the winter 1965–66. Luchterhand, 1966.

Critical Work on Grass
Most secondary literature is in the form of essays or extended reviews of his books. There is a monograph, *Günter Grass,* by K. L. Tank in the series *Köpfe des XX Jahrhunderts,* Colloquium Verlag, Berlin; also a special issue on him in Georgi Verlag, Aachen, and an essay in H. M. Enzensberger's *Einzelheiten.*

Hans Magnus Enzensberger

Hans Magnus Enzensberger

by PATRICK BRIDGWATER
(University of Leicester)

Born November 11th, 1929 at Kaufbeuren (Allgäu). Childhood in Nuremberg. Air-raids and evacuation. Called up into the *Volkssturm* by the proclamation of October 18th, 1944. After the war, "black market and matriculation". Worked as interpreter and barman. Studied literature, languages, and philosophy at Erlangen, Hamburg, Freiburg i.B., and at the Sorbonne (1948–1955). Vacations spent tramping through Europe. Dr.Phil. (Erlangen) *summa cum laude*, 1955, for thesis on Brentano (see Bibliography). 1955–57: programme-editor in Alfred Andersch's "Radio Essay" department of *Süddeutscher Rundfunk* in Stuttgart. Short spell as guest-lecturer at the Hochschule für Gestaltung in Ulm. Visit to USA and Mexico in 1957. From 1957 to 1960 lived at Stranda in Norway. Then spent a year, also as freelance writer, at Lanuvio near Rome. In 1960–61, he worked as a reader for his own publishers (Suhrkamp) in Frankfurt/M. Since then he has again been living in Norway, on the island of Tjöme in Oslo-fjord. *Preis der Hugo Jakobi-Stiftung*, 1956; *Kritikerpreis für Literatur*, 1962; *Georg Büchner-Preis*, 1963. Member of *Gruppe 47*, and a leading member of the "literary Opposition".

From Auschwitz to the Wirtschaftswunderland

IN his essay "In Search of the Lost Language", Enzensberger has repeated that post-war poetry must be able to face Theodor W. Adorno's radical judgement that to go on writing lyric poetry after Auschwitz was barbaric. Although after Auschwitz and Hiroshima poetry was more *necessary* than ever before, it was Auschwitz (and the other symbolical man-made hells) that made the "seraphic tone" type of poetry seem a barbarous anachronism. After 1945 poets could not ignore the fact that "ein Gespräch über Bäume fast ein Verbrechen ist/Weil es ein Schweigen über so viele Untaten einschliesst" (Brecht).[1]

German poetry in fact faced up to Auschwitz in the same way that poetry has always faced up to things: by expressing it. The answer to Adorno's judgement is Paul Celan's austerely masterful "Todesfuge" (1948). The story of how German poetry developed from the *Nullpunkt*[2]-clichés of the immediate post-war years to the achievements of the mid-fifties has often been told, and most brilliantly by Enzensberger himself in the essay quoted above. The story is partly one of coming to terms with the political realities of life, and it is here that the poetry of Ingeborg Bachmann is a landmark, for in her best poetry politics have become an essential reality of poetic life, an essential aspect of human experience. Orphic inwardness has given way to the "public poem". So by the time Enzensberger's poems began to appear in 1956, the apocalyptic atmosphere and verbal paralysis of the post-war decade had been overcome, though Paul Celan was leading himself into a private verbal solitude from which he only emerged with *Die Niemandsrose* (1963). German poetry had in fact begun to exist again. As Enzensberger says, "a new degree of freedom had been won", and this was reflected in the "disillusionment and grotesquerie, refracted vision and parody, understatement and *humeur noir*", the total lack of solemnity of his own poetry and that of Günter Grass. The time for sensitivity and sophistry was past. It was again a time to face facts, which again meant above all the political facts of life. The world in which Enzensberger grew up was the world of Auschwitz; the world in which and of which he began to write was that of the materialistic *Wirtschaftswunder*. It is no wonder that he got off to such an "angry" start.

Certainly when his first poems appeared, Enzensberger was very much of an "angry young man" and experimental poet. Of all the poets of his generation—the second generation of young poets to come of age poetically since 1945—he was the one who had most clearly followed Günter Eich's advice :

"Tut das Unnütze, singt die Lieder, die man aus eurem Mund
        nicht erwartet!
Seid unbequem, seid Sand, nicht das Öl im Getriebe der Welt !" [3]
            (Günter Eich, *Ausgewählte Gedichte*, 1961, 51)

But in less than a decade he has established himself as "a leader of the German avant-garde, the new left, and the expatriates" (*Encounter*, April 1964, p. 16). More importantly, he has dropped the puerilities and frivolities of his early work, and has established himself as one of the most gifted poets and most responsible critics of his generation. No other poet or critic of his generation—and in 1966 he is still only 37—combines Enzensberger's technical ability with such an acute awareness of what are the *relevant* issues of our time. Though he is in a sense "a leader of the German avant-garde", he would hardly regard himself as such. He has no time for the follies of "concrete poetry" or for the ultra-literary and self-consciously experimental wing of the avant-garde. He is well aware that poetry is always essentially a continuing process and part of a tradition, and rightly stresses that all poetry is by definition both "pure" and "committed". If he has mostly stressed the question of commitment, this is understandable; after all, to write a poem is to commit oneself precisely. But to what poetic aim and view of poetry is he committed?

Poetic Aims

Enzensberger has not hesitated to make public his view of poetry and his own changing aims as a poet, and there is a close connexion between his aim and the poetic quality of what he writes at any given time.

The record begins with the then 28-year-old poet saying that he wants his poems to hurt certain people (see Hans Bender's *Nachwort* to *Junge Lyrik 1957*, Munich, n.d.). His immature statement, characteristic of the "angry young man" that Enzensberger deliberately set out to be, is Brechtian in its use of the word "Gedichtschreiber" for "poet". But the statement itself is less than and other than Brechtian. While Brecht defined his poetic aim by writing:

> "Die Schlechten fürchten deine Klaue.
> Die Guten freuen sich deiner Grazie.
> Derlei
> Hörte ich gern
> Von meinem Vers." [4]

Enzensberger's enemies remained unnamed and to some extent imaginary. Of Brecht's "Grazie" there is as yet no sign. And in any case wanting to hurt people is an extraordinarily bad and silly aim for a poet. Given this aim, it is only surprising that his early verse was not worse.

The first two collections—*verteidigung der wölfe* (1957) and *landessprache* (1960)—came complete with "instructions for use". In the former, his aim is naturally still much the same as that recorded in *Junge Lyrik 1957*, though more generally and slightly less irresponsibly worded. He likens his poems to leaflets or advertisements addressed to all and sundry. The characteristic "angry poems" are intended to increase, if only slightly, the amount of anger in the world; he said elsewhere at this time that he wrote many poems simply because he was angry. This clearly means he is already implicitly rejecting Benn's influential thesis of the "absolute" self-expressive poem addressed to no one, and is declaring himself a successor to the "functional poets" or social realists of the 1920s. After all, Brecht declared in 1927 that poetry consisted of the communication of ideas or sentiments from which others should benefit; and Erich Kästner, a "negative" satirist with whom Enzensberger also has much in common, added in 1928 that poems should be spiritually useful. In the poem "telegrammschalter null uhr zwölf" Enzensberger's own view of poetry in 1957 is made even clearer: "...hier gilt allein/die harte poetik fester tarife:/con-densare!.../...klartext bitte" [5] (V. 18). From the beginning En-zensberger was evidently opposed to the obscurity and subjecti-vism of much contemporary verse; he clearly favours the sort of concentrated, austere, "political" poetry made famous by Brecht. But despite its clarity and political relevance—Enzensberger is never irrelevant—his first collection has two main weaknesses. He does not always write "hard poetry at a fixed rate of charges"; his poetry is too often written at a flat rate of charges, his anger directed at all comers; and in any case it is not clear by what standards the rate of charges is fixed. And his "klartext" is not always poetically articulated and patterned. Another poem, "gol-dener schnittmusterbogen zur poetischen wiederaufrüstung" (V. 82f) confirms that in 1957 Enzensberger did not have the ability to match his poetic aims. "Poetic Re-Armament"—it is a striking phrase. The reader might expect a plea for an up-to-date com-mitted form of poetry, a contemporary version of the social realism of the 1920s and 1930s. But the poem itself lacks stamina and substance, is too negative, contains little more than a series of digs at other poets; parody outweighs commitment.

The instructions for the use of *landessprache* (1960) made it clear that Enzensberger's aim had changed. While still stressing that his poems are intended for use, he now says that they do not aim to arouse, increase or spread anger; the reader is simply requested to consider whether he agrees or disagrees with the poems. The silly aim of annoying people has gone. What remains is the more genuinely Brechtian determination to provoke the reader to agree or disagree. If this is clearly at variance with the idea that the poem with which one can argue is no poem, Enzensberger evi-dently shares Eliot's view that "the poetry does not matter". This is precisely the trouble: in his early work the poetry has been allowed to matter too little. His view of poetry is too narrow; he still appears to confuse the poet's function with that of the politician and sociologist. Is poetry useful in the way he thinks it is? And is it as useful as he believes it to be? In claiming that poetry should be useful, Enzensberger leaves important questions unanswered. Though he set up shop as a "political poet", he has never shown much awareness of the manifold problems of "political poetry", despite the essay in *Einzelheiten* on poetry and politics.

His third book of poems, *blindenschrift* (1964) contained no "instructions for use", a significant change. But an essay, "Scheren-schleifer und Poeten", published in 1961, makes it clear that his view of poetry has again altered. He now says that the task of poetry is to point out "states of affairs" (Sachverhalte) which can-

not be shown to exist, or to which attention cannot be drawn, by
any other means (television, press, etc.), By pointing out such
states of affairs, he declares, the poem can change them; with the
help of a poem the reader may succeed in producing truth, or
rather finite, limited, contingent truths (since poems are themselves finite, limited, contingent). Poetry, he concludes, is essentially "ein Prozess der Verständigung des Menschen mit und über
ihn selbst."[6] The immature provocativeness has now completely
gone. If the practical effectiveness of poetry is still perhaps over-
rated and certainly not made clear (what are the "states of
affairs" that can be changed?), the important point is that Enzensberger has finally realized that poetry is concerned with truths, is
a unique means of coming to terms with, and discovering, oneself
and reality. It is no chance that his subsequent third collection
(blindenschrift) is by far his best yet, no chance that real poetry has
resulted from a mature view of poetry and a genuinely poetic aim.
The angry young man has given way to the poet, and satire
accordingly gives way to poetry.

This present view of poetry has been reached through a deliberate rejection of Gottfried Benn's theories. In the essay "Scherenschleifer und Poeten", Enzensberger makes it clear that he has
no time for those whom he calls belated adepts of Benn's Aus-
druckswelt[7]—poets who have nothing to say and say it in accord-
ance with the rules of Benn's aesthetic! He specifically rejects the
basic points in Benn's poetic theory, namely that form is all important, that poetry must always be about the poet himself, and
that the lyric poem is "monologic art" (Benn got the term from
Nietzsche), addressed to no one (see Benn, Probleme der Lyrik, 5th
ed., 1958, pp. 20, 23, 39). His own views on these subjects are clear :
poetry is concerned with truths, "content" is as important as
"form", and poems are addressed to someone, written for someone; there is no such thing as absolute speech (—Benn's "absolute
poetry"). He insists on the same point of view in the essay "Welt-
sprache der modernen Poesie" (in Einzelheiten), where he stresses
that even modern poetry expresses something, and something that
concerns us. This is clearly an explicit rejection of Benn's egocen-
tric formalistic aesthetic; as such it parallels Brecht's rejection of
Rilke and George, and Auden's rejection of Eliot; it is the repudia-
tion by a "life" poet of the idea of "literary" poetry. Indeed, in
his Encounter article Enzensberger implicitly condemns Benn for
seeing art as a "purpose in itself, . . . an aesthetic substitute religion
beyond all social and moral responsibility". But if he is clearly a
"life" poet, he does not—now—make the fundamental mistake of
confusing poetic reality with material reality. He has stressed (in
alternative, Oct. 1964, p. 26) that reality is not "realistic", an

apparent echo of Kafka's view that true reality is always unrealistic.

It is refreshing to have a young poet asking himself what he is writing and why, timely to find someone insisting that poetry must have a use, even if he has tended to oversimplify the labyrinthine question of exactly *how* it should be useful. Enzensberger insists that poetry is not only self-expression. His view of poetry is now essentially a pragmatic one : poems, he says, must be "beautiful" so that people will pay attention to them (meaning : pay attention to their moral).

Despite Gottfried Benn's view that works of art are phenomenal, historically ineffective, of no practical consequence, precisely this being their greatness (see his "Können Dichter die Welt ändern?"), there is a real sense in which Enzensberger's poetry *is* more useful than that of most of his contemporaries—more useful because it is, *and can be seen to be*, about things that matter, and therefore increases our awareness of the world in which we live. It is time to consider his poetry more closely.

Poetic Progress

The poems in Enzensberger's first collection are divided into three sections : friendly poems, sad poems, and angry poems. The angry poems have received most critical attention, yet are the weak point of the collection. Attention has been focused upon them because they draw attention to themselves. But in their haste to welcome the work of this young committed poet, the critics mostly overlooked the real critical issues here. Alfred Andersch's view that in *verteidigung der wölfe* (1957) Enzensberger produced the great political poetry ("das grosse politische Gedicht") lacking since Brecht's death the previous year, is simply not true. The fact of the matter is that in the first two collections by this young "political poet" there is *not one* good—let alone great—"political poem". There are some effective satirical texts, and there are a few very good personal poems. Andersch was in such a hurry to champion this young writer that his literary judgement went haywire. Such critics are at least partly to blame for the weakness of Enzensberger's second collection. One reason why he continued to write bad ("angry") poems in *landessprache* must have been that they had been widely mistaken for good poems. Enzensberger is in fact a poet who made a very considerable name for himself by writing bad poems; his political standpoint blinded some of his German reviewers—who nearly all share his left-wing views—to a marked lack of poetic form in his early work; his admirable recent poems, in which he is committed above all to poetry, have received nothing like the acclaim of the earlier "angry" ones. There has rarely been such an obvious case of a writer being widely admired for quite the wrong reason.

As an outstanding example of an "angry poem", let us consider the title poem of the first collection, "verteidigung der wölfe gegen die lämmer" (V. 90f). Michael Hamburger has compared this poem with Gregory Corso's "Bomb", concluding that "Enzensberger's poem is a serious and responsible contribution to social criticism, based on a fundamental insight into our lupine century: it is the love of the lambs for the wolves that has made it a lupine one" (in *New Departures*, 2/3 1960, p. 122). Enzensberger has certainly made "a serious and responsible contribution to social criticism"—but has made it in his book *Politik und Verbrechen*, and not in this poem. To attack the lambs for their love of the wolves admittedly makes good sense in this totalitarian century, and particularly in Germany where there were 13 million "lambs". But can defending the wolves be called "serious and responsible"? Is this a poem that can withstand Adorno's charge of barbarism? Personally, I should call it provocative and *irresponsible* precisely. It is, of course, meant to be provocative; but is not this a tactless and tasteless sort of provocation? There is a fine contentious rhetoric in the poem— "seht in den spiegel: feig/scheuend die mühsal der wahrheit,/dem lernen abgeneigt, das denken/überantwortend den wölfen..."[8]— but the naughty, clever satirist is more in evidence than the poet. What is the point of the poem, and to whom is it addressed? Is this one of the many early poems Enzensberger wrote, as he admitted, simply because he was angry? Presumably it is addressed to the "lambs" and is intended to enrage them. But how many of the "lambs" read Enzensberger's or any other poetry? How many of those who do would take the poem as being addressed to them? How many of the very few (if any) who did so take the poem would feel the right sort of rage? Enzensberger may have been fully justified in sneering "ihr ändert die welt nicht."[9] But in 1957 he did not realize that he would not change the world politically either. Certainly the holier-than-thou attitude implied by the way in which he talks down to his audience from a personally uncommitted position would be unlikely to achieve any useful effect whatsoever. "Verteidigung der wölfe gegen die lämmer" is better as a statement or satirical text than as a poem. As a poem it is formless and fails to do justice to the insight on which it is based; there is no poetic pattern, only a series of pre-poetic statements. Enzensberger's own remark that some sorts of political poem are either politically ineffective or have no connection with poetry (see *Einzelheiten*, 349), can and should be applied to many of his own "angry poems". Equally relevant here is his view expressed in "Entstehung eines Gedichts" that a purely political poem is by definition not a poem at all. Enzensberger suggests that political poetry will invariably miss its target if it makes straight for it; the political element must as it were seep in through the cracks between the words, behind the poet's back, of its own accord. If this is true, and surely it is, then many of his own poems are thereby condemned. There is a world of difference between "verteidigung der wölfe ..." and, say, Brecht's "political" poems of 1953. From this point of view Enzensberger's poem fails because it is too openly and unsubtly political. The ambiguity of many of Brecht's later political poems, the fact that the political element exists between the lines, is their greatest virtue. Just as the great war-novel is frequently the one which treats war indirectly, so the great political poem is most often the allegorical poem in which the theme is treated not explicity but implicitly.

Much the same criticism could be levelled at most of the "angry poems" in *verteidigung der wölfe*. Two other representative and much-anthologized poems are "ins lesebuch für die oberstufe" (V. 85) and "anweisung an sisyphos" (V. 70). The former is clever, cynical, self-nullifying. The latter is very well written, but the poet's anger is too abstract, too rhetorical : the poem is a piece of satirical "fine writing"—it's magnificent, but is it poetry?

No, the real poems in his first collection are the lyrical "friendly poems" such as "lock lied". Here Enzensberger is writing in *his own voice*, which he does not do again until *blindenschrift* :

> "meine stimme ist ein sanftes verlies
> lass dich nicht fangen
> meine binse ist ein seidener dolch
> hör nicht zu
> ki wit ki wit ki wit" (V. 7)[10]

But even better, I think, are the poems in which real emotion is directly involved. For the over-sophisticated twentieth-century poet perhaps the most difficult poem to write is the one involving deep personal emotion such as the love-poem or elegy, where there are two obstacles : the triteness of the subject, and the emotional reticence of the self-conscious poet. Two highly unusual but also highly successful attempts to come to poetic terms with such emotions are Hans Arp's "Kaspar ist tot" and Kurt Schwitters' "An Anna Blume". A poet's success in expressing the oldest of emotions —love and grief—is usually a fair measure of his quality. Enzensberger is more sophisticated than most; how does he fare in this respect? One of the "friendly poems" in *verteidigung der wölfe* is particularly relevant here. It is the poem with the laconic Anglo-Saxon title "call it love" (V. 19). The throwaway title at once suggests that we are faced here with the same apparent reticence and would-be toughness as in Brecht's "Ich habe dich nie je so geliebt". But Enzensberger's title is not just a smart, cynical, "top of the pops" title; it also contains the only direct reference to love in the whole poem, and it deliberately uses the foreign word to avoid the banal "Liebe". The setting of the poem is uncompromisingly modern : an April evening in the city. The poem shows, with a minimum of words, how those seeking after love in its cheapest form are themselves suddenly overcome by the anarchic holy spirit of love (the "dove of white gauze"). The whole poem is almost reluctant to voice its "old-fashioned" theme, and even the final, laconic "schön ist der abend"[11] is ambiguous. This is an objective love-poem in the sense in which Heym's "Der Krieg" is an objective war-poem; it is also a highly successful depiction of the shy advent of love in an age of thoughtless promiscuity. Both title and poem show that Enzensberger is fully aware of the difficulties of the genre. There is a twofold irony in the title, for "call it love" sounds like something from the hit-parade, yet "love" here refers to "one lost beyond the mountains . . . exiled upon the crumbling stars"; it is the unnamed word—"die Liebe"—which would have the connotation of commercialized "love". If there appears to be some doubt in the poet's mind whether he is writing in what Charles Olson has called "field composition", this is nonetheless an excellent poem in which poet and satirist have for once co-operated most effectively.

A more subjective love-poem is "befragung zur mitternacht" (V. 45) which the poet classifies, naturally enough, among the "sad poems" of his first volume. The poem at first sight appears to be a straightforward restatement of one of the baffling questions of love : "wo bist du?"[12] This is one of those unanswerable and "meaningless" questions which are the poet's professional concern; it was this question ("Wo bist du, wenn du neben mir gehst")[13] to which Günter Eich's admirable love-poem "Gegenwart" gave permanent poetic expression. Enzensberger's "befragung zur mitternacht" seems to carry far more personal feeling than the "angry poems" with their howls of protest. The trouble is that the feeling in question is not only self-conscious, but self-centred, and this means not so much that we are faced here with a specifically modern love-poem, as that the poem is not really a love-poem at all; it is a would-be love-poem.

In both his first two collections Enzensberger only reveals genuine aesthetic emotion in love-poems such as "call it love", and in poems expressing grief. In the last category belong the two most moving poems in *verteidigung der wölfe* : "klage um ingo ledermann" (V. 57) and "erinnerung an den tod" (V. 58f). A few lines of the former must be quoted :

"er ist tot der die orgeln schlug, der sie liebkoste.

. . .

du kannst es mit keinem teilen, mit keiner witwe,
mit keinem hund. der die brunnen kannte, die orgel schlug.
mit einem mund voller klagen, mit einem munde voll sand." [14]

This is genuinely felt and admirably written. The best poems in *verteidigung der wölfe* are in fact those dealing with such basic human experiences; it is only in such poems that Enzensberger expresses himself fully poetically. It is a pity that the angry "public" poems dominate the first two collections. Not until *blindenschrift* do the poet's personal emotions and political themes coincide and fuse, or else achieve a fruitful tension.

Like most first collections, *verteidigung der wölfe* showed more promise than achievement. It was a remarkable collection bound to attract attention. The young poet succeeded in his self-proclaimed aim of increasing the anger in the world. But taken as a whole, the collection is not an artistic success; it contains—inevitably—more failures than poems. If it was the failures which were applauded, that was not Enzensberger's fault exactly, though it was certainly his fault that he allowed himself to be misled by this applause. The fact remains, however, that the poet's social involvement leads to indiscriminate social criticism more often than to poetry. There is plenty of energy, but the energy is rarely articulate. There is too much here that is exaggerated, puerile, and essentially unoriginal: Brecht, Benn and W. H. Auden cast too long a shadow. But there are as many good poems here (e.g. "lock lied", "call it love", "klage um ingo ledermann") as in most first collections, and even the failures are ambitious and remarkable failures, failures because of the poet's lack of maturity rather than because of any lack of talent. Indeed, few first volumes have suggested so much latent talent. That this talent did not lead to any real poetic achievement until 1964 is explained by Enzensberger's lack of self-criticism, and by the failure of too many of his reviewers to apply proper literary standards in their discussions of his first volume.

Landessprache (1960) marks no real advance on *verteidigung der wölfe*, though the process of self-discovery which was to figure so fruitfully in *blindenschrift* four years later begins in a poem like "anwesenheit" (L. 81f): "ich,/ich gehe nicht fort, ich bleibe,/... hier bin ich . . ." [15] But the phrase "hier bin ich" is only orchestrated poetically when it recurs in "lachesis lapponica" (Bl. 78). For the present Enzensberger is caught between past and future, waiting for the present:

"ich bin ein einstiger mann.
einst ist mir niemand erschienen,
einst wird er wiederkommen. ich harre
und warte nicht, sondern harre nur" (L. 82)[16]

However present reality is discovered not in this collection, but in the next, which goes on from just this position. No, essentially *landessprache* is the mixture as before : the poet has become the victim of the satirist's success. His anger is a studied pose which barely disguises the fact that at this time he really has little to say. There are no "friendly poems" : these only reappear in the third collection.

The best poems in *landessprache* are the cooler poems in which, paradoxically it might seem, real personal emotion is seen. Such a poem in which the poet's anger is kept cool, and in which real feeling is certainly present, is "das ende der eulen" (L. 30f), one of a number of Enzensberger's poems concerned with the threat of thermo-nuclear war. This is a good poem because of its particularity and form, and because the poet's (perfectly justifiable) anger is here controlled. The poem is informed by a compassion that is all too often lacking in his earlier "angry poems". That this compassion is directed not towards man, but towards "otters and seals ... the old owls of the earth", is itself significant. Mankind is seen as planning the act that will leave no trace—no trace of itself or of life on earth. The poet's pity is directed not towards the orphans or any other human victims of the possible apocalypse, but towards the world which is older, more numerous, and innocent : the animal world, and particularly the world of the oldest of all creatures, the creatures of the sea (his preference for sea-imagery very likely derives from living in Oslo-fjord). The end of the owls stands for the end of all wisdom, and in the context the end of wisdom means the end of life. Although the poet's pity is withheld from his fellow-men (who are collectively guilty), this pity is itself a sign of man's continuing humanity. There is an entirely fruitful tension between the theme and its treatment producing an admirably humane poem on man's contemporary inhumanity.

The same genuine emotion, the same humanity, and the same particularity, is seen in the poem "ehre sei der sellerie" (L. 62f), the title of which is reminiscent of W. H. Auden's "In Praise of Limestone" and Pablo Neruda's "Oda a la cebolla" ("Ode to an Onion"). This poem about "the delicate earth-heart, celery,/more human than man" is vitiated by its gratuitously provocative tone and by an unnecessary "shock-effect"—a parody of the Ave Maria—but remains one of the best poems in *landessprache*. Another good poem of a totally different kind is the macabre "die hebammen" with its ironical undertones of Georg Heym's "Der Krieg"; the poem suggests the apparent pointlessness of life through effectively disciplined, if cynical, treatment of the midwife-figure. This is a far cry from the echoes of Benn's "Biologie des Todes" in *verteidigung der wölfe*.

These three poems—"das ende der eulen", "ehre sei der sellerie", "die hebammen"—are the best in *landessprache*, yet in Enzensberger's *Gedichte* ... (1962), a selection from his first two volumes, two of these three poems, and one of the best poems in *verteidigung der wölfe* ("call it love"), do not appear, while other poems from *landessprache*, such as the derivative "lebenslauf" (an imitation of Brecht's "Vom armen B. B.") and the silly-sentimental "plädoyer für einen mörder", do appear. The implication is that Enzensberger is not the best judge of his own work—his lack of self-criticism has already been noted—or that he feels obliged to reprint the "successful" poems regardless of their quality. Two of his weakest poems appear in *landessprache*; they are "schaum" and "gewimmer und firmament", both apparently modelled on Allen Ginsberg's "Howl"; their howls of rage are as undisciplined and therefore unpoetic as Ginsberg's. Again the angriest poems are the weakest. Yeats' criticism of Ezra Pound, whom he accused of "raging at ... figures out of a child's book of beasts" (*Oxford Book of Modern Verse*, ed. W. B. Yeats, 1936, xxiii–xxiv) could be justly applied to not a little of Enzensberger's first two collections. While Enzensberger is certainly no "uneducated revolutionist"—far from it—the objects of his scorn and anger do at times appear to be imagined whipping-boys, "figures out of a child's book of beasts", rather than real flesh and blood philistines. And Yeats' view that Pound's work had "more style than form" (ibid.) is certainly applicable. No one could accuse Enzensberger of lacking style; he is a brilliant stylist; but the very diversity of his imagery and vocabulary sometimes seems to replace poetic form, for the dialectical development of a given theme. Too often in his first two collections the images, ideas or slogans are strung together in an uncritical manner, resulting in a satirically effective collage rather than a poetically effective pattern, a pre-poetic statement rather than a poetic enactment.

Enzensberger's best collection to date is quite certainly *blindenschrift* (1964). This is his most personal and most genuinely original collection. The weaknesses of the first two volumes are largely overcome here. His poetry now has "form" as well as "style". In the first poem, "küchenzettel" (Bl. 7f), there is a concentration on particulars and a dialectic treatment of the theme which were often lacking previously. The theme of the poem is, appropriately, the rediscovery of reality, the most ambitious and successful treatment of which we find in the poem "lachesis lapponica" discussed below. In this latter poem we read "hier ist nichts los . . . hier bin ich",[17] and in "küchenzettel" too the rediscovery of reality is accompanied by the rediscovery of self. The sign of continuing life in the last two lines ("links unten ganz in der ecke/seh ich einen katzenteller")[18] parallels the equally simple but equally promiseful ending of Brecht's "Gedanken über die Dauer des Exils" ("Sieh den kleinen Kastanienbaum im Eck des Hofes,/Zu dem du die Kanne voll Wasser schlepptest!").[19] What makes the poem remarkable in the context of Enzensberger's previous work is the genuine *personal* (as opposed to social) commitment, the genuine poetic elaboration of the theme, the ultra-simplicity of form, and the theme itself: the acceptance of life as it is and has always been. Here there is a genuine poetic pattern and development (as opposed to the unpatterned slogans of the earlier work); this pattern may be an obvious and elementary one, but this elementary quality is itself a part of the process of self-discovery; there is nothing artful about the simplicity of this poem, though it is simplicity of a more rudimentary, less subtle sort than in "lachesis lapponica". Both theme and form suggest that Enzensberger has now learnt from the "Taoist" lyrical poet Brecht, and from Günter Eich. The title and dedication of another outstanding poem in *blindenschrift*, "abgelegenes haus" (Bl. 12), presumably expresses a general debt to Günter Eich (cp. his *Abgelegene Gehöfte*, 1948). I have already suggested that Eich's advice in his poem "Wacht auf, denn eure Träume sind schlecht" ("seid Sand, nicht das Öl im Getriebe der Welt!")[20] was Enzensberger's starting point. Eich is, of course, the master of understatement, of which Enzensberger frequently makes effective use. Now he seems to have learnt from Eich's poetry as a whole, whose constant theme is the discovery of reality and therefore of self. The poem "abgelegenes haus" is again a poem of acceptance. The voice of terror coming from the tiny transistor is a most effective collage:

> "karibische krise . . . wäscht weisser
> und weisser und weisser . . .
> einsatzbereit . . . stufe drei . . .
> *that's the way i love you . . .*
> montanwerke kräftig erholt . . ."[21]

This collage (W. H. Auden has made similarly effective use of the radio) is no uncritical juxtaposition; it is a genuine snatch of the invisible voice of terror that fills the earth's atmosphere, and as such an intrinsic part of the poem. But—and this would have been unthinkable in the earlier poems—this voice of terror reassures the poet, for it shows that life is continuing. Life is accepted (cynically, but still accepted) and turned into poetry.

An early stage in the change of attitude that underlies both "küchenzettel" and "abgelegenes haus" is seen in "historischer prozess" (Bl. 55), where self-awareness leads to acceptance of the positive aspects of life rather than enumeration and rejection of the negative aspects. Like Günter Eich's famous "Inventur", this is essentially a stock-taking poem. The poet realizes that when all is said and done he is at least free, and that this freedom can be exercised in various elementary ways; and in this lupine century, even this is much. With this realization comes a new humility and sense of integration. The poem is again made all the more impressive by a radical simplicity, that most desirable of all poetic virtues.

Not all the poems in *blindenschrift* follow the pattern of these three poems. There are still "angry" poems and a few poems in which the various familiar weaknesses are still evident. In "auf das grab eines friedlichen mannes" (Bl. 28) the all too familiar anger is cool; the "gestic" language is effective; but the poem is weak, for the second and third stanzas are unnecessary, and what remains is a slight, cynical observation (the peace-loving man has got his peace now : he's dead). In "purgatorio" (Bl. 36) the pattern is a clever, satirically rather than poetically effective one; the result is an excellent satire or statement. Another poem, "bibliographie" (Bl. 24f), shows that Enzensberger has not yet been able to escape fully from the baleful influence of Benn's cerebral smartness, and several other poems shows that despite his outspoken rejection of Benn's aesthetic, he has not yet achieved a properly critical attitude towards Benn's poetic technique. The poet is still at times the victim of his own cleverness. But "küchenzettel" and "weiterung" show that he has finally come to terms with Brecht and learnt from his lyrical poetry; "weiterung" (Bl. 50) is a critical revision of Brecht's "An die Nachgeborenen" in the new context of the thermo-nuclear "flood". The trend in this latest collection is clear : he is finally returning to the manner and attitude of the best of his earliest poems, the "friendly poems" of *verteidigung der wölfe*. He has finally overcome his own success and rediscovered his own voice. Several things appear to have contributed to this. Living in Norway has probably greatly helped by keeping him away from the publicistic machine that would have further encouraged his satirical anti-self. His whole attitude to life has changed thanks to increasing self-criticism and maturity; and his whole view of poetry has changed too, so that he is now concerned with truth rather than provocation. He has probably been helped by his rediscovery of the poetry of William Carlos Williams, Brecht

(the private, lyrical poetry), Günter Eich, Erich Fried and Paul
Celan. He may well be indebted to William Carlos Williams for
the precise colloquialism and concentration on particulars of his
latest collection, while the syntactical experiments of Fried and
Celan seem to have helped him to articulate and develop his
themes. But without his new-found positive and poetic attitude to
life, no merely poetic influences could have transformed his work.
Williams, Brecht, and Eich have probably helped him to this new
acceptance of life.

The outstanding poem in *blindenschrift*, and by far the best
Enzensberger has yet written, is "lachesis lapponica" (Bl. 76–79).
The "new richness and suggestiveness of texture" of this poem has
been noted by a reviewer who wrote : "Here Herr Enzensberger
has succeeded in co-ordinating and controlling tensions at once
personal and cosmic, particular and general ... The confrontation
with solitude in bare Scandinavian landscapes seems to have provided the social involvement with a necessary dialectic complement." (*TLS*, September 3rd, 1964). Another way of putting it
would be to say that the social involvement has been provided with
a necessary poetic complement, and rejected in favour of poetic
involvement. The poem is aptly named : "lachesis" ("the
measurer") was one of the *moirai* or fates. The real theme of the
poem is the poet's discovery or rediscovery of his poetic self in
the silent empty wilderness of Lapland, that same "grey moor"
to which we already owe "das ende der eulen". The poem consists
of a fateful dialogue between the poet engaged in measuring
intangibles, and his satirical anti-self whose words are italicized and
whose identity is made quite clear in the poem; earlier the
satirist's impersonal voice had been embodied in the figure of
"niemand". The tension between poet and satirist, which had
been implicit in much of his earlier work, has here become explicit, has itself become the theme of this most impressive poem;
and beneath this conflict between lyric poet and social realist or
satirist can be seen another conflict : between poetry and socia*list*
realism, West and East. On this level this is the best *political* poem
Enzensberger has written. Here commitment is caused by a
particular experience—something poetically necessary but previously often lacking—and this experience is none other than the
poetic discovery of self : "hier stehe ich."[22] The "here" is
described in exact detail, which detail is more significant than the
inexact slogans and cynicism of the satirical anti-self. Social and
personal (poetic) involvement do not so much coincide and fuse as
clash fruitfully. The crazy bird in the poet's head shrieks for a
socially committed "standpoint", shrieks out for "victories"; but
the poet is no longer "fighting", is now involved in the "whiteness

in the wind" rather than in any abstract anger. The poet has the
last word : Enzensberger has outgrown his satirical earlier work
and is now committed to the "particulars of poetry/that difficult
art" (William Carlos Williams). In this poem there is a critical self-
awareness and a subtlety and precision of language that is quite new
and wholly admirable. This excellent poem is the clearest sign yet
that Enzensberger is capable of developing from a highly promis-
ing poet into a major one.

Critical Achievements

Enzensberger's actual achievement to date is arguably greater as
a critic than as a poet. He is also the editor of a number of admirable anthologies including : *museum der modernen poesie* (1960),
the most important of the post-1945 anthologies (covering the
period 1910 to 1945) and a notable contribution to the continued
internationalization of German poetry; *Allerleirauh. Viele schöne
Kinderreime* (1962), a most attractive anthology modelled on
Iona and Peter Opie's *The Oxford Nursery Rhyme Book* (1955);
and William Carlos Williams, *Gedichte* (1962), timely in that it
appeared at a time when Williams' immense poetic achievement
was being acknowledged by Enzensberger's contemporaries in the
USA, and particularly interesting in view of Williams' apparently
considerable influence on Enzensberger.

His first critical work was *Clemens Brentanos Poetik* (1961), a
highly successful translation "from Germanistic into German" of
his doctoral dissertation. In the present context it is sufficient to
say that this is not only the best analysis of Brentano's poetry to
date; it is an admirable piece of work by any standard, clearly the
work of a first-class critical intelligence. But Enzensberger has made
his real critical achievement in two later works, *Einzelheiten* (1962)
and *Politik und Verbrechen* (1964).

Einzelheiten is an outstanding volume of committed, non-
academic criticism. Enzensberger writes trenchantly on a wide
variety of subjects such as the language of *Der Spiegel*, the
sociological implications of the paperback industry, the "literary
Establishment" ("literarische Regierungspartei"), the "Aporien der
Avantgarde", the language of modern poetry, the poetry of
William Carlos Williams and of Pablo Neruda, etc. He concludes
with a manifesto on poetry and politics. Though sound in its basic
attitude, this concluding essay fails to do justice to the complexity
of its subject, the most important in the book and one which
closely concerns Enzensberger himself as a poet. He is concerned
here almost exclusively with the history of the "Herrscherlob",[23]
though he admits that in a sense almost all poetry is political

poetry. What he does not consider adequately is the anti-government or anti-establishment political poem or satire. For this the most important questions are (i) to whom is this sort of political poem addressed? (ii) what effect can it hope to achieve? and (iii) where exactly does the boundary fall between "political poetry" in this sense and "poetry"? In view of his own poetic practice, one might expect Enzensberger to face up to these questions. He does not, and is least objective where questions concerning his own work are concerned. But *Einzelheiten* is a most impressive achievement for a young critic. It shows his formidable range and critical intelligence, also a real awareness of the topics that matter. In many ways this is a landmark in recent German criticism, which is by far the weakest point in German literature since the war, a point which has indeed been illustrated by the critics' reactions to Enzensberger's poetry. How many other recent German critics have been so genuinely critical, and how many possess, or have possessed, such *esprit*?

Politik und Verbrechen, Enzensberger's latest and best critical work, is an attempt, as he puts it, to clarify a connection by which all may perish, but for which no one is responsible : the connection between politics and crime. As such it is a logical development from *Einzelheiten* and his poetry. Of all the things that matter today, nothing matters more than this : under what circumstances can and does political responsibility become criminal irresponsibility? What is the connection between idealism and criminality? What is "treason"? These and many other related questions Enzensberger examines in detail and with full documentation. His themes and conclusions are presented more generally in the first and last chapters, "Reflexionen vor einem Glaskasten", and "Zur Theorie des Verrats"; the rest of the book consists of brilliantly written case-histories. He has clearly been stimulated by Margret Boveri's *Der Verrat im 20. Jahrhundert*, and has equally clearly been influenced by Elias Canetti's masterly study of the connections between political power and paranoia, *Masse und Macht* (1960). Now that "civilization" has reached the stage where life on earth could be destroyed by a paranoiac or "Träumer des Absoluten"[24] (Karl Marx) in the wrong place, Enzensberger's investigation is timely. It is only a few years since a critic wrote in the *Times Literary Supplement* (October 13th, 1961) that Enzensberger was "in danger of becoming fixed in a permanent pose of flippancy." The danger was a very real one; the satirist was the victim of his own success, and the poet was the victim of the satirist's success. But *Politik und Verbrechen* shows that Enzensberger has developed into a constructive social critic. There is nothing frivolous about producing a fully documented and highly readable study of the type of personality that could perform if not the final act of destruction, then at least the greatest crime of all— and perform it in the name of "freedom". Like Canetti's *Masse und Macht* and Broch's *Massenpsychologie,* it is a relevant and responsible contribution to life in our politically irresponsible century.

TRANSLATIONS

1. A conversation about trees is almost a crime/because it includes a silence about so many misdeeds.

2. zero-point.

3. Do what is unprofitable, sing the songs people don't expect to hear from your mouth!/Be troublesome, be sand not oil in the gears of the world!

4. Bad men are struck with terror by your claws./Good men are struck with wonder at your grace./This I/should like to hear/said of my verse.

5. Here is valid only/hard poetry at a fixed rate of charges:/condensare!.../... text-in-clear, please.

6. A process of coming to terms with oneself by oneself.

7. World of expression.

8. Look in the mirror: cowardly,/shunning the hardship of truth,/unwilling to learn, abandoning thought/to the wolves.

9. You'll not change the world.

10. My voice is a gentle snare/do not get caught/my reed is a silken dagger/do not listen/kee wit kee wit kee wit.

11. It's a nice evening.

12. Where are you?

13. Where are you when you walk beside me?

14. He is dead who played the organs, who caressed them/... you can share it with no one, with no widow,/with no dog. He who knew the fountain, played the organ./With a mouth full of griefs, with a mouth full of sand.

15. I,/I do not go away, I remain here,/... here I am.

16. I am a one-time man./Once nobody appeared to me,/one day he will come again. I am waiting/and not expecting, just waiting.

17. Here nothing's wrong ... here I am.

18. Right down in the left-hand corner/I see a plate for the cat.

19. Look at the little chestnut tree in the corner of the yard/to which you carry the jug of water.

20. Be sand not oil in the gears of the world.

21. Caribbean crisis ... washes whiter/and whiter and whiter .../ready to fly out ... phase three .../that's the way I love you .../mining shares back to par ...

22. Here I stand.
23. Eulogy to the ruler.
24. Dreamer of the absolute.

SELECT BIBLIOGRAPHY

a. *Enzensberger's main works*

Poetry

verteidigung der wölfe, Frankfurt/M. (Suhrkamp), 1957.
landessprache, Frankfurt/M. (Suhrkamp), 1960.
Gedichte—Die Entstehung eines Gedichts, Frankfurt/M. (Suhrkamp), 1962 (=suhrkamp texte, 10; repr. 1963 in new series: edition suhrkamp, 20).
blindenschrift, Frankfurt/M. (Suhrkamp), 1964.

Criticism

Clemens Brentanos Poetik, Munich (Hanser), 1961.
"Scherenschleifer und Poeten", in *Mein Gedicht ist mein Messer*, ed. Hans Bender, List-Bücher, 1961 (not in original 1955 ed.).
Einzelheiten. Essays, Frankfurt/M. (Suhrkamp), 1962. (the concluding essay, "Poesie und Politik", repr. edition suhrkamp, 1965, under title *Einzelheiten II*).
"In Search of the Lost Language", *Encounter*, Vol. XXI, No. 3, Sept. 1963.
Politik und Verbrechen, Frankfurt/M. (Suhrkamp), 1964 (see also: Hannah Arendt—Hans Magnus Enzensberger, "Politik und Verbrechen. Ein Briefwechsel", *Merkur*, XIX. Jg., Heft 4, April 1965).

Editions, Translations, etc.

Zupp. Kinderbuch, Olten (Walter), 1958.
Clemens Brentano, *Gedichte, Erzählungen, Briefe*, Frankfurt/M. (Fischer-Bücherei), 1958.
museum der modernen poesie, Frankfurt/M. (Suhrkamp), 1960 (repr. dtv, 1965).
Allerleirauh Viele schöne Kinderreime, Frankfurt/M. (Suhrkamp), 1961.
William Carlos Williams, *Gedichte*, Frankfurt/M. (Bibliothek Suhrkamp), 1962.
César Vallejo, *Gedichte*, Frankfurt/M. (Bibliothek Suhrkamp), 1963.

Translations of Poems

See: *New German Poets*, ed. Jerome Rothenberg, San Francisco (City Lights Books), 1959; *Modern German Poetry 1910–1960*, ed. Michael Hamburger & Christopher Middleton, London (MacGibbon & Kee), 1962; *Twentieth-Century German Verse*, ed. Patrick Bridgwater, Harmondsworth (Penguin Books), 1963; *Contemporary German Poetry*, ed.

Gertrude Clorius Schwebell, N.Y. (New Directions), 1964; *Encounter*, April 1964; *TLS*, September 3rd, 1964; etc.

b. *Criticism of his work*

Alfred Andersch, "Kritik" (=rev. of *verteidigung der wölfe*), *Frankfurter Hefte*, Feb. 1958.

Patrick Bridgwater, "The Making of a Poet: H. M. Enzensberger", *German Life and Letters* (in the press).

Reinhold Grimm, "Montierte Lyrik", in Heinz Otto Bürger & Reinhold Grimm, *Evokation und Montage. Drei Beiträge zum Verständnis moderner deutscher Lyrik*, Göttingen (Sachse & Pohl), 1961.

Hans Egon Holthusen, "Die Zornigen, die Gesellschaft und das Glück", in his *Kritisches Verstehen*, Munich (Piper), 1961.

Walter Jens, "Paukenschlag und Kantilene", *Die Zeit*, August 5th, 1960.

F. Stroh, "Hans Magnus Enzensberger: Kritiker und Poet", *Moderna Sprak*, LVI, 3, 1962.

Martin Walser, "Einer der auszog, das Fürchten zu verlernen", *Die Zeit*, September 15th, 1961.

Werner Weber, "Nachwort" in HME, *Gedichte—Die Entstehung eines Gedichts* (see above).

East German Literature

East German Literature

by HELMUT WINTER

(S. Fischer Verlag, previously Lektor at the University of Bristol)

I

IT has been said that German literature is not a means of man's orientation in a particular historical and social situation (as English literature very often is) but is rather a way of questioning the position of the individual, of justifying and defining it. German literature would tend to create a world of ideas which is considered superior to any kind of reality. Such a definition fits contemporary West German as well as East German literature only with considerable reservations. While contemporary western literature usually equates isolated individual experiences to reality, most East German writers try to comprehend their experiences and reactions in a broader sociological connection determined by the responsibilities of the individual towards society. This attitude has a remarkable tradition in German literature, going back over Schiller and Hutten to Walther von der Vogelweide. Following the line of committed writers such as Heine, Büchner, Tucholsky, or Fallada the immediate forerunners of East German literature are Arnold Zweig, Anna Seghers, Johannes R. Becher and Bertolt Brecht, who all returned after their emigration to East, not West Germany.

Johannes R. Becher (1891–1958) has had hardly any influence in spite of all his official acclaim. However Bertolt Brecht (1898–1956) had a stronger effect, and his work still overshadows East German literature. As no East German dramatist has yet found a style independent from him (except, perhaps, Peter Hacks, living in East Germany only since 1955), East German drama at present is hardly worth consideration. The developments in the novel and lyric poetry are the most interesting ones.

The novelists can comparatively easily be grouped by generations. After the bourgeois novels of the older generation represented by Arnold Zweig and Anna Seghers, the outstanding antifascist novel to appear was *Nackt unter Wölfen* by Bruno Apitz. The most noteworthy portrayals of social changes in East Germany came from Erwin Strittmatter and Erik Neutsch, the most revealing presentations of problems resulting from Germany's partition from Hermann Kant and Christa Wolf. Among the more signifi-

261

cant lyric poets are on the one hand the almost unpolitical Peter
Huchel and Johannes Bobrowski, on the other committed young
poets such as Günter Kunert, Wolf Biermann and Volker Braun.

II

Writers like Goethe or Thomas Mann outlived the attitudes of
their earlier works, and the same could be said for Arnold Zweig
(born in 1887) who is revered in East Germany as a classic. The
saddler's son from Glogau studied philosophy and psychology and
then wrote with *Der Streit um den Sergeanten Grischa* (1927) one
of the greatest literary successes of the 1920s. The book was concerned with the First World War, and its main figures also
appeared in Zweig's next novels which together form the *Grischa*
cycle. With *Feuerpause* (1954), *Die Zeit ist reif* (1957) and *Traum
ist teuer* (1963) he rounded off his portraiture of the German
scene between the two wars.

Junge Frau von 1914 is the love story of a banker's daughter
who, against her parents' wishes, marries the penniless writer
Bertin. Through various experiences she slowly matures into a
woman. *Erziehung vor Verdun* is about Bertin's front line
experiences and the tragic death of his two best friends. *Grischa*
tells of a Russian prisoner of war who escapes, is caught, court-
martialled and shot—just as in John Wilson's *King and Country*
a handful of brave men desperately and vainly try to fight against
the merciless machinery of wartime justice. *Einsetzung eines Königs*
narrates how in 1918 the main character Winfrid amid the dis-
orders around the Latvian throne develops into a democrat.

The language of Zweig's massive period panorama is initially
clearly influenced by impressionism and *l'art pour l'art*; later a
detailed and yet economic narrative style predominates, reminiscent
sometimes of Fontane's later novels. Consciously opposed to the
German classical novel, Zweig does not follow the patterns of
individual lives but rather develops his plots from the interplay of
cause and effect. The artistic value of a novel is, however, rarely
determined by exact descriptions of historical situations. The
Grischa cycle is also an attack on Prussian militarism, but that is
not all its scope. The reader is moved by the continual clash of
ideals, the inhumanity of military discipline, unhappy love, corruption, and political intrigues, and thus Zweig's novels become in
their best moments parables of human life.

After 1933 Zweig, a Jew, had to emigrate. He settled down in
Haifa and wrote *Das Beil von Wandsbeck* (1943), one of the most
sensitive books about the Germans under Hitler. In 1948 he decided
to return to East Germany because he believed his antifascist and

socialist ideas would have their greatest effect there. He was
appointed president of the East Berlin Academy of Arts and since
then his literary activities have been mainly concerned with peti-
tions against rearmament and such like. His three post-war books
have not reached the level of his earlier works because obviously
he is now too far from their subject of Germany 1910 to 1930.
Like Brecht, Arnold Zweig could not see his way to using the
changed situation in East Germany as literary material.

His narrative method has often been compared with that of
Thomas Mann. It is, however, completely rational and down to
earth. His language has a visual rather than musical structure;
colourful and tactile it names reality rather than evokes it. If for
many critics he has outlived his fame as a keen-eyed observer of a
significant period of German history and as a penetrating analyst
of human character, his influence on the younger East German
writers is quite unmistakable.

Anna Seghers' work, highly honoured in Eastern Europe, is but
little known in the West. She comes from a bourgeois background,
studied the history of art and Chinese civilization and became a
member of the communist party in the late twenties. Her first
story *Aufstand der Fischer von St. Barbara* (1928) which brought
her, at the age of 28, the Kleist prize, deals with the desperate
struggle of Breton fishermen against their employers and already
shows her characteristics as a writer. The language is compact and
sober and reveals the stresses behind man's use of power. At the
end of the story we read :

> Aber längst nachdem die Soldaten zurückgezogen, die Fischer
> auf der See waren, saß der Aufstand noch auf dem leeren, som-
> merlich kahlen Marktplatz und dachte ruhig an die Seinigen.[1]

Her next major work was the *Novelle, Auf dem Wege zur
Amerikanischen Botschaft* (1930). A man, accidentally involved in
a protest march against the execution of Sacco and Vanzetti, cannot tear himself away from the demonstration and is one of the
first to be shot down by the police.

In 1933 Anna Seghers had to emigrate. *Das siebte Kreuz*, her
greatest success, published 1941 in English and a little later in
German, was mainly written in France and Mexico. It tells of the
flight of seven prisoners from a concentration camp. The com-
mandant has set up seven crosses for the fugitives, all except one
finding their victim. Anna Seghers is clearly influenced by modern
narrative methods in the way she gives a panorama of Nazi Germany through meticulously worked out individual episodes. Her
strength does not lie as with Thomas Mann in turns of intellectual
irony or as with Heinrich Mann in satirical classification of char-

acters but in a clear delineation of a situation in all its different aspects. The quality of the novel lies in its uncommonly strong appeal to the imagination of the reader who is not on the side of the last fugitive because he is a communist, but because he is a victim of a dictatorship. Anna Seghers attacks the Nazi terror and with it every type of terror. The marxist critics objected to the purely topographical description of the various social strata in Nazi Germany. In a famous correspondence with the author Georg Lukács claimed that contemporary literature must follow the tradition of realist writers such as Thomas Mann, Romain Rolland or Maxim Gorky. They must describe society in its totality from one critical standpoint and thus point out the way for the reader to follow. (Lukács' anxiety seemed only too easily understandable faced with the fascist tendencies of such writers as Montherlant, Pound or Ernst Jünger.) Anna Seghers, however, defended her technique of montage and documentation on the grounds that this was the most suitable for her work. In later novels her marxist position becomes clearer. In 1944 she published *Transit*, a depressing book about German refugees waiting for their visas in Marseilles. In 1948 appeared *Der Ausflug der toten Mädchen*, a tale of her early days in Mainz, punctuated with episodes from the Nazi period. The abrupt, direct, Kleistian style and the ingenuity of the intricate construction have a forceful effect. *Die Toten bleiben jung* (1949) is another attempt to depict the interwar years by the changes of human character which are not random developments, but express a moral attitude (or lack of it) and a determined relationship towards society and traditions. The story develops the concept of the infallibility of the communist idea, but as yet with difficulty and not without concessions to the demands of narrative form. The novel *Die Entscheidung* (1959) has only little in common with the best of Anna Seghers' work. It deals with the acceptance of communism by a young generation of workers in an East German steelworks against the temptations of West German capitalism. The book is largely propaganda; such material is today handled by the younger East German writers with more conviction and effect.

Stefan Heym's *Kreuzfahrer von heute* (1950), Dieter Noll's *Die Abenteuer des Werner Holt* (two vols., 1960–63), Max Walter Schultz' *Wir sind nich Staub im Wind* (1962) and Günter de Bruyn's *Der Hohlweg* (1963) are all less significant antifascist novels than Bruno Apitz' *Nackt unter Wölfen* (1958). This book bears witness to the author's sufferings and moral conviction. Apitz, born 1900 in Leipzig as the twelfth child of an oilcloth printer and a laundress, became a stamp-cutter, an antiquary's assistant and an actor, was imprisoned in 1917 on account of antiwar propaganda and after 1933 spent nine years in various concentration camps.

The novel opens with a description of a muster parade in Buchenwald in April 1945. The Jewish prisoner Jankowski has brought into the camp a half-starved child hidden in a case. He manages to bring the case through to the cloth store of the camp where some of the prisoners hide the child in a corner. Höfel, a member of the international communist underground organization in the camp led by a Soviet prisoner, is responsible for training the group in the use of arms. The child has to be removed from the cloth store so as not to endanger the conspiracy. Fearing the arrival of the invading armies the SS is on the point of evacuating or destroying the prisoners; the conspirators decide it is time to act. Höfel reacts out of instinct against the command by the Soviet prisoner to throw the child out. Apitz intensifies the situation so that either 50,000 prisoners can attempt to save themselves at the last moment, or a handful of prisoners can protect the life of a half-starved child and risk all else. Höfel, suspected by the SS, is thrown into a bunker and tortured, but reveals nothing. In the last hours of the war the conspirators show their hand and the rage of the prisoners explosively breaks out. Overrunning the guards they stagger exhaustedly out of the camp to meet the Americans, carrying in triumph the living child.

The themes of the novel are the protection of life against oppression and the troth of conspirators. The oppressive atmosphere of Buchenwald stands out clearly, yet one might ask if this effect could not have been achieved by documents or statistics. However, the fate of living beings always calls more strongly to the reader's sympathy who automatically identifies himself with the prisoners. They suddenly represent all oppressed people, just as the SS stands for all dictatorship in Anna Seghers' work. These are no longer private and individual feelings, and the effect of reading such a novel is to sharpen one's senses for the decisive moments of life in general rather than to offer a more precise attitude towards everyday problems. The symbolic force of the characters makes them more than individuals caught in the atmosphere of the concentration camp, and this rests to a great extent on the compelling conflict between the prisoners. The actual value of the book lies in its vivid portrayal of oppression which goes further than mere accusation and tries to see the events in their historical context. The anger it arouses comes from no abstract idea or neurotic sensitivity but is the natural result of the realistic narrative method of the author. Such a novel, even if it is formally traditional and linguistically plain, can find in a moment of existence moral significance for the whole of life. It is in this respect that *Nackt unter Wölfen* goes further than other concentration camp novels, even beyond Anna Segher's *Das Siebte Kreuz* or Ernst Wiechert's *Der Totenwald*.

III

Post-war East German literature still stood clearly under the influence of the great bourgeois writers and of those in exile. War and resistance novels by Theodor Plivier (1892–1955), Willi Bredel (1901–64), Ehm Welk (1884–1964) and Bodo Uhse (1904–63) were now written. Simultaneously an increasing trend of literature dealing with the social changes in East Germany arose, at first still strongly modelled on Soviet writers such as Fedin, Gladkov, Ostrowski and Fadejev and still on a relatively modest level (e.g. *Menschen an unserer Seite* (1951) by Eduard Claudius; *Tinko* (1954) by Erwin Strittmatter; *Roheisen* (1955) by Hans Marchwitza).

After the short liberalization of intellectual life during 1956–57 the so-called hard prose (*"harte Prosa"*) dominated for a short time, the style of Hemingway, seen at its most interesting in Karl Heinz Jakob's *Beschreibung eines Sommers* (1961) and in the short stories of Karl Mundstock (born 1915), Harry Thürk (born 1927) and Hans Pfeiffer (born 1925).

The most recent development began with the *"Bitterfelder Weg"*, a movement of *"schreibende Arbeiter"* which laid the foundation for the new educative and social novel. The first attempts were Anna Seghers' *Die Entscheidung* (1959), Herbert Nachbar's *Hochzeit von Länneken* (1960) and Bernhard Seeger's *Herbstrauch* (1961). One of the most controversial of these books was *Spur der Steine* (1964) by Erik Neutsch, a journalist born in 1931. The variety of problems in the construction of a socialist society in East Germany is depicted over 900 pages against the example of the setting up of a large chemical plant. The main characters are the young party organizer Horrath who enthusiastically tries to make this an outstanding example of socialist progress, but allows himself to be implicated in an extramarital relationship with the young and attractive woman engineer Katrin Klee and consequently is demoted by the party to a casual labourer; Balla who under Horrath's influence develops from a work-obsessed, politically disinterested daredevil into a consciously socialist foreman, and finally the woman engineer Klee who keeps the relationship with her party secretary secret but proves at the end to be of greater moral and political consequence than Horrath. Numerous secondary characters are grouped around these three, e.g. the bourgeois,

highly talented but politically narrow-minded engineer Hessel-
barth or the roughneck veteran worker Paul Klee (sic).

Balla is really the hero of the book. Clearly he is meant to
represent the new relationship of the individual to a young socialist
society. The new society enables him to develop his personality,
and this in turn brings about the progress of that society. Neutsch's
book recalls with its themes the Soviet novelist Galina Nikolajeva's
The Battle (1962) which incited violent discussions in East Germany. Here too there is an illegal love relationship which disturbs
the moral code of society, although it influences those concerned
in a positive way. In *Spur der Steine* the many complications which
appear in the early phases of a socialist society are reflected in all
kinds of episodes (for example the collectivization of agriculture,
bourgeois ideology, etc.), and this is partly why the novel is so
popular in East Germany. But for all its richness of detail it never
exhausts the fullness of life, the quality of experience being sometimes sacrificed for quantitative description of the chemical plant.
This comes out above all in the language which is very often static
and mechanical. It is the variety of levels of language which
makes for the richness of realist literature, because this expresses
best of all the dialectical interplay of ideas and character. Some
symbolic scenes in the book are successful, however, for instance
Kati's and Balla's experiences on a Soviet building site. An episode
like this, although complete in itself, can throw a new light on the
individual moment. Neutsch's novel is certainly no great work
of art, but an honest, positive book that in spite of its weaknesses
impressively catches the atmosphere of the struggle towards a new
social order in East Germany.

If Neutsch's kaleidoscopic work may be compared with Martin
Walser's *Halbzeit*, the mirror image of West German society, then
corresponding to Günter Grass's novels would be the writing of
Erwin Strittmatter. Both Grass and Strittmatter work more or less
consciously in the tradition of the picaresque novel (just as Herbert
Jobs with his books *Der Findling* (1957), *Der Zögling* (1959), and
Der Vagabund (1963) and Manfred Bieler, one of the most promis-
ing young East German authors, with his satirical novel *Bonifaz*
(1963)).

One of the first to recognize Strittmatter's talent was Bertolt
Brecht who produced with his own company the hitherto completely unknown journalist's first play *Katzgraben* (1954). (Brecht's
production notes for *Katzgraben*, incidentally, contain some remarkable new formulations of his aesthetic theories.) After Brecht's
death Strittmatter, who meanwhile had become president of the
East German writers' association and had had a great success with
Tinko (1954), published two novels which proved him to be one

of the most original East German writers. Whereas *Der Wunder-*
täter (1957) still follows closely the model of the picaresque novel,
Ole Bienkopp (1963) marks a new phase in Strittmatter's work.

It tells of a farm labourer's son who tries after the war to introduce new ways of work in his village. In spite of countless difficulties, often with his own, communist, party, he gradually succeeds in setting up something like a collective farm. However, the
party condemns his singlemindedness as not correspondent to their
current teaching and has him removed. Although after a shattered
marriage he once again finds happiness with the young farm hand
Märtke, his will has been broken and he dies, too late to see the
eventual acceptance of his ideas.

Immediately after the book's publication there were conflicting
arguments, as for the first time an officially recognized writer had
here unashamedly attacked incisive political decisions. After a
lively debate it was finally decided to accept the novel primarily
as an important humorist *Entwicklungsroman.* Like its prede-
cessors *Ole Bienkopp* is full of colourful dialogues, carefully con-
toured characters and an unbridled fancy for comedy of situation.
The naïve narrative approach for which the author is continually
criticized is a legitimate and frequently used literary technique; one
only has to think of Eichendorff's *Taugenichts* (or, more recently,
of Salinger's *Catcher in the Rye*). Although *Ole Bienkopp* takes
place in a village near Berlin it is by no means a regional novel.
Already on the first pages Strittmatter's extraordinary visual
descriptive power is clear, his language being direct, compact, and
full of peasant imagery. From the beginning he sets himself within
the mental horizon of his heroes and thus makes them convincing.
A decidedly visual technique can easily become monotonous, and
the reader needs time to accustom himself to Strittmatter's style
which in its simple artistry sometimes touches on whimsy. Yet for
the most part he gives an impression of great density, based above
all on careful arrangement of details. The proof of a good novelist
is his handling of long scenes with large numbers of people which
are always calling for dramatization; for example, a good writer
will always split up a marriage or a death-bed scene into its small,
living fragments. Strittmatter throws into perspective the tragi-
comedy of Bienkopp's marriage together with the often sardonic
farce of parish pump politics by means of apt settings which only
occasionally appear construed.

It is astonishing that the theme "divided Germany" has been
so seldom used by writers in East and West. Leaving aside plays
like Gerd Oehlschlegel's *Romeo und Julia in Berlin* (1953), Herbert
Reinecker's *Nachtzug* (1963) or Theodor Schübel's *Wo liegt Jena?*
(1965) which make sentimental second-rate tragedies out of this

material, the most note-worthy attempts to portray this theme are in West Germany the novels *Mutmassungen über Jakob* (1959), *Das dritte Buch über Achim* (1961) and *Zwei Ansichten* (1965) by Uwe Johnson. He uses the most modern and the most fashionable literary devices and succeeds in impressing the average reader without fully enlightening him.

In East Germany there are more books about the partition, although of varying quality. The most successful novel on this subject so far (two others are Brigitte Reiman's *Die Geschwister* (1962) and Juri Brezan's *Eine Liebesgeschichte* (1963)) is Christa Wolf's *Der geteilte Himmel* (1963) which caused an immediate and considerable sensation and was adapted as an equally controversial film.

The book describes the love story of a young girl, Rita, who has grown up in the country and has got to know the chemist Manfred during the holidays. She moves to the town and there begins her training as a teacher, during which she has to do practical work in a waggon factory. For several weeks she works in a group where she is the only woman, and is so taken up with the countless problems of the group and the factory that she and Manfred lose contact with one another, he having just graduated and joined a new project in a chemical works. In addition Rita is ill at ease in Manfred's home, for his parents embody a rigid conservatism. When Manfred comes across difficulties in his work and has to watch while Rita falls more and more under the spell of her young local party secretary he flees from life in East Germany to West Berlin. Rita is confused and disappointed, but eventually visits Manfred in Berlin. In the decisive scene of the book in a restaurant on the Kurfürstendamm, it becomes clear from the way in which they talk past one another that they have become too much involved in their respective environments to be able to come together. Manfred explains to her :

> Ja denkst du denn, ich wäre nicht auch mal voller Hoffnung gewesen? Ich hätte nicht auch mal gedacht, mit den Wurzeln des Übels würde man auch das Übel aus der Welt ausreißen? Aber es hat tausend Wurzeln. Es ist nicht auszurotten. Edel vielleicht, sich weiter daran zu versuchen. Aber ohne Überzeugung wird Edelmut zur Grimasse.[2]

He tries in vain to entice her with descriptions of his new and brilliant position. Rita goes back to the East, exhausted by all the excitement and seriously ill. She breaks down, attempts suicide and is put in a sanatorium. The book ends optimistically with Rita, now well again, visiting one of her colleagues and giving him encouragement.

Christa Wolf (who before this had only published the *Moskauer Novelle* (1961)) once said that the main problem of many young people is always the tension between the ideal and reality, between waiting for happiness and experiencing it. This is indeed an accurate description of the individual's problems in East Germany. The main theme of her novel is Rita's way to herself and to a happy life. It is both the attraction and the limitation of the book that it shows this developing awareness (or, in other words, this gradual phasing-out of Rita's love) as a provisional stage on the way to acceptance of the socialist ethos. The author's ideal and aim shows up all too clearly; Rita as a new woman, no longer with spontaneous thoughts and feelings (in contrast to the pessimistic, fickle Manfred) lives and sees through the way of the world, overcomes estrangement and in spite of all opposition applies herself fully to the development of socialism. This is expressed through a number of more or less skilfully combined symbols and motifs which give substance to the plot and raise it above its commonplace implications. In this respect Christa Wolf's novel has been compared with Uwe Johnson's *Mutmassungen über Jakob*. Both books begin with a similar episode, someone walking across the railway line and meeting with an accident in the mist. Johnson's hero apparently has realized that he cannot live in East Germany; Christa Wolf's decides to live there but falls giddily on the rail, momentarily helpless and desperate. For both the railway is a symbol of the threatening mechanism of official-dom. While Johnson tries to record the reality of life in both parts of Germany through inner monologues and a narrator's frag-mentary sketches, Christa Wolf describes in traditional and at times even trite language the conflict of people who must live in East Germany and in spite of all shortcomings make the best of their lives. The unusual popularity of the novel is again partly explained by the many critical asides about the more unpleasant sides of life in East Germany.

The book lacks, however, artistic vitality to be truly significant. The material is too obviously organized, the motifs and symbols are too clearly scattered through the novel. One of the greatest dangers for books of this kind is that they press life into too narrow a pattern. The other extreme can be seen in Johnson where the author gives too many aspects of life and obviously cannot quite keep control of them.

IV

Like the prose literature East German lyric poetry initially was modelled on the works of those in exile. Bertolt Brecht, Johannes

R. Becher and Erich Weinert during their exile had developed social lyric into an effective political weapon. In particular Brecht's wartime poems with the stupendous skill hidden in their simplicity and in their indirect line of argument exercized a decisive influence on the language of East German lyrics. In the first postwar years it became clear, however, that the aggressiveness and sharp aim of lyrics written in exile could not simply be transferred to poetic descriptions of the new situation in East Germany. Becher's *Deutsche Sonette* (1952) or Louis Fürnberg's *Das wunderbare Gesetz* (1956) showed astonishingly clearly that indiscriminate praise of social changes necessarily lowers the level of lyric poetry. Even Brecht's political poems at the time were often shockingly primitive.

In the late fifties political poetry such as Georg Maurer's *Dreistrophenkalender* (1961), Günter Deicke's *Gesetz* (1958) or Armin Müller's *Schwarze Asche—weisse Vögel* (1958) became somewhat freer and more individual, but only very recently has committed East German lyric poetry again found a place on the European scene.

Two poets have a particular place in this development, having but little to do with political lyric, Peter Huchel and Johannes Bobrowski.

Peter Huchel, born 1903 in Berlin, has above all made his name for many years as the editor of the East German periodical *Sinn und Form*. Under him this became one of the best literary magazines in Germany, standing on a par with the West German *Akzente* and leaving the official East German *Neue Deutsche Literatur* far behind. The fame of Huchel as a lyric poet (which is much higher in West Germany than in the East) rests on a slender, widely scattered number of poems which so far have appeared in two collections : *Gedichte* (1948) and *Chausseen, Chausseen* (1963).

Huchel began with poems about his childhood in the village of Alt-Langerwiesch in Mark Brandenburg, in which the poet withdraws into a world of dreams and memories :

> Damals ging noch am Abend der Wind
> Mit starken Schultern rüttelnd ums Haus.
> Das Laub der Linde sprach mit dem Kind,
> Das Gras sandte seine Seele aus.[3]

Huchel is both solitary and deeply rooted in the landscape and life of the countryside. Free from expressionist fervour he follows his own way; for him poetry has always to renew itself from the language of the people, and if the poet uses the language of work without ornamentation he will find new ways for poetry. His own language is simple, never private, always to the point :

> Wenn aus den Eichen
> Der Tau der Frühe leckt,
> Knarren die Türen, rädern die Speichen
> Vom Schrei der Hähne geweckt.
> Noch unterm Laken
> Des Mondes schlafen die Wiesen, kühl und hell.[4]

Many of his poems deal with mythical figures such as "the maid" whom Huchel continually invokes. In such moments logic often parts from feeling, and the mood which Huchel conjures up with skilful assonances and numerous comparisons with "like" is their outstanding feature. Sometimes their effect comes from the poet's all too direct response to his experiences.

Huchel was silent from 1933 to 1945. In the poems he published after the war there is hardly any trace of the nature lyrics of his earlier years. He now sees nature as death and decay, horror and destruction. His images at this stage remind one of the use of metaphor by Rupert Brooke or Wilfred Owen. His landscapes are in ruin and overgrown :

> Sie gingen durch Pfahl und Stacheldraht
> Vorbei am glosenden Tank
> Und über die ölig verbrannte Saat
> Hinunter den lehmigen Hang.[5]

After a few enthusiastic poems about the reform of agrarian economy in East Germany (*Das Gesetz*) which Huchel wrote while he was artistic director of the Berlin radio, and after an exotic cycle *Malaya*, he returned again to the themes of his youth. His most recent poems have a resigned tone of tired aloofness :

> Der Jäger schleppt nun heim die Beute,
> Das kiefernästig starrende Geweih.
> Der Sinnende sucht andere Spur.
> Er geht am Hohlweg still vorbei,
> Wo goldner Rauch vom Baume fuhr.
> Und Stunden wehn, vom Alter weise,
> Gedanken wie der Vögel Reise,
> Und manches Wort wird Brot und Salz.[6]

Huchel's poetry is now less formal, preferring free rhythms and only occasionally returning to strophe and rhyme. What sometimes is easily accepted in West Germany as the lyric of hidden revolt, appears on closer inspection to stand in the debt of Hölderlin and Trakl. Huchel is not concerned with traditional themes of nature

or philosophy but drifts moodily around the ruins of a world which
has become strange to him and which terrifies him :

> Wohin du stürzt, o Seele,
> Nicht weiß es die Nacht.
> Denn da ist nichts
> Als vieler Wesen stumme Angst.[7]

Within the realization that his poetry cannot alter the world
around him Huchel has recognized the limitations of his position;
this is an attitude which makes his lyric far more typical of the
literary situation in West Germany than in East Germany. This
seems also to be another proof for the almost inevitable development of an unpolitical lyric poet to isolated resignation in a totalitarian state. In comparison with Oskar Loerke or Wilhelm
Lehmann, Huchel has concentrated less on pure invocative nature
poetry than on poems more directly concerned with man. However much he may be compared with Trakl or even Jessenin, he
is above all a guardian of poetic integrity in East Germany.

Any poet showing this quality in the East is thereby certain of
an interested public in the West. Together with Peter Huchel one
usually finds in recent West German lyric anthologies Johannes
Bobrowski who adds to his interest by working for a decidedly
christian publishing house in East Berlin. Born 1917 in East
Prussia and, incidentally, a relative of Joseph Conrad, he first
became well known when he won the prize of the Gruppe 47 and
the Viennese Alma Koenig prize in 1962. He died in 1965.
His two volumes of poetry *Sarmatische Zeit* (1961) and *Schattenland Ströme* (1962) appeared in both East and West Germany and
were received by critics on both sides with applause—based indeed
on different motifs. His novel *Levins Mühle* (1964) and the short
stories *Mäusefest* (1965) had a similar reception.

In the volume *Schattenland Ströme* is the poem

> *Dorfmusik*
> Letztes Boot darin ich fahr
> keinen Hut mehr auf dem Haar
> in vier Eichenbrettern weiß
> mit der Handvoll Rautenreis
> meine Freunde gehn umher
> einer bläst auf der Trompete
> einer bläst auf der Posaune
> Boot werd mir nicht überschwer
> hör die andern reden laut :
> dieser hat auf Sand gebaut

Ruft vom Brunnenbaum die Krähe
von dem ästelosen : wehe
von dem kahlen ohne Rinde :
nehmt ihm ab das Angebinde
nehmt ihm fort den Rautenast
    doch es schallet die Trompete
    doch es schallet die Posaune
keiner hat mich angefaßt
alle sagen : aus der Zeit
fährt er und er hats nicht weit

Also weiß ichs und ich fahr
keinen Hut mehr auf dem Haar
Mondenlicht um Brau und Bart
abgelebt zuendgenarrt
lausch auch einmal in die Höhe
    denn es tönet die Trompete
    denn es tönet die Posaune
und von weitem ruft die Krähe
ich bin wo ich bin : im Sand
mit der Raute in der Hand[8]

This may be most easily thought of as a Volkslied or just a Bänkel-
lied. We hear of the tree on the village square, of moonlight and
local music. Looking closer, the poem seems too dark, the images
and sudden changes a little too construed for a Volkslied, its
rhythm too refined and balanced. There is something of a fairy
tale about the three verses and something sad, as if the village
band was blowing a dirge for the poet watching his own funeral.
Is it these mournful ceremonies which give the poem its meaning?
The four stressed rhymed pairs are only broken after the fifth
line by a kind of refrain which differs from the rhythm of the
other lines with its feminine ending. The frequent repetitions give
the poem an incisive, almost monotonous quality. The outside
world remains impersonal and anonymous, separate from the narrator. With alliteration, mostly pure rhymes and syntactical con-
structions such as "fährt er und er hats nicht weit" Bobrowski
strengthens the heavy forward-moving rhythm. The images are
taken from village life : the coffin as a boat, four oak boards
broad and white.

Villages in general play an important role in Bobrowski's lyric.
Just as Huchel feels at home in Mark Brandenburg, Bobrowski
did in the district between the rivers Weichsel and Wolga, in
Sarmatia, as it was once called. It is this background that gives his
poetry a particularly Eastern timbre. It is noteworthy, by the way,

how strong the traces of Eastern landscapes are in modern German literature, one thinks of Celan and the Bukovina, Grass and Danzig, or Lenz and Masuria. Bobrowski's poetic form is more strongly individual than Huchel's. He has, for example, revitalized the ode that praises famous men in his poems on Chatterton, Villon, Gongora, Josef Conrad and Dylan Thomas. *Dorfmusik* is a rare example of his rhyme poetry, for usually he uses free rhythms, especially favouring enjambements and inversions. The splitting up of complete sentences is his basic formal technique; single words thereby gain a particular significance. His poems are indeed often secretive but never unapproachable, and in bearing witness to a world that in spite of all its shortcomings he holds to be inhabitable, they reach out far beyond all the fashionable poetry of doom.

V

The youngest generation of lyric poets in East Germany concern themselves almost excusively with their immediate surroundings. For a long time they could not free themselves from Brecht's overpowering influence, and even with one of the most talented, Günter Kunert, born 1929 in Berlin, one can often detect Brecht's unmistakable idiom. Kunert's poems are symptomatic for the more recent development in East German lyric because they do away with all the old clichés, draw away from officially encouraged optimism and face up to the problems of today. With great skill they employ techniques which allow for interpretations on different levels. In his parables (e.g. *Wie ich ein Fisch wurde*) Kunert presents a sceptical view of man's achievements :

> Denn aufs neue wieder Mensch zu werden
> Wenn man's lange Zeit nicht mehr gewesen ist,
> Das ist schwer für unsereins auf Erden
> Weil das Menschsein sich so leicht vergißt.[9]

Heinz Kahlau, born in 1931, also does not shy away from formulating his attitude towards his environment, creating his distance from it in critical metaphors. It is no longer just the working man who stands at the centre of his poems, but also the lonely, doubting one. Brecht's seed of dialectical thought has flourished in Kahlau's poetry; from examples and anecdotes he has developed his own use of imagery which is precise and rich in expression.

Just as in West German literature about the year 1960 a change towards the problems of the individual made itself felt, so at about the same time East German literature turned the other way. After the writers had come to terms with the new social changes, the first literary proofs of a new national consciousness could be noticed (cf. Strittmatter, Neutsch, Wolf). The as yet most original expression of this is found in the poems of Volker Braun, born in 1939, a former builder's labourer who after studying philosophy now works with the Berliner Ensemble. Braun first made his name with the poem *Jugendobjekt* (which is now in his first collection of verse *Provokation für mich*, 1965) where we read :

> Ja, für Butter, mit diesen erbärmlichen Handbaggern
> schaufeln wir
> Uns die Brust voll Ruhm und Hoffnung, schaufeln ein
> Vaterland her,
> Eh sie noch richtig hochkommt, die Sonne, über den
> Gräben im Rhinluch . . .[10]

With all the poem's critical distance one cannot miss the author's pride in East German success and the pioneering spirit. Braun's talent shows up clearly in the remoulding of his models Whitman and Majakovski when, for instance, he writes :

> Unsre Gedichte sind Hochdruckventile im Rohrnezt der
> Sehnsüchte,
> Unsre Gedichte sollen uns Wiesen zeigen unter den
> Brückenbögen der Gedanken,
> Unsre Gedichte sollen die Schauer der Angst von der
> Haut jagen,
> Unsre Gedichte sollen die Brüste mit Sonne panzern.[11]

With this emphatic language Braun seems to be well on the way to becoming East Germany's Jevtushenko.

Wolf Biermann, the *chansonnier*, finds the most telling expression for the mood of East German artists when he sings with ambiguous simplicity :

> Mein Vaterland, mein Vaterland hat eine Hand aus Feuer,
> hat eine Hand aus Schnee,
> und wenn wir uns umarmen, dann tut das Herz mir weh.[12]

VI

Summing up we may say that the drama is undoubtedly the least developed literary form in East Germany. (One might perhaps mention Strittmatter's socialist peasant plays *Katzgraben* and *Holländerbraut*, Baierl's version of Mother Courage *Frau Flinz* and most recently Hacks's *Moritz Tassow* or Lange's *Marski*.) The revitalized *Bildungs-und Entwicklungsroman* dominates the prose; the committed poem addressed to the general public and, in a quiet backwater, the modern poem describing nature and private experience are the outstanding types of lyric. In contrast to West German developments literary experiments are neither officially favoured nor generally popular, a preference being given to the rejuvenation of old forms. Linguistically there are remarkable differences between East and West German literatures. In as much as East German books offer a reliable picture of current usage, they reveal on the one hand a certain infiltration of official jargon and on the other a welcome freedom from the worst products of the linguistic americanization in West Germany. One cannot yet speak of two basically different German literatures, even though the already mentioned encouragement of an East German national consciousness could gradually lead to this. It must not be forgotten that East German writers are always under close scrutiny in their own country.

German literature generally lacks the tradition of the work of art as a political instrument, already fulfilling itself in the duality of art and society. Since the Second World War German writers have apparently finally given up any attempt to formulate a new understanding of the human situation. They are no longer concerned to comprehend the world in its meaning (or absurdity) but only to use language to describe it sceptically and as factually as possible. It would be wrong to consider East German literature at the moment as more than an artistic statement of a changed historical and social situation.

TRANSLATIONS

1. A long time after the soldiers withdrew and the fishermen were out to sea revolt still squatted down on the bare market place empty in the heat of summer and thought back on its children.

2. Don't you think I too once had hope? That I once believed one could uproot evil from the world by tearing out its roots? But evil has a thousand roots. It cannot be uprooted. Very noble to go on trying, but without conviction it becomes too farcical.

3. Then in the evening the wind blew shaking its shoulders around the house, the linden leaves spoke to the child, the grass breathed out its soul.

4. When from the oaks seeps the dew of morning, then the doors creak, then the wheels turn, called by the cock's early cry. The meadows sleep still beneath the sheet of the moon, cool and bright.

5. They went through the posts and barbed wire fence and past to the glowing tank, and over the oily burnt up seed down the hill's bare clay slope.

6. The hunter now drags home his prey, the antler's pine branch staring spread. The thinker seeks another track, slips quietly past this narrow path where floated golden mist from trees, and hours drift by, wise with

their age, and thoughts like those of birds migrating and words turn into bread and salt.

7. The night knows not to where you fall, o soul, for there is nought but many creatures' silent fear.

8.   *Village Music*

Now my last boat floats away
hat no longer on my head
four white boards of joined oak
in my hand a twig of rue
all my friends around me go
    one blows there upon the trumpet
    one blows there upon the trombone
boat don't sink beneath this weight
hear the others calling loud
this one built his house on sand

By the well the crow now calls
from the branchless tree, o woe,
from the bare and barkless tree
take away his funeral shroud
take away his twig of rue
    but again the trumpet blares
    but again the trombone blares
no one laid their hands on me
all now say he slips from time
and his journey is not far

Now I know I float away
hat no longer on my head
moon on eyebrows and my beard
finished and forever fooled
hark once more to sounds above
    for again the trumpet sounds
    for again the trombone sounds
and from far the crow now calls
I am where I am, in sand
with the rue twig in my hand

9. For to once more become man again, if for a long time one has not thus been, that is for our kind on earth so hard, because man forgets his humanity with ease.

10. Yes, for butter we shovel with these miserable spades, shovel out a fatherland, our breast full of fame and hope, before he fully comes up, the sun, over the Rhinluch ditches...

11. Our poems are high pressure vents in the piping system of our longings, our poems shall give us meadows beneath the bridge vaults of thoughts, our poems shall drive out the shudder of fear from our skin, our poems shall arm the breast with sunlight.

12. My fatherland, my fatherland has a hand of fire, has a hand of snow, and when we embrace, then my heart cries woe.

SELECT BIBLIOGRAPHY

Novels

1951 E. Claudius; *Menschen an unserer Seite* (Reclam Vlg, Leipzig).
1952 E. Welk; *Mein Land, das ferne leuchtet* (Hinstorff Vlg, Rostock).
1954 B. Uhse; *Die Patrioten* (Aufbau Vlg, Berlin).
     L. Renn; *Trini* (Aufbau Vlg, Berlin).
     F. C. Weiskopf; *Lissi* (Dietz Vlg, Berlin).
1955 H. Marchwitza; *Roheisen* (Tribüne, Berlin).
1956 F. Fühmann; *Das Gottesgericht* (Nation, Berlin).
1957 H. Jobst; *Der Findling* (Tribüne, Berlin).
1958 B. Apitz; *Nackt unter Wölfen* (Mitteldt. Vlg, Halle).
1959 A. Seghers; *Die Entscheidung* (Aufbau Vlg, Berlin).
     W. Bredel; *Eine neues Kapitel* (Aufbau Vlg, Berlin).
     H. Marchwitza; *Die Kumiaks und ihre Kinder* (Tribüne, Berlin).
1960 D. Noll; *Die Abenteuer des Werner Holt I* (Aufbau Vlg, Berlin).
1961 K. H. Jakobs; *Beschreibung eines Sommers* (Vlg Neues Leben, Berlin).
1962 F. Fühmann; *Das Judenauto* (Aufbau Vlg, Berlin).
1963 Ch. Wolf; *Der geteilte Himmel* (Mitteldt. Vlg, Halle).
     E. Strittmatter; *Ole Bienkopp* (Aufbau Vlg, Berlin).
     M. Bieler; *Bonifaz* (Aufbau Vlg, Berlin).
1964 E. Neutsch; *Spur der Steine* (Mitteldt. Vlg, Halle).
     J. Bobrowski; *Levins Mühle* (Union Vlg, Berlin).
1965 H. Kant, *Die Aula* (Rütten & Loening Vlg, Berlin).

Poetry

1948 P. Huchel; *Gedichte* (Aufbau Vlg, Berlin/Stahlberg Vlg, Karlsruhe).
1952 J. R. Becher; *Deutsche Sonette* (Aufbau Vlg, Berlin).
1953 B. Brecht; *Buckower Elegien* (Aufbau Vlg, Berlin).
     H. Cibulka: *Märzlicht* (Mitteldt. Vlg, Halle).
1955 A. Bostroem; *Terzinen des Herzens* (Insel Vlg, Leipzig).
1956 L. Fürnberg; *Das wunderbare Gesetz* (Aufbau Vlg, Berlin).
     S. Hermlin; *Dichtungen* (Aufbau Vlg, Berlin).
1957 E. Arendt; *Gesang der sieben Inseln* (Rütten & Loening Vlg, Berlin).
1958 G. Deicke; *Die Gesetze* (Aufbau Vlg, Berlin).
1961 J. Bobrowski; *Sarmatische Zeit* (Union Vlg, Berlin).
     G. Maurer; *Dreistrophenkalender* (Vlg Volk und Welt, Berlin).
1962 F. Fühmann; *Die Richtung der Märchen* (Aufbau Vlg, Berlin).
1963 P. Huchel; *Chausseen, Chausseen* (S. Fischer Vlg, Frankfurt/Main).
     J. Bobrowski; *Schattenland Ströme* (Union Vlg, Berlin).
1964 G. Kunert; *Erinnerung an einen Planeneten* (Carl Hanser Vlg, München).
     H. Kahlau; *Der Fluß der Dinge* (Aufbau Vlg, Berlin).
1965 V. Braun; *Provokation für mich* (Mitteldt. Vlg, Halle).
     G. Kunert; *Der ungebetene Gast* (Aufbau Vlg, Berlin).

Plays

1953 F. Wolf; *Thomas Müntzer* (Reclam Vlg, Berlin).

1954 E. Strittmatter; *Katzgraben* (Aufbau Vlg, Berlin).
      H. Kipphardt; *Shakespeare dringend gesucht* (Henschel Vlg, Berlin).
1955 H. Hauser; *Am Ende der Nacht* (Henschel Vlg, Berlin).
1956 P. Hacks; *Die Schlacht bei Lobositz* (Aufbau Vlg, Berlin).
1957 H. und I. Müller; *Die Lohndrücker* (Reclam Vlg, Leipzig).
1958 H. Pfeiffer; *Laternenfest* (Henschel Vlg, Berlin).
1959 E. Strittmatter; *Die Holländerbraut* (Aufbau Vlg, Berlin).
1961 H. Baierl; *Frau Flinz* (Henschel Vlg, Berlin).
1962 P. Hacks; *Die Sorgen und die Macht* (Henschel Vlg, Berlin).
1963 H. Kleineidam; *Millionenschmidt* (Reclam Vlg, Berlin).
1964 H. Hauser; *Barbara* (NDL 2/1964).
1965 H. Lange; *Marski* (Suhrkamp Vlg, Frankfurt/Main).
      P. Hacks; *Moritz Tassow* (E. Friedrich Vlg, Velber).

Secondary literature

Ad den Besten. *Deutsche Lyrik auf der anderen Seite*. Eckart 1959 (3).
H. P. Anderle. *Mitteldeutsche Erzähler*. Köln 1965.
H. P. Anderle. *Die Literatur der DDR*. Sammlung Metzler, Stuttgart 1966.
R. C. Andrews. Re-education through literature: *E. Strittmatter's Tinko*. German Life and Letters (14).
R. C. Andrews. *Anna Seghers Die Entscheidung*. German Life and Letters (15).
Bibliographie zur Kulturentwicklung in West und Ost. Deutsche Studien 1963 (2).
H. J. Geerdts. *Literatur unserer Zeit*. Rudolstadt 1961.
German Writing Today. Times Literary Supplement 23.9.1960.
P. Hamm. *Glü ist schwer in diesem Land. Zur Situation der jüngsten DDR Lyrik*. Merkur (19) (4).
L. u. N. Krenzlin. *Bitterfeld einige Fragen der Literaturtheorie und Ole Bienkopp*. Weimarer Beiträge 1964 (6).
J. Peddersen. *Die literarische Situation in der DDR*. In: Handbuch der Deutschen Gegenwartsliteratur, hsg. H. Kunisch. Nymphenburger Vlg, München 1965.
M. Reich-Ranicki. *Deutsche Literatur in Ost und West*. Piper Vlg, München 1963.
Rischbieter/Wendt. *Deutsche Dramatik in West und Ost*. Velber 1965.
J. Rühle. *Literatur und Revolution*. Köln 1960.
D. Schiller. *Die Entwicklung der Lyrik in der DDR* 1945–60. Weimarer Beiträge 1962 (2).
D. Schlenstedt. *Zum Problem des Menschenbildes in der jüngsten sozialistischen Literatur*. Weimarer Beiträge 1962 (3).
D. Schlenstedt. *Motive und Symbole in Christa Wolfs Erzählung, Der geteilte Himmel*. Weimarer Beiträge 1964 (1).
Schriftsteller der DDR. Leipzig 1961.
Skizze zur Geschichte der deutschen Nationalliteratur von den Anfängen der deutschen Arbeiterbewegung bis zur Gegenwart. Weimarer Beiträge 1964 (5).